Every Child a Reader

MONTH-BY-MONTH LESSONS TO TEACH BEGINNING READING

Helene Coffin

■SCHOLASTIC

New York • Toronto • London • Auckland • Sydney
Mexico City • New Delhi • Hong Kong • Buenos Aires

Dedication

*In loving memory of my mother and father, Mary and James Doyle,
who always believed in me and taught me that anything is possible.*

CREDITS

"Change" by Charlotte Zolotow from RIVER WINDING by Charlotte Zolotow. Copyright © 1970 by Charlotte Zolotow. Used by permission of Scott Treimel, NY.

"To a Red Kite" is reprinted from MURAL ON SECOND AVENUE AND OTHER CITY POEMS by Lilian Moore. First published in I THOUGHT I HEARD THE CITY. Copyright © 1971 by Lilian Moore. Reproduced by permission of the publisher, Candlewick Press, Somerville, MA.

"Lunchbox" by Valerie Worth from PEACOCK AND OTHER POEMS by Valerie Worth. Copyright © 2002 by George Bahlke. Reprinted by permission of Farrar, Straus and Giroux, LLC.

"Apple Joys" by Eve Merriam from FRESH PAINT by Eve Merriam. Copyright © 1986 by Eve Merriam. Used by permission of Marian Reiner.

"The Pickety Fence" by David McCord from ONE AT A TIME by David McCord. Copyright © 1965, 1966 by David McCord. By permission of Little, Brown and Company.

"First Day of School" by Aileen Fisher from ALWAYS WONDERING by Aileen Fisher. Copyright © 1991 by Aileen Fisher. Used by permission of Marian Reiner on behalf of the Boulder Public Library Foundation, Inc.

"But Then" by Aileen Fisher from UP THE WINDY HILL by Aileen Fisher. Copyright © 1953, 1981 by Aileen Fisher. Used by permission of Marian Reiner on behalf of the Boulder Public Library Foundation, Inc.

"If You Find a Little Feather" and "Keep a Poem in Your Pocket" by Beatrice Schenk de Regniers from SOMETHING SPECIAL by Beatrice Schenk de Regniers. Copyright © 1958 by Beatrice Schenk de Regniers. All copyrights renewed. Used by permission of Marian Reiner.

"Wide Awake" by Myra Cohn Livingston from WIDE AWAKE AND OTHER POEMS by Myra Cohn Livingston. Copyright © 1959, 1987 by Myra Cohn Livingston. Used by permission of Marian Reiner.

"May" text copyright © 1965 by John Updike. All rights reserved. Reprinted from A CHILD'S CALENDAR by permission of Holiday House, Inc.

"Invitation to the Wind" from DANCE WITH ME by Barbara Juster Esbensen. Copyright © 1995 by Barbara Juster Esbensen. Used by permission of HarperCollins Publishers.

"January" and "June" from ONCE AROUND THE HOUSE by Bobbi Katz. Text copyright © 2006 by Bobbi Katz. Reprinted by permission of Houghton Mifflin Harcourt Publishing Company. All rights reserved.

"Yellow Butter" from THE LLAMA WHO HAD NO PAJAMA: 100 FAVORITE POEMS by Mary Ann Hoberman. Text copyright © 1981 by Mary Ann Hoberman. Reprinted by permission of Houghton Mifflin Harcourt Publishing Company. All rights reserved.

"Big" from ALL TOGETHER by Dorothy Aldis, Copyright © 1962 by Dorothy Aldis and renewed 1967 by Roy E. Porter. Used by permission of G.P. Putnam's Sons, A Division of Penguin USA. All rights reserved.

"Brooms" from ANYTHING AND EVERYTHING by Dorothy Aldis, copyright © 1955. Used by permission of G.P. Putnam's Sons, A Division of Penguin USA. All rights reserved.

"Prediction" and "The Wind Woman" by Barbara Juster Esbensen. From SWING AROUND THE SUN by Barbara Juster Esbensen. Text copyright © 1965 by Lerner Publications Company, © 2003 by Carolrhoda Books, Inc. Reprinted with the permission of Carolrhoda Books, a division of Lerner Publishing Group, Inc. All rights reserved. No part of this text excerpt may be used or reproduced in any manner whatsoever without the prior written permission of Lerner Publishing Group, Inc.

"I Like Peanut Butter" and "I'm Small" by Lilian Moore from I'M SMALL AND OTHER VERSES by Lilian Moore. Copyright © 2001 by Lilian Moore. Used by permission of Marian Reiner.

"Cow" is reprinted from TURTLE IN JULY by Marilyn Singer, by permission of the author.

"It's Time for Spring" by Bobbi Katz. Copyright © 1991 by Bobbi Katz. Reprinted by permission of the author, who controls all rights.

"Things to Do If You Are the Rain" by Bobbi Katz. Copyright © 1982 by Bobbi Katz. Reprinted by permission of the author, who controls all rights.

Editor: Lois Bridges

Production editor: Amy Rowe

Cover designer: Brian LaRossa

Interior designer: Sydney Wright

Copy editor: Marla Garfield

ISBN-13: 978-0-545-05897-1

ISBN-10: 0-545-05897-X

4360 4767 10/10

Copyright © 2009 by Helene Coffin

CONTENTS

ACKNOWLEDGMENTS

We learn from each other, and I have been very fortunate to have learned from so many in my life and teaching career. It is important for me to take this time to show my gratitude.

First, I must recognize the two people who encouraged me to write this book and who both made it possible for this book to become a reality. Nancie Atwell, the founder of the Center for Teaching and Learning (CTL), has been my mentor, my fiercest champion, and my agent. Since I have worked at her school, she has pushed me to undertake writing my lessons for a broader audience, to try new approaches to teach reading, and to present my ideas at national conferences. Nancie was the starter, my ignition, behind this book, and I am profoundly grateful to her. I also want to thank my twin sister, Maureen Hodge. Maureen was my taskmaster, my adviser, the one to offer me the hard critiques, and the one who devoted limitless time to read, read, and reread my manuscript. She talked on the phone with me for hours, bossing me and making sure I met my deadlines. Maureen was my strength and the "wind beneath my wings."

Lois Bridges, my editor, has also been a blessing during this undertaking. For her immediate responses, terrific and specific feedback, and, most importantly, her positive energy throughout the process, I am most grateful. And Amy Rowe, my production editor, deserves special kudos for her expert guidance in my journey to publish this book.

But, this book began many years before I wrote it. Two former colleagues and my dearest friends at the West Bath School, Diane Morris and Lori Sawyer, were instrumental in offering praise and support in my teaching of reading. To Cathy Folan, my former principal, and to Livy Williamson, a literacy consultant at West Bath, I give my sincere thanks for bolstering me and daring me to think I might have something worthwhile to share with other teachers.

I wish also to acknowledge my colleagues at CTL. These have been the people I have taught with, shared ideas and materials with, and pulled shoulder-to-shoulder with in our common goal to make students better readers, thinkers, and learners. All of you—Sally MacLeod, Katie Rittershaus, Glenn Powers, Jill Cotta, Ted DeMille, and Pam Brackett—thank you for your daily influences and your rallying behind me as I wrote this book.

I also have my CTL friends and cheerleaders to thank. When I was stressed and overwhelmed by this huge undertaking, these people renewed my spirit by their continual supportive deeds and kind words. Carrie Bolander, Michelle Buehner, Donna Guenther, Liz Hall, Roberta Jordan, Corinne Larson, Maggie Limm, Sheryl MacDonald, Kelly Moss, Sally Powers, and Renée Roy, hugs and kisses to all of you.

And, there is my husband "W." For your overwhelming patience living without a wife for two summers and for the comforting pride you take in me, my teaching, and this work, I simply say, I love you . . .; and you can take me out to dinner now; my book is off to press.

I will end my acknowledgments with a special word about all the students I have taught over the years. Without them, there would be no book and no reason to write it. It is the love I have for my students that causes me to continually reflect and struggle to improve my teaching. They are the true inspiration for this book. Thank you, my little darlings.

FOREWORD

I can't count the times I've shut off the lights and locked the doors on Helene Coffin. You'd think by now I'd have learned that she's still somewhere in the building, hard at work. Helene won't head for home until she has reflected on the day's teaching and learning and tried to anticipate every minute of tomorrow's. She *authors* the time she spends with her kindergarten classes—invents, considers, chooses, rethinks, edits, appraises, reappraises. She is my definition of a professional educator. Her heart beats to the rhythms of the professional's mantra: *only a hundred and eighty days, only a hundred and eighty days.* Her thoughtfulness, sense of purpose, and joy in teaching are legend.

Reading poetry is one of the tasks that keep Helene at school beyond sunset. She skims collections of poems written for young children until she finds the next keeper—a poem she loves and predicts her students will fall in love with, too. At our school, the small, fresh images and stories that Helene selects have become the heart of the "word work" that helps turn beginning readers into fluent readers.

Each morning Helene gathers her kindergarten class around a chart stand and invites them to enter a world of wonderful words—of sensory and evocative diction, of language compressed to its essence, of ideas, feelings, experiences, and themes that ring true for 5- and 6-year-old boys and girls. Children love the poems for their meanings and for the reading lessons they convey, as the class practices strategies that enable them to make the wonderful words their own. Through these intense, loving workouts—combined with daily reading workshops and writing workshops in which children tell, hear, choose, read, and write reams of great stories—all of Helene's kindergartners will be reading by June. That's nothing new for this remarkable teacher.

Helene's career began in 1970 in a tiny rural school here in Maine. She moved next to a big, open-concept facility; in 2004, before we lured her to CTL, she was teaching at a local, one-class-per-grade K–6, with classes averaging 17–21 students. No matter the setting, all of her students, except those with severe special needs, were readers by the end of kindergarten.

Outside of the classroom, Helene keeps abreast of new developments in research and pedagogy. Inside her classroom, she observes, experiments richly,

Every Child a Reader

reflects, revises, and nurtures. Teaching is both her calling and her favorite intellectual challenge. When I suggested poetry as a medium for kindergarten word studies, she was intrigued and courageous. She hit the books in search of perfect poems, and she began to weave among them a curriculum of reading strategies: voice-print matching, letter identification, sight words, prediction based on semantics and syntax, sounding out, attention to punctuation, identification of known words inside unfamiliar ones, phonograms, suffixes, consonant digraphs, compound words, you name it.

The result is a double blessing. Children learn to read with more exuberance than Helene has ever witnessed, and they achieve fluency and independence sooner in the school year than ever before. But they also carry away in their hearts and minds a repertoire of beloved poems to savor in years to come as they relate the new experiences of their lives to the verse they voiced and internalized in kindergarten.

My suggestion to teachers of beginning readers who also feel intrigued and courageous about the potential of poetry is to approach this book by focusing on one perfect poem at a time, along with the relevant word work and activities that Helene designed and refined to make the most of a class's time: she is such a meticulous planner that the degree of detail she provides may seem daunting if you attempt a cover-to-cover perusal. The lessons do progress in a sequence, from concepts of print through higher-level skills and strategies. Trust that the lively poems and the specificity of her advice about teaching them have achieved wonders among our school's population of regular kids.

At the end of a long day at CTL, in an otherwise still building, I often hear evidence of the presence of my friend Mrs. Squeaky. It's Helene, as her black marker squawks and squeaks its way across the lines of a sheet of manila chart paper. In the morning, a new, perfect poem will be loosed on an eager bunch of kindergarten readers. She is already anticipating their excited reactions—just as I am anticipating the excitement of the primary-grade teachers who will meet Helene, her students, and the delightful poems that helped them become readers in the pages of this smart, inspiring book.

Nancie Atwell
Center for Teaching and Learning
Edgecomb, Maine

INTRODUCTION
Our Gateway to Reading

As a kindergarten teacher with more than 25 years of teaching experience, I thought I knew how to maximize the literacy-learning potential of my young students—that is, until four years ago, when I took on the kindergarten position at the Center for Teaching and Learning (CTL), Nancie Atwell's school in Edgecomb, Maine. It was Nancie who introduced me to the amazing power of poetry.

In addition to using the typical resources a literacy-rich classroom would utilize (e.g., big books, leveled readers, and read-alouds), for years I also relied on song lyrics I printed on chart paper to nurture kindergartners' motivation to read. Although most of my students became independent readers by June, I have to admit that teaching reading through songs was often frustrating. Rather than focusing on the printed words, the children would get caught up in the melodies and simply sing what they had memorized. The singing was fun for the children, but it wasn't helping them to read as I had hoped. Their engagement was aural rather than visual.

Then Nancie encouraged me to include poetry on charts as part of my reading program. To be honest, I reacted with skepticism. Poetry . . . in kindergarten? I thought my kindergartners would never enjoy reading poems as much as they loved singing songs. Oh, how wrong I was!

Reading poetry became a joyful experience for every child in my classroom; they all became engaged in the process of reading and discussing great poems by such contemporary children's poets as Aileen Fisher, David McCord, Lilian Moore, Beatrice Schenk de Regniers, and Charlotte Zolotow. Not only did I see genuine enthusiasm for our daily poetry reading, my students' confidence levels soared. They began to view themselves as readers early in the school year—many by December.

Today my kindergarten literacy program still includes the shared reading of big books, songs on charts, class messages, author studies, other read-alouds, independent reading, and writing workshops. But a new, integral piece of my kindergarten literacy program is the daily reading of poems on charts. I've found that integrating reading instruction and poetry maximizes every kindergartner's opportunity to succeed at decoding and comprehending text.

Through the vivid diction of good poems, language comes alive for my young students. The strong rhythms, the rhyming patterns, the repetition of words and phrases, the enticing sounds of language, and the small, fresh, meaningful stories engage my students. Their individual voices resound as one big voice when they read poems aloud with me each day. Since poetry is read at a slower pace than other texts are—a pace that's enforced by line and stanza breaks—children can focus on specific words as the pointer touches each word. And because each line contains only a few words, children are able to be successful at voice-print matching more quickly. In addition, the brevity of poetry entices a beginning reader to reread again and again.

Poetry is a powerful vehicle for enhancing fluency, expression, comprehension, and a love of the printed word. It has become instilled in my students' hearts as well as in their minds. When I asked my class at the end of last year to name a favorite poem, I was stunned when all of them raised their hands and volunteered not only to name their favorite poems, but also to recite them from memory. Their presentations touched me deeply, but there was one recitation that left me speechless: Jacob, a kindergartner who had transformed from a rambunctious little guy before he entered kindergarten into a gentle, sweet boy I adored, recited a 25-line free-verse poem called "If You Find a Little Feather" by Beatrice Schenk de Regniers. There was no rhyming pattern to help him remember the words, but because its meaning had such a powerful effect on him, Jacob recited it flawlessly and with such feeling—just as if he were the bird talking.

And how rewarding it is to hear children recite their favorite poems with confidence and great intonation. Nancie heard my students reciting their favorite poems and asked me if they would perform them at our last-day school ceremony. I was a bit hesitant, because it was such short notice. However, my students' immediate reaction was, "Sure!" Even the most timid, Abram, reassured me he would be okay. And he was right! During our K–8 Move-Up Ceremony, he stood before a packed audience of children, teachers, and parents and boomed the words of his favorite poem, "Fat Father Robin," by David McCord. To me, this is the ultimate testament of the power of poetry. At that moment, I realized my students had learned to appreciate and even love poetry.

An Overview of My Literacy Program at CTL

As you might surmise, my kindergartners read throughout the day. I purposely begin each day with a 15–20-minute Poetry Time because they are fresh, alert, and eager to learn. My students gain much self-confidence and skill from the variety of meaningful word studies I develop from the poems we read together.

In addition to poetry sessions, I build in other opportunities for reading during the day. In a 45-minute reading workshop, I include a choral reading of a daily class message, the study of different authors' works—both fiction and nonfiction—the shared reading of big books, and the independent reading of just-right books. Individual students also read aloud to me during reading workshop, which allows me to easily meet individual needs.

My students are even read aloud to at lunch by me or an older student, and I often connect different topics in history, science, and math through literature. At rest time, I read aloud from a chapter book to help develop children's listening comprehension.

Then, because reading does not end when the school day does, all my students take home self-selected books to read and have a family member read to them every night. On Fridays, they also take home poetry notebooks to share with their families over the weekend.

Although all these reading activities contribute to the literacy development of my students, I believe the use of poetry has made the single most powerful impact on my students' progress and my reading instruction. The poem "Change" by Charlotte Zolotow, which my students and I read together every June during the final days of kindergarten, describes not only my students, but it also describes me. My students have thrived as readers, writers, and thinkers. Now I can't imagine a day without the songs of poetry filling our hearts and minds.

Reading Throughout the Day

8:45–9:30 Circle Time

During this block, I implement certain literacy routines each day: the "Special Helper's" name exercise (i.e., naming the letters and sounds in a classmate's name), the recitation of the letters and sounds on the alphabet chart, the reading of sight word cards, the reading and discussion of poems, a word study, and a picture book read-aloud.

9:30–10:15 Math

To begin the calendar routine, students identify the letters and sounds in the name of the current month. I often read aloud to introduce or reinforce certain math concepts.

10:35–11:15 Reading Workshop

At the beginning of reading workshop, students participate in the shared reading of the class message. After they read the class message, I present a mini-lesson to the class (e.g., author studies, cloze activities, or "making words" activities). The final segment of reading workshop is independent reading. During this particular time, students select their just-right books to take home each day for their required 30-minute reading homework, and then they read or browse their selections while I listen to individuals read aloud so that I can assess their progress, advise them about their just-right book selections, and teach or reinforce different reading strategies.

11:15–12:00 Writing Workshop

Students learn about writing conventions and craft by writing simple memoirs, poetry, and letters. They write spelling approximations by segmenting sounds and recording the corresponding letters for the sounds they hear in words. Students also have portable word walls they use to spell high-frequency writing words correctly. At times, I read aloud stories to demonstrate a specific craft.

12:05–12:25 Lunch

Every day at 12:15 a seventh or eighth grade student reads a story aloud while the kindergartners eat their lunches.

1:00–1:30 Rest Time Read-Aloud/Reading Buddies

During rest time on Monday through Thursday, the kindergartners listen to chapter books, which help to strengthen their listening comprehension. On Fridays, the kindergartners meet with their fourth-grade reading buddies to read poems aloud from their poetry notebooks, practice sight words on their individual word rings, and listen to stories read by their fourth-grade reading buddies.

2:00–2:20 Choice Time

During this block, the kindergartners often participate in a variety of reading activities.

Reading Homework

Each student from kindergarten through eighth grade is required to read 30 minutes every night of the week for homework.

How I Teach Reading With Poetry

My kindergartners' day at CTL starts with Circle Time. Within this learning block, I dedicate 15 to 20 minutes to reading and discussing new poems as well as old favorites, because it sets the tone for my classroom. The wonderful poems we read, work with, and discuss help create a warm, supportive environment conducive to acquiring a love of written language and the building of a community.

Although these learning times are joyful, positive, and relaxed, one cannot enter this zone without an action plan. This plan includes four main components:

☀ Behavioral expectations

☀ Routines and procedures

☀ The just-right poem

☀ Poetry notebooks

Behavioral Expectations

First and foremost, it is essential to establish behavioral expectations along with set routines and procedures. At the start of the year, I focus on my management, or what I refer to as "audience behavior"—*what it sounds like* and *what it looks like*. Before any learning activity, we review together what a good audience member looks like: Eyes are focused on the speaker; hands are to self; lips are zipped; ears are listening; "ischium" (i.e., bottom) is glued to the mat; and the student is sitting "crisscross applesauce"(i.e., legs are bent in position, one over the other). For at least the first month of school, I point to picture symbols of an eye, a hand, an ear, and a cross-legged stick figure whenever we review appropriate behavior during our meetings to capitalize on both the auditory and visual modalities.

As my students begin to demonstrate good audience behavior with few reminders from me, I then transfer to them the responsibility of making sure the audience is ready for any student who goes in front of the class to read material on the chart stand or to speak to the whole group. Students assume this responsibility well, and audience members always respond quickly to a peer's redirection if it's asked politely.

Key to my management are the round braided seat cushions I use to provide personal spaces for my students. Calmness reigns whenever my students sit on their mats. When they gather on the rug for a lesson, there's a sense of order and structure. To me, the time it takes to teach my students how to get their mats in turn from the pile, how and where to place their mats, how to sit on their mats, and how to neatly stack the mats after a meeting ends is time well spent. When students know a teacher's expectations, fewer disruptions occur and the flow of the lesson is maintained, resulting in more time for learning.

Routines and Procedures

The inclusion of high-frequency word practice (i.e., words that carry little meaning but tie a sentence together) as part of your daily routine is critical, because these common words comprise 50 percent of all the written words students will encounter in their reading. If students are able to immediately recognize these words, they can solve the puzzle of other words through meaning, grammar, or graphics. From the poems that I'll introduce in a particular week, I select four or five words for children to focus on and practice. Since I expect them to learn these words with automaticity, we practice reading aloud our sight-word collection, which includes every sight word that's been introduced. We then continue to practice reading these words long after they are instantly recognized, as an insurance they won't be forgotten.

At the end of each trimester, I evaluate each student's ability to read the collection of sight-word cards. This assessment helps me determine which words every member of my class reads with automaticity. Then, I remove these particular words from the word card collection because they no longer need to be reviewed, and retain only those words that need more practice.

The Just-Right Poem

Even with CTL's strong library, finding appropriate poems for kindergartners takes a lot of time. I've spent countless evenings and weekends scouring poetry anthologies and collections in search of poems that will click with my students. The content of the just-right poem must be engaging to a 5-year-old, and the vocabulary used in it must be sufficient to teach reading but not so sophisticated as to overwhelm a beginning reader. At the start of the year, the poems I choose are short and feature much repetition. As the year progresses, the vocabulary becomes more difficult and the predictable pattern less explicit.

From the first day of school in September to the last day in June, the poems we read address topics I know my students will connect with. Without a personal connection, there is no engagement. Without engagement, there is no learning. Therefore, choosing poems to which young students can relate is key to ensuring enthusiastic readers and successful learners.

It is important not only that children identify with the poems you choose, but that you like them as well so you can present them with enthusiasm. Children will listen with rapt attention to a poem that is read aloud with feeling.

When I've found a poem I think my students will enjoy, I study it and ask myself the following questions:

* Is it too lengthy?

* Is it meaty enough to be worthwhile?

* Is the vocabulary adequate or too difficult?

* How many previously learned sight words does it contain?

* Are there any new sight words I may use?

* Does the poem feature enough repetition or a strong rhythm to help children learn the words?

* Which skill or concept could be introduced or reinforced in our word work?

Once I've made a selection, I print the poem on large chart paper. On Monday, I introduce it by reading it aloud with love and enthusiasm. Then the children take time to share their personal connections to the poem's topic. For example, they may relate their fears about beginning kindergarten or their lunch-box disasters. At the end of the discussion, I invite children to read parts of the poem with me—either by chiming in or by supplying rhyming words. On the second day, we read the poem together and then concentrate on a particular skill or concept (e.g., finding words that are the same, different digraphs, or a specific phonogram).

Children quickly and naturally learn to read the words of poems they embrace. From this initial step of memorizing words, I begin to guide them to independence as readers. This process requires me to reflect each afternoon, when I prepare for the next day's learning, about what my students can do and what they need to know next. I build on their success by introducing an appropriate skill when they are ready for it. But that doesn't mean that old skills are forgotten. We continually practice previously taught concepts of print, so beginning readers can learn to respond to print automatically. I've learned that a new lesson should be introduced only when the class is ready for it. It's far better to proceed slowly in the beginning in order to build children's confidence. By knowing one's students and their individual needs, a teacher will recognize the appropriate time to introduce a new skill or concept.

In September, students enter kindergarten with varied literacy experiences. Since some children start school with limited knowledge about printed language, I always spend much of the early fall focused on print concepts. These include the following skills:

- Directionality

- Differences between letters and words

- Distinctions between uppercase and lowercase letters

- Letter recognition

- Punctuation

- One-to-one matching

- Alphabetic principle (i.e., the ability to associate sounds with letters and use sounds to form words)

Without these fundamental understandings, reading acquisition cannot be achieved. As soon as my students understand the basic print concepts, I begin to teach new skills at a faster pace because my students' rate of performance accelerates.

To maintain a high level of interest in reading poetry, it's important to move on to a new poem after two days even if students aren't ready for a new skill, and even if they can't read the poem fluently yet. I often return to poems to reread them as "old favorites" and reinforce previously taught skills. Children will reread particular poems if they love them!

Poetry Notebooks

We read more than 80 poems together during the school year. I purchase three-ring, 1½-inch binders to serve as poetry notebooks for my class, so there will be room to include every poem we read throughout the year. Each week, I type up our new poems, place them in plastic sleeves, and add them to the children's binders. We revisit "old favorites" from the notebooks during Poetry Time on Fridays.

Students also read aloud their personal old favorites to peer reading partners during our activity blocks, and they reread new poems and old favorites to fourth-grade reading buddies each Friday afternoon.

At CTL, every student from kindergarten through eighth grade is required to read or be read to for 30 minutes each night. In addition to borrowing storybooks each day from our classroom library, on Fridays my students take home their individual poetry notebooks. They become personally invested in their poetry notebooks and can't wait to share the poems with their families. Parents are able to observe their children's reading development. The poetry notebook is often the first book kindergartners can successfully read independently. This accomplishment greatly boosts their confidence, and they become enthusiastic and willing readers of poetry. Other genres naturally follow. Many parents have told me how much their children enjoy reading their poetry notebooks aloud from cover to cover—a positive experience for the entire family.

I also ask that, during the weekends, children illustrate their favorite poem of the week. Their illustrations should clearly depict the poem's meaning. When my students return their poetry notebooks on Mondays, I check to see if they have illustrated their favorite poem, and determine if details need to be added to their illustrations to clarify the meaning of the poems.

On the last day of school in June, when I present their notebooks to the children and announce that they can keep them forever, smiles radiate around the room. They treasure these notebooks, and I know their families love them as well.

By implementing these essential components, your students will thrive. They will come to love poetry and most important of all, they will become confident, independent readers.

About This Book

For this book, I've chosen 40 poems that have proven most effective in leading children to literacy. These poems are arranged in order of skill progression:

☀ Concepts of print

☀ Sight words

☀ Predictions based on semantic, syntactic, and graphic cues

- ☀ Phonograms: *-ing, -all, -ill,* and *-ick*

- ☀ *r*-controlled vowels: *er, ir, ur, ar,* and *or*

- ☀ Endings: *-s, -ing,* and *-ed*

- ☀ Compound words

Throughout the book, different skills are revisited to help reinforce the knowledge students have acquired.

Most of these poems are my students' "old favorites" that they read again and again. Others are my own personal favorites, because I've either enjoyed presenting them or I've been able to design effective word studies with them.

I encourage other kindergarten teachers to type these poems, photocopy them, holepunch them, and place them in notebooks for their students to share with their families. Not only are the notebooks a great home-school connection, but they also allow children opportunities to practice their newfound skills independently.

Accompanying each poem from September to June, I've provided a brief rationale regarding my choice, followed by detailed lessons that promote a specific skill needed for children to become fluent, expressive readers, and concluded with a personal reflection. I chose this particular format to show how I plan my teaching by taking a teacher through all phases of a lesson design. More importantly, I wanted to demonstrate how a reflective practitioner thinks.

I embrace the reflective process, because it enables me to continuously monitor my students' needs and interests, and adapt my curriculum to provide more effective lessons. Reflection stimulates me and keeps my instruction fresh and interesting as I continue to learn new knowledge and grow as an educator.

These lessons have helped my students to:

- ☀ Develop an understanding of print concepts

- ☀ Learn consonants and vowels

- ☀ Learn digraphs and consonant blends

- ☀ Learn sight words

- ☀ Learn new vocabulary

- ☀ Make predictions based on semantics, syntax, and graphic cues

- ☀ Recognize rhyming patterns

❋ Understand contractions and compound words

❋ Learn how punctuation gives voice to reading

❋ Develop fluency and expression

I've also included two comprehensive checklists (pages 331 and 332) that I use to note the reading behaviors of my students. These record forms allow me to track my students' progress in reading easily.

Teaching children how to read is a rewarding yet challenging journey. Learning to read through great, child-centered poems helps to make the journey a joyful experience. It has all the ingredients for success: fun, repetition, rhythm, simple but vivid vocabulary, and personal meaning. Happy reading!

SEPTEMBER

LESSON ONE
Concept of a Word

First Day of School

I wonder
if my drawing
will be as good as theirs
I wonder
if they'll like me
or just be full of stares
I wonder
if my teacher
will look like Mom or Gram
I wonder
if my puppy
will wonder
where I am!

—*Aileen Fisher*

What I Was Thinking

When I found "First Day of School," I knew my students would easily identify with the feelings of the child in Aileen Fisher's poem, and that it would also be a great way to get them hooked on poetry, as it contains a predictable pattern with a strong rhythm that facilitates its memorization.

To introduce the poem, I thought I'd recite it aloud from memory instead of reading it aloud from the chart, using a pointer. Before school began I practiced saying its words until I was able to recite it fluently and with feeling, so my students could experience Fisher's meaning and not become distracted by the print.

Materials

"First Day of School" by Aileen Fisher, handwritten on manila tag chart paper in large, neat print and attached by rings to a wooden chart stand

Pointer (I use a simple, red, chunky wooden pointer so it does not become a distraction.)

What This Lesson Looks Like

✺ Gather your students around the chart stand. Explain: "Under the chart stand is a neat pile of round mats. Please make a line, and when it is your turn to take a mat, please take the top mat on the pile, and find a place you'd like to sit during Poetry Time. Make sure you can see the chart clearly and leave a little room between you and your neighbor so that you have personal space."

✺ Tell your students what you remember about your own first day of school, how nervous you were because you didn't know what school was going to be like, and so on. Then explain: "I'm going to recite a poem about someone's worries on his or her first day. Listen as I recite this poem aloud. It's written by one of my favorite children's poets. Her name is Aileen Fisher, and the title of her poem is 'First Day of School.' "

✺ Stand beside the chart and face your class. Glance at the words if you need to, but try to maintain the flow, rhythm, and tone of the poem. It's much more effective if you can say the poem—that is, recite it from memory. Speak with expression, emphasizing the repeating phrase, "I wonder."

✺ After reciting the poem, ask: "Were you nervous about starting school? What kinds of questions or worries did you have?" Let children share their personal feelings about the first day of school.

✺ Explain to your students: "Now I'm going to *read* the poem again. As I say each word, I'll touch it with the pointer. Watch me." Read the poem slowly, but with expression, using the pointer.

✺ Finally, tell your students: "I'm going to read this poem one last time." Explain: "When the pointer touches the last word in each line, I'd like you to chime in and say the word." If the children have difficulty with supplying the appropriate words, support them by giving the beginning sounds or beginning blends.

Fisher's poem was a gift from heaven! While I was performing the poem, I saw the shy smiles of my young audience transform into big grins. This poem was meaningful to my kindergartners because they shared similar fears and questions about this big event in their lives. When the children discussed their own fears about starting kindergarten, they became less anxious because they discovered that many of their classmates expressed identical worries. At that moment, a community of learners formed—children who cared about one another.

LESSON TWO
Voice-Print Matching

What I Was Thinking

Although Aileen Fisher's "First Day of School" contains repetition and rhyme and addresses a perfect topic, I was concerned that the relatively large number of words in the poem would inhibit my students' ability to voice-print match with success. To ensure a successful experience, I asked my students initially to practice touching the repetitive phrase *I wonder* with the pointer. I knew that they'd be ready to use the pointer to *read* the poem as soon as they gained more awareness of printed language and knew the words from memory. I didn't want to set them up for failure by expecting too much too soon. I knew I'd need to create a safe environment and build a rapport with my students for learning to occur.

What This Lesson Looks Like

❀ Tell your students: "Today we're going to read 'First Day of School' again." Show them the pointer and explain its function. "As I touch a word, I'll read that word aloud. Touching each word helps me to make sure that I read one word at a time and don't get ahead of myself. For each word we say, there's a word printed here on the chart. I want you to focus on each word as I touch it with my pointer." Read the poem slowly, pointing to each word as you read it aloud. Make certain to maintain this deliberate pace so you can help children begin to grasp the concept of voice-print matching (i.e., one-to-one matching).

✦ Explain to your students: "Now I'm going to read the poem aloud once more, but this time, I want you to join in. I'm going to read most of the poem by myself, but when I stop reading aloud, I want you to say the word I point to, if you can. Remember to focus on each word that I point to and be ready to chime in when I stop." Then reread the poem to the class, but this time leave out the word *wonder* each time it appears in the poem, as well as the phrases *good as theirs, like me, of stares, Mom or Gram,* and *where I am.*

✦ Tell your students: "The poet, Aileen Fisher, used repetition to strengthen the poem's rhythm. Can someone tell me the two words she repeated over and over?" When someone correctly responds with *I wonder,* touch and read *I* and *wonder* in the first line. Ask, "What helped me know where the word *I* ended and *wonder* began?" When someone responds with *a space* or *white space,* say, "That's right: just as there's a space between you and your neighbor, there's a space between two words." Point to the space between *I* and *wonder* as you define the term so your students will see it as well as hear that crucial word, *space.*

✦ Now point again to the words in the first line and read them aloud as you touch them with your pointer. Then sweep your pointer quickly across the first line from left to right so the children can see what comprises a line. "These words that I just read from left to right make up a *line.*" Ask, "Can you find *I wonder* in a different line of this poem? I'm looking for someone whose eyes are zeroed in on *I wonder* in a different line." Let the child you choose use the pointer to touch each word as he or she reads. Ask, "Can you point to the space between the two words?" Continue this procedure until no lines are left that contain the phrase *I wonder.*

✦ For the final reading, ask your children to read along with you. Say, "Keep your eyes on the pointer so you'll be ready to say each word as I touch it. In this way, we'll be reading together in one big voice."

✦ Reflection ✦

When we completed this activity, Ridgely raised his hand and said, "I see the word *wonder* again." He reached for my pointer to show his classmates his discovery. He found the word, touched it, and read it aloud. He beamed with pride. And I knew what my next lesson needed to focus on: finding other words that are the same.

I was amazed by Ridgely's visual discrimination skills, and admittedly, I was tempted to use this "teachable moment" to find other words that were the same, but I recognized it was time to stop. I had pushed hard enough for one day. They were tired and ready to get up and move. Believe me, it's far better to have eager kindergartners who are ready to take in new information than weary ones who can't or won't focus. Maintaining a high energy level and enthusiasm for learning to read is key to success. Slow and steady wins the race!

LESSON THREE
Voice-Print Matching Review

What I Was Thinking

Before I introduced a new skill, I decided to review what the children had already learned about line spaces, and one-to-one matching. By reviewing their knowledge of these concepts, I could not only check my students' understanding, but I could also boost their confidence.

Since I wanted to ensure another successful lesson, I knew I should begin by choosing a child who demonstrated good understanding of printed language. He or she would serve as a role model for this particular lesson to demonstrate voice-print matching. Then I only call on a few others who raised their hands to volunteer, because I didn't want to force children who weren't ready to brave this challenge. I also knew that time was an issue. I needed to establish the policy that I'd choose no more than three children to execute any one task in which the whole class was involved.

Materials

Class list attached to a clipboard

Green, yellow, and red fine-point pens

What This Lesson Looks Like

✿ Tell your students, "Today, a few children will get an opportunity to lead their classmates in reading the poem 'First Day of School' by Aileen Fisher.

They'll use the special pointer to touch each word as it's read. I can choose no more than three volunteers to demonstrate different reading skills, because if we took time to allow everyone to have a turn, we wouldn't have time to participate in other fun activities. But I promise you'll get a turn, because I keep a checklist of the children who've already had the opportunity of performing a poem."

✻ Hint: Make sure to keep this class list handy so you can check off a child's name as soon as he or she has completed a turn. If the child performs a particular skill successfully, I check the name with a green pen; if the skill is performed with some support from me, I check the name in yellow; and if the child needs much support from me to be successful, I check his or her name in red, as a reminder to me that this particular child needs much more practice.

✻ Invite your students, "Please read the poem aloud *chorally* with me. *Chorally* means to read together. Remember to read with feeling and to use your big reading voices. Keep your eyes on my pointer so you don't get ahead of yourself. And remember, there's a word in print for each word you say." To emphasize this point, tap the pointer in the air as you pronounce each word in this last sentence.

✻ After the shared reading of Fisher's poem, ask: "Who knows where we started to read this poem? Raise your hand if you know." Choose a capable volunteer to use the pointer to indicate the title. "That's right. We started by reading the title of the poem: 'First Day of School.' "

✻ Tell them: "Say the words in the title slowly with me so we can keep track of the number of words in the title." Hold up a finger for each word you say. Ask, "How many words are in the title?" To check your students' accuracy, repeat the words in the title slowly, holding up one finger for each word. Call upon a different volunteer to use the pointer to touch each word in the title. Ask the student, "What helped you know where one word ended and the next word began?" If he or she can't recall the term *space*, ask the child to show you a space, and point out other spaces in the title.

✻ Remind your students of what they already know: "You showed me where we started reading: at the top of the page. In a poem, this top line is called the *title*. Then you showed me how to use the pointer to read each of the four words in the title." Use the pointer as you reread the title. Ask, "If I want to continue reading this poem all the way to the last line, who knows where I go after I have read the title? Show me with the pointer."

✷ Choose a capable volunteer to touch each word with the pointer as you and the class perform a final reading of the whole poem, from beginning to end. This is challenging, so be certain to choose a child who is willing to take this risk, and whose abilities make you fairly confident. Tell the student: "I'll support you when you begin by gently guiding your hand that holds the pointer. Just as your mom or dad supports you when you ride a two-wheeler for the first time, then lets go when she or he thinks you can do it by yourself, I'll support you as long as you need my help. And I'll let go when I think you can successfully touch and read each word."

❧ Reflection ❧

I keep my students engaged and eager, but I continue to reinforce the concepts we've worked on so far: directionality (e.g., top to bottom, left to right), return sweep, one-to-one matching, and the terms *space* and *title*. Since many of the children already memorized this poem, their reading was more fluent and expressive. I predict that our next poem "lunchbox" will become an old favorite poem that will be reread throughout the year.

LESSON FOUR
Prediction and Concept of a Word

> **lunchbox**
>
> They always
> End up
> Fighting—
>
> The soft
> Square
> Sandwich,
>
> The round
> Heavy
> Apple.
>
> *—Valerie Worth*

What I Was Thinking

I wanted to read a poem that contained very few words so that my students would experience success in voice-print matching. I also wanted my students to discover how a poet's choice of words enhances a poem's rhythm, and how the use of simple, descriptive vocabulary effectively creates a strong image. The poem "lunchbox" by Valerie Worth fit the bill.

Materials

The poem, "lunchbox" by Valerie Worth, printed neatly on manila tag chart paper attached by rings to a chart stand

What This Lesson Looks Like

✾ Introduce your students to the poem by reading its title. Use the pointer to sweep under the word from left to right as you read it aloud: "lunchbox."

✾ Invite your students to predict what they think this poem is about. Students may share their predictions with a partner or with the whole group. If you invite your students to share their predictions with a partner, tell them: "Use your 'whisper' voices. You must listen carefully when your partner is speaking, because you may be chosen to share your partner's predictions with all of us. When you and your partner have finished sharing, focus your eyes back on me, as a signal to me that you've finished sharing. A prediction is just a guess. We won't really know what the poem is about until we read it. But it's fun to guess, and good readers make predictions whenever they read. Now, turn to a neighbor and share your prediction." Allow a few minutes for children to share their predictions with their neighbors.

✾ Read the poem to your students. Use the pointer to touch each word. Focus on reading with inflection, and try to maintain the poem's rhythm. Be aware that touching each word can lead to a word-by-word intonation, which can stilt the fluency, making it difficult for children to comprehend the poet's meaning. If your pointing does affect your fluency, reread the poem again, but this time use the pointer to sweep across each line as you read it.

✿ After reading, discuss the meaning of the poem with your students. Ask, "What does this poem mean to you? What pictures came to mind as I read this poem aloud? What words did Valerie Worth use to describe the sandwich? What kind of sandwich do you think was in the lunchbox? What words did she use to describe the apple? Since she described the apple as heavy, do you think the apple was big or little? Did the apple or the sandwich win the fight? How do you know?" Invite your students to share their lunchbox stories.

✿ Explain, "I'm going to read aloud the poem one last time, and I welcome you to join in." Choose a student to come up to the chart to collaborate with you in pointing to the words in the poem as the class reads it aloud chorally. Remember to gently guide the student's hand with the pointer. As soon as you believe that he or she understands one-to-one matching, allow the child to use the pointer independently.

❧ Reflection ☙

The poem "lunchbox" was a big hit. As I read it aloud, I heard children giggle, because they clearly understood its meaning. It was delightful to hear them connect Worth's poem to their own lunchbox skirmishes; almost every student had a tale to relate. Since I want my students to develop a love of poetry, I capitalized on this moment by allowing extra sharing.

When I asked for a volunteer to lead the group by touching the words with the pointer, hands flew up enthusiastically. Children begged to have a turn. Each child selected to lead, masterfully pointed to each word they read. The brevity of the lines ensured success for even the most timid reader. I'm certain we'll return to this poem often and read it as an old favorite.

LESSON FIVE
Concept of a Word and Rebuilding a Poem

What I Was Thinking

I guessed the small poem "lunchbox" would be suitable to rebuild—that is, to cut apart and have the kindergartners reassemble, because there are so few words in each line on which to focus.

I also believed this activity would engage all my students because they'd be taking an active role in rebuilding the poem. It would help them to better understand the concept of word (i.e., a word is comprised of letters, and that for words to be the same they must contain the same letters in the same order).

Materials

Two sets of sentence strips, 10 strips per set (for the title and nine lines of the poem)

One black, one red, and one blue permanent marker

A large pocket chart (set up next to the chart stand displaying "lunchbox")

A 3" x 5" card with the words *lunch* and *box* printed in blue marker in large, neat, lowercase letters

A pair of scissors

> ☀ Use a black marker to write the title and each line of Worth's poem on the sentence strips of one set.

> ☀ Insert each black strip, in order, into the pocket chart.

> ☀ Use a red marker to write the title and each line of Worth's poem on the second set of sentence strips.

> ☀ Use a blue marker to print the words *lunch* and *box* in large, neat, lowercase letters on the 3" x 5" card.

What This Lesson Looks Like

> ☀ Explain to your students: "I've written each line of Worth's poem 'lunchbox' in black marker on strips and inserted them into this pocket

chart in the correct order." Point to the first sentence strip and reiterate: "This group of words written from left to right is called a *line*. How many lines are in this poem?" Count together. Then invite them to read the poem aloud with you from the chart as you point to each word.

- Hold up the second set of sentence strips. Tell them, "I've also written each line of the poem 'lunchbox' on these strips in red marker. I'll cut each sentence strip into word cards with your help. When all the words have been cut apart, we'll work together to rebuild the poem."
- Hold up the first red strip, which contains the title. Say, "Let's read the title of this poem together: 'lunchbox.' How many words did you read?" If someone responds, "Two," explain that he's partially right: "You *said* two words, but *lunchbox* is *written* as just one word. Look at the word: *lunchbox* is made up of these letters: *l-u-n-c-h-b-o-x*." Point to each letter as you spell aloud, and then sweep your hand under the word as you say *lunchbox*. "If it were written as two words, this is what it would look like." Hold up the word card with the words *lunch* and *box* written on it in blue. "This white space separates the two words, so we can tell where one word ends and another word begins."
- Explain: "I'll need your help to cut the red words apart. I'm going to move the blade tip of my scissors along the bottom of the strip. When the tip points to a space, shout, 'Cut!' " Dramatize the task to keep them completely engaged. When you have completed the cutting exercise, ask your students to count the number of words that were cut apart.
- Announce: "There are enough words for everyone to participate in rebuilding the poem. I'll shuffle the words before passing them out. Each student will be given one card. When you get your red card, try to find its match on a black strip so you'll be ready to place your card in the pocket chart. For example, I have a red word card with the letters *a, p, p, l, e*. Can anyone find the black word on the chart that matches these letters?" When someone is able to point to the correct word, check the student's accuracy by verifying that each letter is the same and that it is in the same sequence on each card, using both cards to check for the match (i.e., *a . . . a; p . . . p; p . . . p; l . . . l; e . . . e*). "That's right! The

letters in both words are exactly the same, so the word printed on my red card is the same word as the one that's on the black sentence strip."

✿ Explain: "I'll point to each word as I read the poem. When I touch and read the same word you have, hold up your card for me to see. If you're correct, I'll ask you to place your word card directly on top of the same word that's printed on the sentence strip in the pocket chart. I'll continue to read until everyone has found a match."

✿ Reread the poem in red as a whole group.

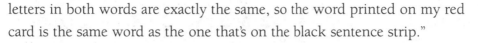

❦ Reflection ❦

My students loved participating in this activity, especially watching me sever the strips each time as they said, "Cut!" The volume of their voices strengthened until it reached a frenzied level. Although I had to caution the students to speak a bit softer, their enthusiasm remained until the last word was scissored off.

When we rebuilt the poem, most of my kids demonstrated good visual discrimination skills. They could easily match up the same words. However, I noticed many of them experienced difficulty identifying lowercase letters when we stopped to check the accuracy of their matches. I noted to myself that I needed to include more letter-recognition practice. I didn't want to drill my students, but I needed to find opportunities for incidental learning and take advantage of these moments.

When we came to the word *the* in the rebuilding of the poem, the two children who had this word held their cards up. As I always do, I became very dramatic and told them there was a problem because two children had the same word, and I had touched only one word. First, we checked their accuracy, and then we looked carefully at the poem for another *the*. They were so excited when they discovered the word *the* in a different location! That's when I decided that I would introduce our first high-frequency word: *the* during the next word study.

LESSON SIX
Word Concept Review and High-Frequency Words

What I Was Thinking

I knew my students were ready for high-frequency words, and they didn't need to know letter sounds to be successful in recognizing these words. They understood what a word was, and that's all they needed to begin. Learning high-frequency words would help them feel more successful, and it would allow them to attend to other clues to solve unfamiliar words they encountered in their reading.

Now that my students had experienced rebuilding a poem, I wanted an opportunity to observe their understanding of the print concepts we had explored together so far. To accomplish this, I thought that working in pairs would allow me a chance to observe, and it would give less capable students support whenever it was needed. I knew I had to make accurate decisions about the pairs of students who would work together. Then I remembered I had my color-coded checklist. Armed with this valuable information about my students, I'd be more likely to make better groupings—that is, I'd be able to match a more successful student with someone who required support.

Materials

Enough packets of words to the poem "lunchbox" for paired students. To make the packets:

* ❈ Type the poem "lunchbox" in red, Times New Roman font. Use the 22-point font size for the title and the nine lines of the poem.

* ❈ Make a color photocopy for each pair of students.

* ❈ Use a paper cutter to cut apart each word in the poem. (I cut one copy at a time to avoid confusion.)

* ❈ Gather the word cards for one copy of the poem and store them in a small manila envelope.

* ❈ Follow this procedure until you have enough packets for partners to use.

An additional photocopy of the poem for each student

A 3" x 5" card with the word *the* printed neatly in large lowercase letters

A list of your students, grouped into pairs (a capable student working with a less capable student)

The observation checklist and coded pens (green, yellow, and red)

What This Lesson Looks Like

✾ Show your students the word card *the*, and read it aloud. Tell them, "This word is found often in printed materials. It's a difficult word to read because it can't be sounded out. That's why it's called a *sight word*. You have to memorize this word by looking at it and seeing it in your mind. How many letters does the word *the* have? Let's say each letter as I point to it."

✾ Tell your students, "Scan the poem 'lunchbox' from top to bottom and left to right in search of the word *the*." Demonstrate how to scan the poem by sweeping the pointer across each line. "Please raise your hand when you've located *the*." Choose a student to point to the word. Give him or her the word card and say, "Match this word card up with the word in the poem." Ask, "Can you check your accuracy by naming each letter?" Assist whenever support is needed. Once the child has located the word, ask, "Can you read it aloud to the class? Remember to start at the beginning of the word and sweep across to the end of the word with your pointy finger as you say *the*." Ask, "Does anyone see *the* in a different place?" Repeat the same procedure with a different student.

✾ Read the poem again to the class. Say, "Look at how the poem is divided into three parts. Each part is called a *stanza*. I'm going to use my pointer to show all the lines in the first stanza, then the second stanza, and then the third stanza." After you've pointed out the three stanzas, divide the class into three groups for a rereading of the poem. Say, "The first group will read just the first stanza; the second group will read the second stanza, and the third group will patiently wait to read the last stanza by themselves." Before the reading, be certain they understand the directions. Ask: "Raise your hand if you are part of the first group . . . the second group . . . the third group. How much will each group read?" Tell your students: "I'll help you know when to read by calling out, 'First group, second group, third group.' Okay? As soon as I see everyone's eyes on the poem, we'll begin reading." When your students are focused, announce: "First group, begin reading."

☀ Next, tell the class: "Now you'll be working with partners to rebuild the poem 'lunchbox.' " Hold up a manila envelope of word cards for the class to see. "Inside each of these packets are all the words of the poem, typed in red." Then show them the photocopy of the poem. Say, "You'll work with a classmate to rebuild the poem just like we did yesterday, from the beginning to the end. You must take turns and help each other whenever help is requested. Allow your partner time to find the next word. Raise your hands when you've completed this activity so I can check your work, and then you'll read the poem to me one last time."

☀ Tell them, "Please find a personal space in the room to work with your partner." Then walk around the room and stop for a few minutes at each group to observe and offer assistance. Record your observations on the class checklist.

☀ When students have completed the rebuilding activity and have turned in their packets and poem sheets, give each of them a typed photocopy of the poem to illustrate and include in their poetry notebooks.

⋅ Reflection ⋅

It was interesting to see the different dynamics of the pairs. Some children needed to be reminded to take turns, while others had difficulty waiting for their partners to find a match. I wasn't too concerned because it was still early in the year, but sharing and waiting were two behaviors I would definitely need to address. Still, I was pleased with my student pair matchups. Without a doubt I'll continue to use my observation sheet whenever we work on reading skills.

This activity allowed me an opportunity to interact personally with each child and to record my observations of their understandings. Most of my students could voice-print match with very little support from me by this point. Next, they needed to develop their knowledge of letters and sounds.

LESSON SEVEN

Introduction to Lowercase Letters and CVC Patterns

> **Big**
>
> Now I can catch and throw a ball
> And spell
> Cat, Dog,
> And Pig.
> I have finished being small
> And started
> Being Big.
>
> —*Dorothy Aldis*

What I Was Thinking

To reinforce my students' new skills, I wanted to find a short rhyming poem that contained some repeating words and was one with which they could identify. I was drawn to Aldis's poem because of its simple, meaningful language and brevity.

My previous teaching experience has taught me that while some children enter kindergarten with the ability to spell simple words such as *cat* and *dog*, they capitalize all of the letters when they write the words. I believed that these students would be able to read the words independently *if* they could recognize *cat* and *dog* printed in lowercase. I wondered: "Would someone in this class who already knows the correct spelling be able to recognize these words with only the first letter capitalized?" I imagined the child's face lighting up when he or she located and read them aloud. What an easy way to build self-confidence!

Moreover, I felt that kindergartners would be able to identify with the child's declaration in the poem of "Being Big." When children start school, they perceive themselves differently; they're no longer the babies who went to preschool, but the "big" kids who now go to "big" school.

I knew I had a keeper: a perfect poem for kindergartners to read aloud in the early weeks of *big* school!

Materials

The poem "Big" by Dorothy Aldis, printed neatly on manila tag chart paper attached to the chart stand

What This Lesson Looks Like

- Stand next to the chart stand displayed with the poem "Big," face your students, and remind them: "When I see everybody's eyes focused on me, I'll tell you about the new poem."

- Explain: "Today I want you to listen carefully as I recite this poem. Be prepared to discuss why I thought you'd be able to easily relate to it."

- Recite the poem with feeling.

- Discuss the poem's meaning with your students: "Why does the child feel big? In Dorothy Aldis's poem, the child proudly name some of his or her accomplishments. What can the child do? Can you spell words or catch a ball well? What else can you do now that you couldn't do last year? Do you feel 'big' now that you have started kindergarten? Do you feel that preschoolers are little compared to you?"

- Reread the poem. Choose a student to use the pointer to touch each word as you say it.

- Invite students to join in for the final reading of the poem: "This time, I'd like you to read with me. Please keep your eyes focused on the pointer so we can read in one big voice."

❧ Reflection ❧

I was right! There were a few children who were able to read the words *cat* and *dog* independently. And then there was Carter, who could read easy words and decode simple consonant-vowel-consonant (CVC) pattern words. He spiced up the lesson when he raised his hand to announce that he knew how to read other words in the poem. I gave him the pointer and he began by touching and reading *I* and *a*. Then he explained to his classmates and to me how he had figured out the word *pig*. "I just sounded it out, like this: /p/ /i/ /g/." Some of his classmates looked perplexed, so I used this teachable moment to explain letter-sound correspondences and how sometimes we can use this knowledge to figure out words we don't know by blending the sounds of each letter in sequential order.

Carter's demonstration gave me more insight about my future lessons. As we identified different letters within the context of the poem, I could emphasize the sound associated with each letter. And then I'd blend the sounds in the words for the class to identify. Some of my students were ready for this next step, but those children who were not yet ready would at least be exposed to this new skill. And sooner or later, through continual practice, the light would come on for them, too.

Thoroughly discussing the meaning of the poem and introducing the words *cat, dog,* and *pig* early in the lesson helped the children comprehend the text more easily and read the words more fluently.

LESSON EIGHT
Capital-Letter Identification

What I Was Thinking

The small number of capital letters in the poem "Big" would keep my students focused during the reading activity. In addition, since it takes some time to distinguish letters, I didn't want to highlight too many letters at once.

Materials

A 24" x 36" piece of heavyweight 4-mil plastic sheeting, two-hole-punched at the top and attached to the chart stand as a protective cover to the poem "Big"

A package of different-colored Vis-à-Vis pens

What This Lesson Looks Like

* Gather students in the designated chart area. Tell them, "Today we'll read 'Big' again." Review yesterday's lesson by asking, "What was this poem about?"

✽ Then ask, "Do you remember the two words we found: *cat* and *dog*? Can someone find one of these words in the poem? Please use the pointer to sweep across the word as you read it. How many letters are in the word? Please touch each letter as you count aloud. Now, go back to the beginning of the word and name each letter as you touch it with your pointer." If the student needs support, ask the class to say the letter aloud. But first instruct them: "Keep your lips zipped until I say, 'Audience.' We need to give your classmate time to think." Repeat the same procedure for finding the second word, i.e., *cat* or *dog*.

✽ Reread the poem aloud chorally as you point to each word.

✽ Begin the new lesson by giving your students an opportunity to demonstrate their knowledge of letter names. "Today you're going on a letter hunt. First, I'd like you to find one letter you already know. I'm going to give you a moment to locate a letter you'd like to share with the class." After a few minutes, ask: "Does anybody need more time?" Allow another minute for those children who need additional time to explore the chart. If some children are still struggling, it's a strong indicator they don't know their letters yet. However, they still can be successful during the whip-around by naming the same letter a classmate identified. Explain to your students, "We're going to whip around the class, beginning with the children in the front row and ending with the children in the last row." Point to the child in the first row who will begin. Then, with a sweeping motion, make a zigzag line until you reach the last child in the row. "Keep your eyes on the letter you want to identify so you'll be able to point to it quickly. If you're ready, it won't take us very long for everyone to take a turn. And it's okay if someone else identifies the same letter you found." I've discovered that a more capable child will choose a different letter to identify if his or her first choice has already been shared. If the same letter is identified again and again, it usually means that the whole class doesn't know many letters. And you'll recognize immediately if letter recognition needs to be strengthened. At the end of this activity, acknowledge your students' success in the areas of the lesson that went well (e.g., following directions, being calm and focused, and/or identifying letters).

Note: Be honest with your praise. Children are aware of their strengths and weaknesses, so if the praise isn't genuine, they won't believe you, and their trust in you will diminish.

☼ Explain, "Some of you identified capital letters, while others identified lowercase letters. Capital letters are the big letters. We use capital letters at the beginning of names, at the beginning of sentences, and at the beginning of important words in titles of poems and books. Who sees a capital letter?" Choose a few volunteers to locate and name different capital letters in the poem. Prompt them as needed by saying, "I see a capital letter in this line," then sweep your hand across that line.

☼ Announce, "I notice that some of the words in the poem start with the same capital letter as some of your names. Please raise your hand if you see the first letter of your name."

☼ Choose a child whose name begins with one of the capital letters in the poem. "Please point to the capital letter that starts your name and tell us its name." Reinforce the name of the letter: "You're right. Your name does begin with a [letter name]. Both [name of child] and [word] start with the letter [letter name]."

☼ Repeat the student's name and the word he or she found, but this time, emphasize the beginning sound of each word as you say it. "And they both have the same sound. Listen as I say them again. The letter [name of letter] says [sound of letter]."

☼ Tell that student to choose a colored pen to circle the capital letter on the plastic sheet. If the same capital is located at the beginning of another word, choose someone else to name the letter, and circle it in the same color.

☼ Follow this procedure for all students whose names start with the capital letters found at the beginnings of printed words in the poem. Help children to choose different colors for different letters.

☼ Review the circled capital letters by associating the classmate's name with the letter. Direct the children to name each letter as you touch it with the pointer. As each letter is identified, say: "[Name of letter] is the first letter of [name of child]'s name."

LESSON NINE

Letter Identification and Sound Association, Capital-Letter Review, and New Sight Words

What I Was Thinking

I had several ideas for follow-up lessons on letter recognition. For the first lesson I wanted my students to be engaged throughout, and I knew a hands-on activity using magnetic letters would do the trick. I thought children would be intrigued by them.

Additionally, I believed the word *and* would be a logical choice for a new high-frequency word, since *and* is repeated several times in the poem "Big." I also decided to focus on the words *a* and *I*, because I could strongly reinforce the distinction between letters and words within a meaningful context.

Materials

Five plastic magnetic capital letters: *A, B, C, D,* and *P*

Five jumbo craft sticks (so you can glue a different magnetic letter to the end of each craft stick)

Three 3" x 5" cards with *and, I,* and, *a* printed in large letters

What This Lesson Looks Like

☀ Before rereading the poem, ask your students: "What's the title of our new poem? Let's name the letters in 'Big' as I point to them: *B-i-g*. Can you find this word in a different line? That's right. *Big* is the last word in the last line. Notice that this word begins with a capital letter. Why do think the author of this poem decided to do this?" If no one has an idea, tell your class: "Maybe she wants a big letter on this word because it's a very important word to the child in the poem."

✿ Invite your students to read the poem aloud with you. Remind them to read with feeling.

✿ Say, "Yesterday, you circled all the capital letters in the poem. There were five capital letters in all." Hold up a craft stick attached with the magnetic letter *A*, and say: "There was capital *A* . . ." and follow with the remaining capital letters in alphabetical order, (i.e., *B, C, D,* and ending with *P*). Be sure to repeat the phrase *there was* each time you hold up a stick.

✿ Hold up the sticks and say, "I'm going to mix up the sticks so they'll be in a different order. Now, let's say the name of the letter as I hold each of them up. If you're unsure of its name, I want you to listen to your classmates. If you know it, I want to hear you name it. Let's try to say the letter names in one big voice."

✿ Explain, "We've just reviewed the letter names by saying them together. Now I want five of you to have a chance to match a plastic letter with the same letter in a word on the chart paper poem." Pass out the craft sticks to five capable children. Remember to check off the names of students who participated in this activity. Tell them, "I want you to match your plastic letter with the same letter in print." When a child makes a correct match, ask, "What's this capital letter's name?" Then say, "Listen as I say the word you found. Listen especially to the beginning sound. Be ready to tell me the sound of this letter." Emphasize the beginning sound as you say the word the student found as you sweep your hand across it. Ask the student, "What sound did you hear at the beginning of the word?" Explain, "The letter [name of letter] makes the [sound] sound." Follow this process with the remaining four students.

✿ Check the child's name off the checklist using the coded system previously explained.

✹ Show your students the word card for *and*, and read it aloud. Tell them, "This word is found frequently in books. That's why it's called a *high-frequency word*. How many letters make up the word *and*? Let's say each letter as I point to it. The word *and* can be sounded out. Listen as I blend the sounds: /a/ /n/ /d/." Point to each letter as you make its sound. "Since *and* is found so often in print, I want you to be able to read the word *and* and say, 'Just like that [snap your fingers]!' "

✹ Direct your students: "Scan the poem from top to bottom and left to right in search of the word *and*." Demonstrate how to scan the poem by sweeping the pointer across each line. "Please raise your hand when you've located *and*." Choose a student to point to the word. Give him or her the word card to match up with the word in the poem, and ask, "Can you check your accuracy by naming each letter?" Assist whenever support is needed. Once the student has located the word, ask, "Can you read it aloud to the class? Remember to start at the beginning of the word and sweep across to the end of the word with your pointy finger as you say *and*." Ask, "Does anyone see *and* in a different place?" Repeat the same procedure with a different student.

✹ Tell them, "I chose two more high-frequency words for you to learn. Many of you will be able to read these words because you first learned them as single letters." Hold up the word card *I*. "If you know this word, please read it aloud."

✹ Ask your students to scan the lines of the poem for the word *I*. Give the word card to a volunteer who has located the word *I*, and say: "Match this word to the same word on the chart. Does anyone see *I* in a different place?" Repeat the same procedure with a different student.

✹ Ask, "What helps you know that this is the *word I* and not the *letter I*? If the student is unable to explain the reason, point out the space before *I* and the space after it. Explain: "Spaces separate *words*. A word is made up of letters. There are no big white spaces between the letters of a word."

✹ Follow the same procedure for the word *a*.

☙ Reflection ❧

The five children who participated in the letter-matching activity enjoyed the experience so much that their classmates expressed disappointment when we moved on to the next part of the lesson. I had to remind them that we wouldn't have time to participate in other fun activities if we took time to allow everyone to have a turn. Since I had made a promise they'd all get a turn eventually, I had to remember to begin the next lesson with a review of this hands-on matching.

I saw puzzled looks from some students when the words *a* and *I* were introduced as high-frequency words. It was obvious they hadn't grasped the difference between a letter and a word, and I knew by their apparent confusion this issue needed to be resolved before I moved on to a different skill.

LESSON TEN

Capital Letters and Their Lowercase Counterparts, Plus Review of High-Frequency Words

What I Was Thinking

When I studied the poem "Big" for another possible lesson, I noticed the lowercase letter partners for the capital letters we had discussed. And I knew it wouldn't be too difficult to design more lessons on letter identification if my students needed more practice to master this skill. Using a variety of these interactive learning experiences would facilitate students' recognition of letters.

Materials

Five plastic magnetic lowercase letters: *a, b, c, d,* and *p*

Five jumbo craft sticks (so you can glue one magnetic letter to one end of each craft stick)

Card set of previously introduced high-frequency words: *a, and, I,* and *the.*

The five plastic magnetic uppercase letters attached to craft sticks, from the previous lesson

Plastic sheeting, scrubbed clean

What This Lesson Looks Like

☼ Reread the poem "Big" aloud chorally pointing to each word as you say it. Ask: "Would someone like to come up and read the poem aloud to the class?" Hand the pointer to the student and say, "Please touch each word as you say it." Remind the class about audience behavior and wait time: "You are the listeners. Please focus on your classmate, zip your lips, and listen to him or her read 'Big.' If he or she forgets a word, please keep your lips zipped until I say, 'Audience'. And then, if you know the word, you may say it aloud. But first, let's allow your classmate time to think."

☼ Review the set of high-frequency words: ask your students to read the word aloud as you hold up a card. Then invite them to search for the same word in the poem: "Show me with your eyes that you know where this word can be found in the poem." Choose a student whose eyes appear to be focused on the appropriate location to point to the word on the chart. "Place the word card below the word you found to see if it's the same word." Repeat this process for the other high-frequency words.

☼ Explain to your students, "Yesterday we studied five capital letters: *A, B, C, D,* and *P*." Hold up each craft stick attached to a capital magnetic letter and direct your students to say its name if they know it. "If you aren't sure, I want you to listen to its name as your classmates say it." After the name of the letter is given, direct them: "Make its sound."

☼ Announce: "I'm going to pass out these craft sticks to five different children today. If you receive a stick, please find a matching capital letter printed at the beginning of a word in the poem." When a child makes a correct match, ask, "What's this capital letter's name?" After each child has finished matching and naming the letter, request, "Please give me your craft stick and take your seat."

☼ Check off the child's name using the coded system previously explained.

☼ After all five capital letters have been matched up, explain to your students: "Lowercase letters are important to know because printed language is mainly written with lowercase letters." Hold up the new group of sticks as you say: "Today's lesson will focus on the lowercase counterparts for these capital letters. That means that both the capital and the lowercase letter have the same name."

☼ Explain: "Some capital and lowercase letters look the same, except for their size." Hold up the stick attached with the capital letter *C*. "Tell me its name." Then hold up the lowercase *c*. "I bet you know this letter's name. That's right! It's the lowercase *c*." Call upon a volunteer to first locate the capital *C* and then its lowercase counterpart in the poem. Ask the student, "Would you choose a pen from the package and circle both the capital and lowercase letters with that same color each time you see them?"

❉ Follow the same procedure for the capital *P* with another volunteer. But when the student locates the lowercase *p*, ask a new question: "The capital *P* and the lowercase *p* look the same except for what?"

❉ Then explain: "Capital letters sometimes differ from their lowercase counterparts in size *and* in shape." Show your students the stick attached to the plastic capital *A*. "Name this letter. Now I'll show you the lowercase letter *a*." Hold one stick in one hand and the second stick in your other hand so the children are able to see the shapes of both letters clearly. "What kinds of lines form the capital *A*? What kinds of lines form the lowercase *a*?"

❉ Call upon a third volunteer to choose a colored pen that has not yet been used to find and circle all the examples of the capital *A* in the poem. Each time an *A* is circled, the student should say its name aloud: "Capital *A*." After the final *A*, ask the student to find a lowercase *a* to circle. "As you can see, there are many lowercase *a*'s to circle. I'd like other children to have a turn to find some. Thank you for finding the first lowercase *a*. Your classmates can refer back to the lowercase *a* you circled if they don't know what it looks like." Choose a different student to circle as many as she or he sees. Remind the class: "Search the poem for every *a*, because if your classmate misses any, you may know where they are. And if you do, you'll be given the chance to identify them." Follow this procedure for the lowercase *b* and *d*.

❧ Reflection ❧

Although this lesson allowed many students an opportunity to participate, I knew they'd need many different interactive experiences with letters to ensure mastery of this skill. I wasn't concerned about maintaining my students' enthusiasm and focus because my comprehensive literacy program would allow a variety of learning experiences to target specific letters and sounds in different settings. By including a quick activity during Class Message, Special Person Exercise, Reading Workshop, Writing Workshop, and Activity Time, as well as during Poetry Time, all my students would be able to develop proficiency with letters and sounds. I just had to remind myself to be patient; it takes time and continuous practice for children to develop these skills.

LESSON ELEVEN

Savoring "Rich Words"

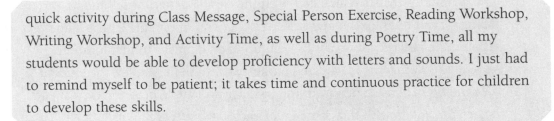

Apple Joys

Twirling the star-shaped stem
Biting into the ruddy globe
Sliding out the satin seeds

—*Eve Merriam*

What I Was Thinking

After we took a trip to a local orchard to pick apples, I looked for and located a poem by Eve Merriam about apples in CTL's extensive poetry collection. This poem appealed to me because of its diction. Exposure to and interaction with rich language enriches children's vocabularies, which in turn facilitates their reading. I liked the words *ruddy, globe,* and *satin* to describe an apple, but I knew some children wouldn't understand the meaning of these words, and even for those who did, they wouldn't use the words in their daily conversations. It seemed a perfect place to start to build vocabulary.

I decided to begin by introducing *ruddy, globe,* and *satin* as new vocabulary, even before reading the poem aloud. I would use the picture of a ruddy-faced person; a world globe; and a piece of satin cloth to pass around for children to touch so that they had many "senses" of the word. I wanted to teach my students more than the meaning of these words. I also wanted to help them appreciate the vivid imagery of poetry by bringing their attention to the rich words Merriam chose to use to describe the apple.

Now that I was ready to present the poem, how would I pull the children in? Then I noticed the three lines were like clues to a riddle. All children like riddles, so, why not present the form as a riddle? I'd cover the word *apple* in the title of the poem, and they'd have to figure out the object Merriam is describing by listening to her words. Then I'd show them a real apple and use it to demonstrate the action within the poem, such as twirling the stem, biting into the apple, and sliding out the seeds, as I read it aloud. I hoped these techniques would increase my students' enthusiasm and motivation to pay close attention to each word.

Materials

The poem "Apple Joys" by Eve Merriam, handwritten in large, neat print on manila tag chart paper attached by rings to a wooden chart stand

   ❈ Completely cover the word *Apple* in the title with a double-thick sticky note to prevent the print from being legible.

A poster titled "Rich Words"

   ❈ Trace the letters in the title of "Rich Words" with Elmer's glue.

   ❈ Then, sprinkle with gold glitter.

A red apple

A world globe

A small piece of satin fabric or ribbon

A photo of a person with a ruddy complexion

Sticky notes

Highlighting tape

Gold glitter

What This Lesson Looks Like

   ❈ Ask your students, "What do you notice about the title of the new poem?" Then follow with: "That's right! I've covered the first word with a sticky note. I thought it would be fun to be detectives and use clues from Eve Merriam's poem to figure out what the object is that she describes so well in her poem."

✿ "Before I read her poem, I want to discuss the meaning of some words that may be unfamiliar." Begin by highlighting the word *ruddy* with highlighting tape. Ask, "Does anyone know what *ruddy* means?" If no one raises a hand, give the definition. "*Ruddy* means 'reddish in color.' For example, somebody may have a ruddy complexion." Show a photo of a person with a ruddy complexion. "This person's face is reddish in color. You can remember that ruddy means red by making a connection between the words *red* and *ruddy*. Both words begin with the letter *r* and say /r/ at the beginning. Listen as I say these words: *r-r-ed* and *r-r-uddy*. Now you have your first clue. What does *ruddy* mean?"

✿ Highlight the word *globe* with the highlighting tape. Ask, "Have you ever seen a globe of the Earth?" If someone responds affirmatively, ask: "What shape is a globe?" Hold up a world globe as you explain: "A globe is anything that is somewhat rounded. For example, a lightbulb is a globe. Can you think of any other objects that are globes? Hmm, possibly another clue for you!"

✿ Highlight the last word, *satin*, with the highlighting tape. Ask, "Do you know what satin is? I'll give you a little clue: it's a fabric, a type of cloth. What does it feel like? Some girls may know because they may own a satin party dress." Allow students to respond with their ideas. If no one responds correctly, explain: "Satin is a silky material that's smooth and shiny." Hold up a piece of satin and run your fingers along its surface as you define the term. "Let's do a 1-2-3 pass with this piece of satin so each of you can feel how smooth this fabric is. A 1-2-3 pass is a short turn. Please pass it to your neighbor as soon as you have stroked the fabric so we can continue our lesson."

✿ Explain: "Each line of Eve Merriam's poem will give you a clue to solve the mystery of the unknown object. Her choice of words will create a picture in your mind. So listen carefully as I read the poem aloud. I'll begin when I see everybody's eyes on me."

✿ Read the poem with a deliberate pace and with emphasis on the word *stem* and the phrases *ruddy globe* and *satin seeds*. After reading the poem, ask, "Can anyone guess the object she describes so well in her poem?" If someone responds correctly, ask, "What words helped you know it was an apple?" If no one knows, point out the three phrases: *star-shaped stem*, *ruddy globe*, and *satin seeds*. "What's red and round, has a stem and smooth, shiny seeds?" As you respond with the word *apple*, remove the sticky note from the title to reveal *apple*.

❈ Hold up a red apple for the class to see. "I'm going to act out each line as I read the poem aloud. Listen and watch."

❈ After the second reading of the poem, ask, "What was I doing first?" Point to the word *twirling*. "Then I was . . ." Point to the word *biting* as they respond. "What did I act out in the last line?" Point to the word *sliding*.

❈ Tell them, "Eve Merriam beautifully describes from beginning to end what she does with an apple. She uses some rich words in her poem. I'd like to begin a list of interesting words we find in the poems we read. Today we talked about three interesting words. Can you tell me one of the words?"

❈ When a child names one of the new vocabulary words, print it neatly on the poster, naming each letter you write. Follow this process with the remaining two words. "Let's read these words together." Sweep your finger across the words as you say them.

❧ Reflection ☙

Using manipulatives to introduce the new vocabulary helped my students grasp the meaning of these new words, and the dramatic presentation of the initial reading of the poem added another dimension of comprehension—finding meaning in action. My students loved being able to look at the photo, spin the globe, and feel the satin cloth, as well as watch me act out each line of the poem.

When I found this poem, I realized it was a meaty one to use, but I was concerned my students would lose interest in the reading of the poem because of the unfamiliar vocabulary that would most likely hinder their comprehension. But I'm so glad I decided to go the extra mile in planning this lesson, because I wanted my students to experience a poem with such richness within just three lines. If I hadn't designed a sensory lesson, my students' understanding would be minimal at best. The sensory experience helped them understand and remember the words. Through these techniques, they were able to see how each word worked in context. By allowing my students to make sense of the words in different situations, they'll be able to apply their knowledge of this vocabulary in their reading. As a result, their reading comprehension will be strengthened.

Although I put a lot of thought into planning this lesson, it was well worth the effort and time. The lesson was effective, and I accomplished what I set out to do: make learning engaging.

LESSON TWELVE
Location of a Target Letter in a Word: <u>S</u>/<u>s</u>

What I Was Thinking

I knew I wanted to target another letter, but I wasn't sure which one would be appropriate until I studied the letters and words in Merriam's poem. Her use of alliteration made the next letter to be targeted an obvious choice—the letter *s*, both uppercase and lowercase. Then I noticed that the letter *s* was at the beginning of some words and at the end of others. That revelation confirmed my decision to use this letter because identifying it would give my students more practice in recognizing where a word begins and ends.

To distinguish the beginning of a word from the ending of a word, I decided to have students circle the letter in green if it was at the beginning of the word and in red if it was at the end of a word. To emphasize this difference I'd use the metaphor of a traffic light—green means "go" or "start," and red means "stop" or "end." Describing the function of a traffic light and relating it to a printed word would help in understanding the concept of a word. The use of green and red creates an effective visual aid because it helps to differentiate the beginning letter of a word from the ending letter.

Materials

Plastic sheeting to attach over the poem "Apple Joys"

One red and one green Vis-à-Vis pen

A plastic magnetic capital letter *S*

Every Child a Reader

"Rich Words" poster

A plastic magnetic lowercase letter *s*

Two jumbo craft sticks (to glue one magnetic letter to one end of each craft stick)

What This Lesson Looks Like

❈ Reread the poem "Apple Joys" aloud to your students. After, discuss the new vocabulary words: *ruddy, globe,* and *satin.* "Yesterday you learned the meaning of some words that were unfamiliar to you. Who remembers what the word *ruddy* means? How did the poet use this word in the poem?" Use the same format to review the vocabulary words *globe* and *satin.*

❈ Point to these words on the "Rich Words" poster. Say, "Let's read these words aloud. When I point to a word, I want you to read it if you know it. If you don't know the word yet, please remember to listen to the word being read aloud by your classmates." After a word is read, ask, "Who sees it in the poem?" Choose a volunteer to point to the word, read it aloud, and name the letters in the word. Give support as needed with the letter identification.

❈ Introduce the term *alliteration*: "Eve Merriam used alliteration in her poem 'Apple Joys.' Alliteration is a poetic device used by poets and authors to make particular words stand out by writing many words in a line that start with the same consonant letter sound. The alliterative words Merriam uses in her poem begin with this letter." Hold up the capital *S* and ask: "Who knows the name of this letter?" Then hold up the lowercase *s* and explain: "The lowercase *s* looks exactly the same. It's just smaller."

❈ Discuss the shape of the letter *s*. Then say, "It looks like a slithering snake. The words *slithering snake* both begin with the letter *s*. Listen again as I say these words." Emphasize the beginning sound in each word as you say it. Then ask, "What sound did you hear at the beginning of these words?"

❈ Explain to your students: "Today you're going to find the letter *s*. If the *s* is at the beginning of a word, I'd like you to make a circle around it in green ink. If the letter *s* is at the end of a word, I'd like you to make a circle around it in red ink. There's a reason I chose the colors red and green. Just as a green light signals a driver to go and a red light signals the driver to stop, the reader starts from the first letter and stops at the last letter in a word. Green means go—you're at the beginning of a word. Red means stop—you're at the end of the word."

☀ Review how a space will help them know if they are at the start of a word or the end of the word. Point to the letter *b*. Direct your students to raise a hand if they know the letter's name. Ask a student who responded with the correct answer: "Is the *b* at the beginning or at the end of the word? How do you know?" Remind your students we read left to right across a line. Use your pointer to sweep across the line. Then point to the space that comes before the word. "A big white space *before* the letter helps the reader know it's the start of a word. The reader knows the word has ended because there is a big white space *after* the last letter. I'm going to move the pointer slowly across the word *biting*. When I reach the last letter in the word, tell me to stop. Watch for the big white space that comes after the last letter in a word, because it indicates that you've come to the end of the word."

☀ Tell your students to raise their hands when they find either an uppercase *S* or its lowercase counterpart in the poem. Choose a capable student to point to the letter. Ask: "Where is the *s* located in the word?" Ask the student to explain his or her response: "How do you know?" Restate the student's answer by thinking out loud. As you explain, move the pointer across the line until you reach the word that contains the letter *s*. "The letter *s* is at the beginning of the word because there is a space *before* the *s*, or the letter *s* is the last letter in the word because there is a big white space *after* the *s*." As you emphasize the word *before* or *after*, point to that particular space with the pointer. Show your students that the pointer moves back to demonstrate *before*, and moves ahead to demonstrate *after*. Tell them: "*Back* and *before* both begin with the same sound: *b*. If your finger moves *back* to touch the space, you know that the space comes *before* the word." Invite the student to circle the letter in the appropriate color. Continue with the explicit modeling with two or three more volunteers. Then, model only when the student is unable to respond.

☀ Comment: "I see many green circles. That tells me there are several words that begin with the /s/ sound." Ask, "In which lines do you see words beginning with the letter *S*?" When a specific line is identified, point and read the *S* words aloud. After the *S* words in both lines have been read aloud, ask: "Does anybody remember the name for the sound technique the poet used to make particular words stand out?" If no one responds, try prompting with the first few letters: "Alli . . ."

❧ Reflection ❧

Every year there are children who confuse the positional words *before* and *after*, and this year was no different. However, by the end of the lesson, most of my students could easily differentiate the beginning of a word from the end of the word, and they were able to explain why they used green or red to circle the letters they found.

I'm glad I decided to reinforce the concept of a word because during the lesson, I watched many children ponder the question I asked about the location of the letter. Although most of them answered correctly, they needed a lot of wait time before responding. Their hesitation demonstrated to me they did not yet have control of this concept.

The different teaching strategies helped all my students gain more insight about the printed word. The children especially enjoyed the traffic light analogy because it made sense to them. For some children who were visual learners, the color-coded circles alleviated their confusion because it clearly defined the beginning letter and the last letter. For some other students who were aural learners, the continual repetition of hearing me think aloud was effective. And I have to admit, I can't think of a better way to enhance my students' understanding of the meaning of alliteration than by including alliterative language (*slithering snake; before* and *back*) as teaching cues.

OCTOBER

LESSON ONE

Introduction of a New Sight Word

> ## My Favorite Word
>
> There is one word—
> My favorite—
> The very, very best.
> It isn't NO or Maybe
> It's Yes, Yes, Yes, *Yes*, YES!
> "Yes, yes, you may," and
> "Yes, of course," and
> "Yes, please help yourself."
> And when I want a piece of cake,
> "Why, yes. It's on the shelf."
> Some candy? "Yes."
> A cookie? "Yes."
> A movie? "Yes, we'll go."
> I love it when they say my word:
> *Yes, Yes, YES!* (*Not No.*)
>
> —*Lucia and James L. Hymes, Jr.*

What I Was Thinking

One afternoon, Nancie Atwell noticed me at my desk browsing through a pile of poetry books in search of a good poem. She asked me if I knew "My Favorite Word" by Lucia and James L. Hymes, Jr. I remember thinking, "I know my favorite word when I teach." That word is *yes*.

Throughout the year I try to instill self-confidence by referring to a banner that hangs in our classroom that reads, "You never know what you can do until you try."

Every Child a Reader

Any time I encourage students to be risk-takers, they know I want to hear the word *yes*: "Yes, I'll try" or "Yes, I can." The word *no* is a forbidden word in my classroom.

When I heard Nancie recite the first few lines of the poem, I knew my students would immediately think of my philosophy. But I also knew they'd soon recognize it's the voice of a child. More importantly, they would be able to make a personal connection with this poem. I envisioned a lengthy discussion about requests they'd like to have affirmed by their parents.

Although the poem was fairly long, I still wanted to give it a try, because I knew it had definite "kid appeal" and it would be a fun poem to read aloud. Because of its length, we'd probably have to spend two or three days focused just on the reading. When children like a poem, they'll read it again and again until they know it by heart, as Nancie had learned it along with her daughter. That's what I predicted would happen with this one. I could imagine hearing the excitement in my students' voices resound with every "Yes!"

Materials

The poem "My Favorite Word" by Lucia and James L. Hymes, Jr., handwritten in large, neat print on manila tag chart paper attached by rings to a wooden chart stand

A 3" x 5" card with *yes* printed neatly in large lowercase letters

What This Lesson Looks Like

✿ Loosely fold up the bottom edge of the chart paper so all the lines of the poem are covered except for the title. Say, "I don't want you to see any of the words in the poem." Then read the title aloud, and say, "I'm covering the words because I want you to make a prediction. What could possibly be the speaker's favorite word?" After a few guesses have been made, give a few clues: "This word has three letters. It begins with the letter *y*. And it's *my* favorite word."

✿ Hold up the card printed with *yes* and tell them: "It's the word *yes*." Point to each letter as you say its name. "Y-e-s." Invite your class: "Now let's spell *yes* together: y-e-s. As I point to a letter, please say its name." Tell them, "My favorite word is *yes*, too, because when I ask you to attempt something new, I like to hear you say, 'Yes, I'll try.' I don't like hearing the words 'No, I don't want to,' because trying is what growing is all about."

✿ Tell your students: "I see the word *yes* in several lines. I'd like you to find a line that contains the word *yes*. Please put your hands on top of your head as soon as you see the word *yes* in a line, and focus on that word so you can find it quickly if you're asked." When many children signal that they have identified the word *yes* in one line, choose a volunteer to match the card with the printed word in the poem. Direct the student to confirm that it's the same word by cross-checking the card with the printed word. Then ask the student: "Is the word *yes* written again in this line? If it is, please point to it and read the word aloud each time you see it in the line." Follow the same procedure with other students who have located different lines containing the word *yes*.

✿ Prepare students for the reading of the poem: "I want you to listen carefully to the poem. Is it a child or a grown-up whose favorite word is *yes*? Be prepared to justify your choice by giving specific information from the poem."

✿ Read the poem aloud with feeling.

✿ After the reading, repeat the question: "Is it a child or a grown-up whose favorite word is *yes*? How do you know?" Elaborate on the students' response with these questions if needed: "There is conversation between the child and someone else. Who is that person? What did the child ask for? How did the parent respond to the requests? Would your mom or dad say 'yes' to those same requests?"

✿ Discuss requests they'd like to have affirmed by their parents. "Tell me something you *know* your parents would never allow you to do or have, and just for fun, I'll pretend to be your mom and respond positively to your request."

✿ Explain to the class, "You're going to help me reread this poem. But you don't have to worry about not knowing all the words. The only word you have to know is this one." Hold up the word card printed with *yes*. "I'm going to read most of the poem, but each time my pointer touches the word *yes*, I'll stop reading and you'll read that word by yourselves. Follow along with your eyes, so you'll be ready to read aloud the word *yes* each time I touch it with my pointer. Are there any questions?"

✿ Reread the poem with feeling. Students will chime in each time you stop at the word *yes*.

❧ Reflection ❧

When I think back to this lesson, I can't help but smile because it was such a fun time for the children—and for me, too! Throughout the lesson, I witnessed complete engagement, active participation, and genuine enthusiasm. There was minimal pressure on the children to perform; I just wanted them to have fun with this poem. It was a rather lengthy one to introduce at this time of the year, so I knew I couldn't be too demanding and expect too much too soon.

If my students could make a personal connection with this poem, and if they spent more time rereading it, I believed they could learn the words. They definitely connected with this poem, so for the next few lessons, the focus would be on learning the words.

LESSON TWO

Sight Vocabulary Practice, Introduction of a New Sight Word, Echo Reading

What I Was Thinking

When I scanned "My Favorite Word" I noticed that all the sight words I had previously introduced to the class were used and repeated throughout the poem. Knowing that children need continual practice with sight words to be able to recognize them with automaticity, I thought "My Favorite Word" would be ideal to use to reinforce their sight recognition skills. By circling the sight words, they would see how frequently these words occur in print.

But the question was: How could I best help my students learn the words without frustrating them in the process? I considered that echo reading might be the answer. To echo read, I'd read a line first and ask my students to repeat that line immediately afterward. After rehearsing this technique in my mind, however, I realized that echoing all the lines in the poem would be too tedious and would affect my students' enthusiasm and focus. This poem was too good to allow that to happen.

Now the question was: How much of the poem *should* they echo read?

Then as I reread it, I could hear the strong rhythm of the first five lines and knew that these lines could be easily learned. Breaking the poem into manageable chunks would be more effective and enhance understanding, but it would require me to design more lessons. Since I knew my students would benefit from this additional oral reading experience, it would be time well spent.

Materials

A 3" x 5" card with the word *no* printed neatly in large lowercase letters

Plastic sheeting to place over "My Favorite Word"

Sight-word cards: *and, I, a, the, yes*

Vis-à-Vis pens

What This Lesson Looks Like

☼ Reread the poem "My Favorite Word" in an animated voice.

☼ Choose a student to summarize the poem's story. Ask, "What's the child's favorite word? Can you find the word *yes* in the poem?" If the student needs support, hold up the sight-word card printed with *yes*. "Circle the word *yes* each time you see it in the poem." If the student is unable to locate every *yes*, choose a capable volunteer to finish circling them.

☼ Hold up the card printed with *no*. Say, "This word is the opposite of *yes*. I don't like to hear you say this word, but if you can *read* this word, whisper it to me." Then ask: "How many letters do see in the word *no*?" Respond with: "You're right! There are two letters." Follow with: "As I point to each letter, say its name."

☼ Say, "I see the word *no* printed in two different lines—in the fourth line and in the last line. Raise your hand when you locate both words." Invite a student to point to the word *no* in both lines. After the student has correctly identified the word in both locations, say: "Choose a different-colored pen to circle *no* in both lines."

☼ Explain: "This poem contains many of the sight words you've been learning. I see the words *and, I, a,* and *the*. Do you see any of these words?

Every Child a Reader

I'll repeat them slowly so you'll have a chance to quickly check the poem: *and, I, a,* and *the*. Please raise your hand if you see one of these sight words." Call on a student to tell you the word he or she sees. "Please point to the sight word you noticed and read it aloud." If the student doesn't point to the correct word, hold up the word card so it can be matched to the proper word. Then ask, "Would you choose a different color to circle _____ each time you see it in the poem?" Follow this procedure for the remaining sight words with different volunteers. If the students are unable to remember all the sight words, hold up one card at a time for the class to read aloud. Then ask, "Who sees the word _____ in the poem?" Continue with the same procedure of pointing to the word, reading it aloud, choosing a pen color, and circling the sight word each time it's seen in print.

✸ Review the circled words by reading them aloud. "I'll track the print with the pointer. When I come to a sight word you've circled, I'll stop and touch it with my pointer; then we'll read the word aloud together."

✸ After the last sight word is read, tell your students, "Notice the number of sight words in this poem. Just by knowing how to read these words, you've learned almost half of the words to this poem. Good for you!"

✸ Introduce the term *echo reading*. "Who can tell me what an echo is?" Restate a student's response by saying, "That's right. An echo is a repeating back of sounds or words. Today we're going to echo read. I'll read a line, and then you'll read the same line back to me. Listen to *how* I read it, because I want you to sound just like me. In other words, I want you to sound like you're talking. I'll read the title first, and as soon as my pointer touches the first word in the title, you'll repeat what I said. Show me you are ready to begin: eyes focused on the chart. Let's start."

✸ After the class has echoed the words in the title, explain: "I'll go back and reread the title, which you echoed, and then I'll read a new line. When it's your turn, you'll echo read the title and the first line. We'll add a new line each time we read, but we'll also reread each line we've echoed. By the time we reach the fifth line, you'll be able to read the five lines without support from me, because you've reread them so many times. But to be successful, keep your eyes on the pointer and listen as I say each word." Follow this procedure to echo read the first five lines of the poem.

✤ Reread the first five lines aloud chorally. If the class read the lines fluently, say: "Now I'd like you to read the five lines independently. I'll just assist with the pointing, but also know that I'll help you read any word if you need me." Otherwise, end the lesson after the choral reading.

> ### ❧ Reflection ❧
>
> Echo reading, combined with the cumulative rereading of the lines, allowed my students to internalize the language easily and effortlessly. Stopping at the fifth line was a good decision because the continual repetition of the lines was beginning to become monotonous. Although this technique was effective, I want to implement a different method for tomorrow's lesson to keep the learning fresh and productive. From experience, I've found children's enthusiasm for a particular strategy tends to wane from overuse. What can I do to keep my students motivated? Using their sight words to facilitate their reading of the next five lines may be the way to go—and it may even help them to view themselves as readers.

LESSON THREE
Sight Words and Reading With Fluency

What I Was Thinking

Because I pushed so hard yesterday to complete the activities I had planned, I didn't want to do another involved word study two days in a row. My students needed time to process the new learning. Besides, I didn't want to be the cause of a kindergarten rebellion! Since the kindergartners were still adjusting to being in school all day, my lessons needed to be perfectly paced. Keeping this in mind, I felt a low-key lesson would allow my students a "breather" before I presented another concept. So for today's lesson, I decided they'd reread the poem and practice sight words.

Materials

The poem "My Favorite Word" handwritten on chart paper, without the plastic cover

Highlighting tape to highlight the following words in the poem: *may, course, yourself, cake,* and *shelf*

What This Lesson Looks Like

☼ Praise your students' accomplishments: "You worked extremely hard yesterday and made good gains in learning this poem. Because of your effort, you now can read the first five lines fluently."

☼ Invite your students to reread the first five lines of the poem aloud, chorally.

☼ After they've finished reading the first section, introduce the focus of this lesson. Tell them: "You made your voices sound like you were talking to me. Now you're ready to focus your attention on the next five lines. It's my turn to read aloud, and your turn to listen. I'll read the next five lines aloud. Please follow the pointer as I touch and say the words." Then read the next five lines aloud.

☼ Explain to your students: "There are several sight words we've studied in these five lines. I want you to watch as I use the pointer to sweep across each line. When I come to a sight word you know, I'll stop and touch it with my pointer. The touch signals to you to read the sight word aloud. Please stay focused on the pointer so you'll be able to read each sight word in one big voice. Show me you're ready to begin: eyes focused on the pointer."

☼ After all the sight words have been identified, explain the students' role for the third step of the lesson: "This time, you'll help me with the rereading of these lines by reading the sight words. I'll read all the other words. When the pointer touches a sight word, I'll stop reading, and you'll read it aloud. Please read the sight word aloud on time. Hesitation will disrupt the flow of the reading. It's important to follow the pointer as I read."

☼ After they've finished this exercise, say, "Now I'm going to challenge you. Not only do I want you to read the sight words, I also want you to read the words I've highlighted with the colored tape. In other words, you'll continue to read the sight words whenever the pointer touches them, but now you'll read aloud the highlighted words, too. Be ready to read whenever I stop reading aloud."

☼ For the final rereading, read the first ten lines aloud chorally. Encourage your students to read with expression again, like they're talking.

LESSON FOUR
Basic Punctuation Introduction

What I Was Thinking

Through repeated readings of "My Favorite Word," my students had internalized its language, and they were able to use proper inflection when they read the different kinds of sentences aloud. It was now the perfect time to discuss how punctuation lets readers know what kind of expression to use when reading a sentence. I had the perfect poem to introduce this concept because it contained the basic types of sentences I wanted to discuss: telling sentences, questions, and exclamations.

But I was concerned that too much teacher talk would affect my students' ability to remain focused and engaged in this introductory lesson. What could I use to keep them interested and involved? Response cards might be the answer. Giving students their own set of cards to use to respond to my questions would allow them to be active learners. And it would allow me an opportunity to quickly assess their understanding of punctuation marks.

During this lesson, my students would identify the different kinds of punctuation marks in the poem and echo read sentences with me to see how end punctuation is used to clarify meaning for the reader. Learning the connection between meaning and punctuation is one of the most important steps students need to make to achieve fluency.

Every Child a Reader

Materials

A set of three colored 2" x 6" response cards for each student: red, yellow, and purple

* At one end of each red strip, make a period with a black permanent marker.

* At one end of each yellow strip, make a question mark with the black marker.

* At one end of each purple strip, make an exclamation point with the black marker.

A set of three colored 9" x 12" posters: one red, one yellow, and one purple

* On the red poster, make a large dot with a black marker. Print the word *period* in large lowercase letters below the symbol.

* On the yellow poster, make a large question mark with a black marker. Print the words *question mark* in large lowercase letters below the symbol.

* On the purple poster, make a large exclamation point with a black marker. Print the words *exclamation point* in large lowercase letters below the symbol.

What This Lesson Looks Like

* Say: "Let's reread the poem 'My Favorite Word' together with feeling."

* Then say: "For the past two days, your reading has focused on the first 10 lines. I'd like you to read those lines without my support. I'll do the pointing and you'll do the reading. But instead of reading as a whole group, we're going to read in two groups." Divide the class into two groups. Point to Group One and say, "You'll read aloud in one big voice while the second group listens. Try to read smoothly and with expression." Look at Group Two and say, "When Group One finishes reading the five lines aloud, you'll read aloud the same lines. Your job right now is to listen to your classmates and focus on the print as they read."

* Then explain to your students: "Today we're going to learn about punctuation marks that come at the end of sentences. These marks help the reader know where a sentence ends and what kind of expression to use when reading a particular sentence aloud. Punctuation helps make the author's meaning clearer. Today you'll be learning about the period, the question mark, and the exclamation point."

✵ Hold up the red poster printed with a period. Ask: "Who knows the name of this punctuation mark?" Explain the function of a period: "A period is a little dot at the end of a telling sentence to indicate that it's the end and to stop your voice for a second. It's often called a *full stop*. That's why I chose a red poster for the period, because red means *stop*!" Then ask, "Look at the poem. Can you find a period? Please put your hand on top of your head when you have located a period."

✵ Invite a student to point to a period in the poem. Ask the student to identify the punctuation mark. Prompt the student if necessary: "It's called a p . . . p . . ." Then repeat the name of the punctuation mark and the type of sentence that ends with this particular punctuation: "A period is used at the end of a telling sentence."

✵ Instruct your students: "Listen to my voice as I read aloud the telling sentence that ends with the period [name of student] found. Then echo what I read." Read the sentence aloud. After the class has repeated the same sentence aloud, ask: "What happened to our voices by the time we reached the last word in the sentence?" Respond with: "Our voices went down."

✵ Choose two other students to locate periods. Follow the same procedure used with the first student.

✵ Hold up the yellow poster printed with a question mark. Ask, "Who knows the name of this punctuation mark?" Explain the function of the question mark: "A question mark is used at the end of a question. I chose a yellow poster because when the traffic light turns yellow, I always ask myself a question: should I go or should I stop?" Ask, "How is a question different from a telling sentence?" After a student responds, restate the student's response: "A question asks us something, while a telling sentence is a statement that tells us something. Search the poem for question marks. How many question marks are there in all? Show me with your fingers."

✵ Invite the first student who holds up three fingers to point to all the question marks in the poem. Ask the student to name the punctuation mark. Prompt the student if necessary: "It's called a qu . . . qu . . ." Then repeat the name of the punctuation mark and the type of sentence that ends with this particular punctuation: "A question mark is used at the end of a question."

Every Child a Reader

✤ Instruct your students: "Listen to my voice as I read aloud the first question that ends with a question mark [name of student] found. Then I want you to echo my reading." After reading the three phrases and the repetition by your students, ask: "What happened to our voices by the time I reached the last word in the sentence?" If your students don't know, respond with: "Our voices went up."

✤ Hold up the purple poster printed with an exclamation point. Ask, "Who knows the name of this punctuation mark?" Explain the function of the exclamation point. "An exclamation point is used at the end of a sentence to show excitement. I chose a purple poster because purple is a bold, exciting color." Instruct your students: "Search the poem for exclamation points. How many exclamation points are there in all? Show me with your fingers."

✤ Invite the first student who holds up two fingers to point to all the exclamation points in the poem. Ask the student to identify the punctuation mark. Prompt the student if necessary: "It's called an excla . . . excla . . ." Then repeat the name of the punctuation mark and the type of sentence that ends with this particular punctuation: "An exclamation point is used at the end of a sentence to show excitement."

✤ Instruct your students: "Let's read the two sentences aloud that end with the exclamation points [name of student] found." Read the sentences aloud, chorally. Then ask, "What happened to our voices by the time we reached the last word in the sentence?" Respond with: "Yes, you're right! Our voices got louder."

✤ Rearrange the order of the posters. Review the punctuation marks as a whole group: "Please name the punctuation mark you see on the poster I hold up." After you hear a correct response, elaborate: "A [name of punctuation] comes at the end of a [type of sentence]."

✤ Pass out a set of response cards to each student. Instruct your students: "Please place your card strips on the floor in front of you. The punctuation mark should be at the top of the strip. When I say 'Show me,' you'll hold up the card that answers my question."

✤ Instruct the class: "Show me the question mark." As soon as most students hold up a strip, show them the yellow poster with the question mark and respond,

"If you're holding up a yellow card, you are showing me a question mark." Continue with this procedure for the period and the exclamation point.

Note: Try to maintain a lively pace to keep your students engaged in this activity. Don't be overly concerned if you find students confusing the symbols. The primary purpose of this activity is to assess the needs of your students by determining which punctuation marks are difficult for them to identify.

✹ Continue the response card procedure with the following directions: "Show me the punctuation mark used at the end of a question . . . of a telling sentence . . . to show excitement." After each direction is given and most students have held up a strip, hold up the appropriate poster and restate the correct response: "The punctuation mark used at the end of a [name of type of sentence] is a [name of punctuation mark]."

❧ Reflection ❧

I was a bit apprehensive about being able to complete every step of this lesson in one day. I knew success depended on how quickly I was able to introduce the three punctuation marks. Although a lecture format would be the fastest methodology to use, for many students it's an ineffective approach, and a lecture doesn't appeal to young children in general. Another hands-on lesson was necessary. I was ready to stop the lesson at any time if I sensed my students had had enough information thrown at them. But that wasn't the case.

Because the kindergartners enjoyed being detectives to find the location of specific punctuation symbols, there was sufficient participation to keep them engaged. I was pleasantly surprised to discover that a number of children already could identify these end marks and were able to relate some information about them with ease. In addition, since my students' fluency and expression had improved through their many readings of the poem, most of my students could hear the different intonations they used to express the different types of sentences.

At this juncture of the lesson, the response cards were a godsend; they kept my students engaged and helped me ascertain what my next lesson should include. Providing clear and consistent cues for holding up the response cards and maintaining a lively pace helped my students persevere.

LESSON FIVE

Attending to Punctuation

What I Was Thinking

Only five more lines to address! These final lines provided a perfect vehicle for enhancing expression and learning to attend to punctuation. I wanted to reinforce my students' learning by providing an opportunity to experiment with the different kinds of end marks. The activity would help them understand the importance of attending to punctuation and how the entire meaning of a sentence can be altered just by changing the punctuation mark.

Materials

A pocket chart

A black permanent marker

A red permanent marker

Scissors

A set of response cards for each child, from the previous lesson

The punctuation posters from the previous lesson

Four sentence strips

❋ On one sentence strip, use a black marker to print the sentence *It's on the shelf.* Scissor off the excess paper.

❋ On another sentence strip, use a black marker to print the question *Some candy?* Scissor off the excess paper.

❋ On a third sentence strip, use a black marker to print the words *Yes, Yes, Yes!* Scissor off the excess paper.

❋ Insert one sentence strip per pocket, beginning at the top of the pocket chart.

❋ Cut the last sentence strip into three 2-inch-long strips.

• On one 2-inch strip use a red marker to make a period.

• On the second 2-inch strip, use a red marker to make a question mark.

• On the third 2-inch strip, use a red marker to make an exclamation point.

- Insert these three strips in the last row of the pocket chart, leaving a large space between each strip.

What This Lesson Looks Like

✿ Read "My Favorite Word" aloud, chorally. Then invite a student who demonstrated fluency and expressiveness to read the poem independently: "I'd like you to read this poem aloud to your classmates. Your expression was wonderful, and you read so effortlessly. Please come up and read so we can hear how you make the words come alive."

✿ Following the reading, explain: "Today we're going to practice using the appropriate expression for each type of sentence. To do this, you need to know what you should do with your voice when you see the punctuation mark at the end of the sentence you're reading."

✿ Tell your students to look at the first sentence strip in the pocket chart: *It's on the shelf*. Point to the end punctuation mark. Ask, "What's this punctuation mark called?" Then say, "Listen as I read this sentence aloud. Be prepared to tell me what my voice sounded like." When a student responds that your voice went down at the end of the sentence, elaborate by saying: "You're right! My voice did go down at the end of the sentence. When we read sentences that end with periods, we usually use our normal voices. Sometimes they have a happy or a sad tone, but they always go down at the end."

✿ Instruct your students: "Reread this sentence using your normal voices."

✿ Draw their attention to the second strip printed with the phrase *Some candy?* by saying: "Look! On this sentence strip I see only two words [point to each word] and there's a _____ _____." Point to the question mark and wait for students to supply its name. "To read a question, my voice needs to go _____." When you hear a correct response, confirm the answer: "You're right! My voice has to go up." Then explain, "I'll read the question aloud first. Then I want you to repeat it immediately after I finish. Listen to the sound of my voice. Make your voice sound just like mine."

✿ Point to the last line, *Yes, Yes, Yes!* and ask them to read it aloud. They should be able to read fluently because the word *yes* is one of their sight words. Comment on their reading by saying: "Your voices got louder and louder.

How did you know what kind of expression to use?" Someone may respond, "Because we've read it so many times." Tell the class, "Yes, that's true. Rereading does improve our expression. Good readers also pay attention to the punctuation." Point to the exclamation point and ask: "Who remembers its name?" Prompt if needed.

✸ Reread each sentence chorally.

✸ After your students have finished reading all three sentences, explain: "By changing the punctuation mark, the meaning of the sentence may be entirely different." Invite a student to choose a punctuation symbol from the bottom row. Ask, "Which punctuation mark did you choose? What should happen to our voices when we read sentences that end with a [name of symbol]?" Instruct the student to find a sentence that ends with a *different* punctuation mark. Explain: "With a [name of punctuation mark], the sentence reads like this." Then ask the student to cover the punctuation mark with the symbol she or he chose. Ask, "What's going to happen to my voice as I read the sentence aloud? Listen as I read the sentence now." Ask, "Did the meaning change?" Continue the same process for the remaining two symbols.

✸ Reread the sentences chorally with the new symbols in place.

✸ Rearrange the symbols for each sentence, and ask: "Who would like to read the first sentence? Look at the new end punctuation before you read so you'll use the appropriate inflection." Choose a capable volunteer to model the reading. When the student finishes reading aloud the new sentence, review what you heard by saying, "I noticed your voice _____." Then invite the class to echo read: "Let's reread the sentence just like your classmate read it." Follow this process for the remaining sentence strips.

✸ Hold up the purple poster displaying a period. Say, "Tell me the name of this punctuation mark. A telling sentence ends with _____." Invite your students to brainstorm: "Let's share different examples of telling sentences." Allow several students an opportunity to share. Then continue the same procedure for the question and the exclamation point.

✸ Pass out a set of response cards to each student. Provide clear guidelines for using these cards (see Lesson Four) and consistent cues for holding up their cards.

✤ Explain to your students: "I'll say a sentence. I want you to show me the symbol that should be used at the end of my sentence. Please remember to wait for my cue: *Show me*. Listen carefully to how I say the sentence."

✤ Say the sentence: "I'm older than you." Instruct your students: "Using your response cards, show me the symbol that belongs at the end of my sentence." Then hold up the red poster with the period drawn on it. "A period goes at the end of this sentence because it's a telling sentence. My voice went down at the end of the sentence."

✤ Now change the sentence to *I'm older than you?* Instruct your students: "Show me the symbol that belongs at the end of this sentence." Then hold up the yellow poster with the question mark drawn on it. "A question mark goes at the end of this sentence because it's a question. My voice went up at the end of the sentence."

✤ Change the sentence one last time to *I'm older than you!* Instruct your students: "Show me the symbol that belongs at the end of this sentence." Then hold up the purple poster with the exclamation point drawn on it. "An exclamation point goes at the end of this sentence because it shows excitement. My voice sped up and became louder at the end of the sentence."

✤ Invite a student to read the poem independently as a closure to the lesson. Explain to your students: "I'd like you to demonstrate what you've learned about end punctuation by reading 'My Favorite Word' aloud with feeling."

◈ Reflection ◈

By building on their prior knowledge, my students developed a better understanding of punctuation through a progression of lessons. By the final lesson, they had a solid understanding of the purpose of end punctuation. Some fine tuning of attending to punctuation cues was needed since some students still confused punctuation marks while others overly exaggerated their reading, making it sound forced. As I write this, I think of Abram, who was invited to read the poem aloud with feeling. He concentrated so hard on using the appropriate intonation that his voice ended up sounding like a squeaky mouse whenever he read a question or an exclamation aloud.

These lessons served only as an introduction to end punctuation. More work needs to be done before I feel my students have internalized this concept and are able to apply their knowledge of punctuation. To deepen their understanding of this concept, I must remember to review the end marks in future poems as I model reading. Through repetition and reinforcement, eventually all my students will be able to attend to punctuation skills automatically.

LESSON SIX

Introduction of New Sight Words

I Like Peanut Butter

I like peanut butter
thick
thick
thick

If it makes my mouth
feel
sticky
stick
stick,

I go for the grape jelly
quick
quick
quick.

—*Lilian Moore*

What I Was Thinking

This poem attracted my attention simply because of the subject matter: it was a simple rhyme about a food that most young children adore—peanut butter! But after I read through the poem and noticed it contained simple vocabulary and rhyming words formed from the same phonogram, I knew I wanted to use it in class, as it would allow me to introduce to my students another reading strategy: rime analogy.

At this stage of their reading development, my students are involved with letters and sounds. Since kindergartners rely on sounding out words for a long time before they are comfortable with using a different strategy to determine unfamiliar words, I knew that most of my students weren't ready to focus their attention on word families, but that didn't mean I couldn't introduce the concept of using rime analogies.

Since only one phonogram is used in the entire poem, and it's a common rhyming pattern that merits introducing, I thought, "Why not!" Some of my more capable students, who were already able to decode one-syllable words, would benefit from learning about word families. These students could begin to analyze the patterns of sounds within words and would soon come to recognize rimes without having to sound them out. When students decode unknown words by analogy, they not only increase their access to words, but they gain access more efficiently. My students who weren't yet ready to attend to chunks of words would be able to see how words with the same vowels and ending letters usually rhyme. And that's a starting point!

Materials

The poem "I Like Peanut Butter" by Lilian Moore, handwritten in large, neat print on manila tag chart paper attached by rings to a wooden chart stand

Four 3" x 5" cards printed with *like, my, it,* and *go*

A pocket chart attached to the chart stand

One black marker and one red marker

Three word strips

What This Lesson Looks Like

❁ Introduce the new high-frequency words: *like, my, it,* and *go*. Read each word aloud as its card is held up. Invite the students to spell the word as you point to each letter. Then say, "Let's cheer the word!" Raise a fist and shout the word. Now invite a student to find the word in the poem. When all the new words have been introduced, ask your students to point out other words they recognize in the poem (Cunningham, 1995).

Every Child a Reader

☀ Read the title aloud: "The title of this poem is 'I Like Peanut Butter' by Lilian Moore." Ask, "How many of you like peanut butter? How would you describe peanut butter to someone who has never eaten it?" Then say, "Let's find out what Lilian Moore wrote about peanut butter."

☀ Read the poem aloud, pausing at the last line of the first and second stanzas to allow time for your students to supply the words *thick* and *stick*, respectively. This is your check to see which students notice words that are the same. Then pause at the second and third lines of the last stanza of the poem for your students to supply the word *quick*. This will give you some indication of their understanding of rhyme.

☀ Ask your students: "What helped you know the words you read aloud?" When a student responds that the words are the same, invite him or her to locate the word *thick* each time it appears in the stanza and identify the letters to spell the word. Then invite a second volunteer to repeat the procedure for *stick*. Point out the word *sticky*, and ask, "Is this the word *stick*? Why not?" Invite a third student to locate the word *quick* each time it appears in the last stanza and ask him or her to spell the word by identifying its lowercase letters.

☀ When the poem ends, ask your students: "Which words did Lilian Moore use to describe peanut butter?" Then ask, "What did she do when the peanut butter became too sticky?" Follow up with these questions: "How many of you like peanut butter *and* jelly too? Why do you like to add jelly? How many of you like just peanut butter without the jelly, even if the peanut butter is thick and starts to stick?"

☀ Invite students to share their own stories about eating peanut butter.

☀ When students have finished sharing their stories, explain to them the purpose of the second reading: "This poem rhymes. I want you to listen for three rhyming words as I read the poem aloud, and be ready to tell me all three of them." Then read the poem aloud.

☀ After the reading, ask, "Who knows the three words that rhyme?" Call on a student to recall the rhyming words in the poem.

☀ As the student names a word, print the word on a word strip. Use a black marker to write the onset and a red marker for the rime. Say the beginning sound as you write it. Follow with the sound of the rime. Then say the word. Insert the word strip into a pocket of the pocket chart. Follow this procedure for the remaining two words.

☀ Direct your students' attention to the words in the pocket holder and ask: "Which part of each word is the same?" Someone may name only one of the letters. If this happens, probe for more by saying: "Are there any other letters that are the same?" When the letters *i, c,* and *k* are identified, explain: "These letters make the /ĭk/ sound. As you can see, this particular chunk of letters is found in other words, too. These three words have the same vowel sound and the same ending sounds. That's why they rhyme."

☀ Instruct your students: "Let's practice sounding out these words by using the /ĭk/ sound pattern to help us. To do this, we'll say the beginning sound first, then /ĭk/, and then we'll say the word. For example, look at the first card. Listen as I sound out the two parts of the word and then say the word: /th/ . . . /ĭk/ . . . *thick.*"

☀ Practice isolating the two parts of each rhyming word. Then blend the sounds to say the word.

☀ Invite your students to chime in during your final rereading. "These rhyming words will help you to quickly remember the words to this snappy poem. I bet some of you already know the words. Please join me as I read the poem one final time."

❧ Reflection ❧

Initially, I was satisfied with this lesson since each part went so smoothly, and no red flags were raised. But as I thought more about it, I realized this introductory lesson didn't allow individuals to demonstrate their facility with rhyme. By having the group supply the word *quick* in the last stanza during the first reading of the poem, I thought I'd be able to judge my students' awareness of rhyme. However, this particular lesson only provided me with a general sense of their awareness of rhyme. Because children need to be able to recognize rhymes before they can generate new rhyming words, I needed to review rhyming words with a lesson that allowed each student to demonstrate his or her facility.

Every Child a Reader

LESSON SEVEN
Phonograms and Orally Generating Rhyming Words

What I Was Thinking

Not only would this lesson strengthen my students' auditory discrimination skills, it would also serve as an introduction to rime analogy. Recognizing these sound patterns would aid in facilitating their development of word-building strategies. Teaching elements of phonics through chunks, rather than individual phonemes, would enable my students to pronounce unknown words more easily.

I wanted to begin with a quick warm-up rhyming activity that would allow me to observe my students' awareness of rhyme. I'd be watching for the following red flags: students hesitating with their responses; students looking at their classmates' signals before responding; and students giving incorrect signals. Then I'd review what they had learned about the rhyming words in the poem to introduce the new activity—generating a list of words with the -ick pattern.

Since I recognized that the first two activities wouldn't be very stimulating, I knew I needed to find an invitation for my students to persevere. A feely box would serve this purpose, because all kindergartners love using a "feely box." It would generate enthusiasm for the final activity—substituting consonant sounds to form new words in the -ick word family.

Materials

Highlighting tape

One red marker and one black marker

A "feely box" (i.e., a plastic peanut butter jar placed inside a colored tube sock)

Chart paper titled with the phonogram -ick

A pocket holder

Five word strips, each printed in red with the phonogram -ick and inserted into five pockets of the pocket holder

Eighteen 2" x 3" letter strips printed in black with the consonants *b, D, f, g, h, j, l, M, n, p, qu, R, s, t, v, y, w,* and *z,* then inserted into the feely box

What This Lesson Looks Like

✿ Read the poem "I Like Peanut Butter" aloud chorally.

✿ Following the reading, ask your students, "Which three words in the poem sounded alike at the end?" As each word is mentioned, locate it in the poem and highlight the ending letters *-ick* with highlighting tape to reinforce the concept of sound patterns.

✿ Connect students' understanding of patterns to words. "We've studied different kinds of patterns in math. What's a pattern?" After a student answers the question, say, "Sometimes words follow a kind of pattern, too. When the same letters repeat in the same order in other words, they make the same sound. The words *quick, stick,* and *thick* contain a particular sound pattern at the end." Ask, "What sound pattern do all three words have?" Point out that the three words end with the same three letters, *i-c-k.* Conclude by saying: "That's how we know they rhyme: because they sound the same at the end of the word."

✿ Invite your students to identify the rhyming words you sound out: "I'll demonstrate how to sound out each rhyming word by blending the sounds together. After each word is sounded out, I want you to tell me the rhyming word." Point to each word as you sound it out.

✿ When all three words have been sounded out, ask, "What sound pattern did you hear in all three words?" Follow with this question: "What did you learn about words that rhyme?"

✿ Begin the word study with a warm-up activity. Explain to your students, "I'm going to read some word pairs. If they rhyme, I want you to signal me with a thumbs-up." Demonstrate this signal as you say "thumbs-up." Continue your directions by saying, "If they don't rhyme, signal me with a thumbs-down." Demonstrate this signal as you say "thumbs-down." Instruct your students, "Show me the signal for rhyming words. Now show me the signal for word pairs that don't rhyme."

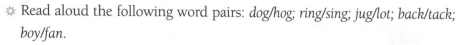

❋ Read aloud the following word pairs: *dog/hog; ring/sing; jug/lot; back/tack; boy/fan.*

❋ If your students had no difficulty with the previous word pairs, include some nonrhyming word pairs that begin and/or end with the same consonants. Students who demonstrate proficiency with these words understand the concept of rhyme: *mop/map; take/talk; snake/wake; hot/hat; nap/zap.*

❋ Introduce the second activity by pointing to the chart paper titled *-ick.* Say, "In the first activity, you heard some words I rhymed. In this activity, you're going to create a list of rhyming words with the *-ick* sound pattern. Let's start our list with the words we already know with the *-ick* pattern." Print the words *thick, stick,* and *quick* in a column under the title. As you print the letters, say the sounds for the onset and the rime. Then repeat the list of words. Ask, "Who can think of another word that rhymes with *thick, stick,* and *quick*?" Continue to model sounding out the onset and rime as you write each word down. When your students have exhausted all words, read the list aloud with your students. As you read each word aloud, emphasize the beginning sound and have your students complete the blending of the word.

❋ Hold up the feely box for your students to see. Explain: "Inside this feely box are letter cards. You'll choose a letter card and place it before an *-ick* word strip." As you say a direction, demonstrate what to do. Pull out a letter card from the feely box and place it in the pocket chart. Follow with this direction: "Then you'll read the word you formed by blending the onset [point to the letter card] and the rime [point to the word strip]." Demonstrate sounding out the word. Then say, "I'll help you say the beginning letter sound if you don't know it. And finally you'll tell me the word you formed. If your word is not a real word, we'll take that card out of the pocket chart and return it to the feely box." If you have fewer than 18 students, don't return any letters to the feely box. Conclude the directions by saying, "Your classmates will continue to have opportunities to form a word until we've found five real words."

❋ After all five words have been formed, read them aloud, chorally.

❧ Reflection ❧

Overall, I was pleased with the results of this lesson as it showed me that many of my students could use the rime analogy strategy to help them decode words, and they could also sound out most consonant letters with automaticity. However, upon closer review, I realized they were successful only with letters that were similar to the pronunciation of the letter names. For example, because they could hear the /b/ sound when they said the letter *b*, it was an easy sound to learn. On the other hand, some of my students confused the /w/ and /y/ sounds because they assumed that these sounds would also be similar to the letter names. To alleviate this confusion, I'll need to develop more focused letter-sound activities.

At CTL, since different classes share classroom spaces, I try to adhere to scheduled blocks of times. Although my students thoroughly enjoyed the feely box activity, I had to stop before they had spelled five real words. As luck would have it, the children kept picking a consonant letter that made a nonsensical word. However, because they still had plenty of practice with sounding out and blending words, terminating the activity didn't bother me. The goal of this lesson had been attained. Since my students knew what to do now, the feely box would be a good choice time activity after lunch for interested students.

Every Child a Reader

LESSON EIGHT
Introduction of Color Words

> ### Yellow Butter
>
> Yellow butter purple jelly red jam black bread
>
> Spread it thick
> Say it quick
>
> Yellow butter purple jelly red jam black bread
>
> Spread it thicker
> Say it quicker
>
> Yellow butter purple jelly red jam black bread
>
> Now repeat it
> While you eat it
>
> Yellow butter purple jelly red jam black bread
>
> Don't talk
> With your mouth full!
>
> —*Mary Ann Hoberman*

What I Was Thinking

As soon as children learn colors and color words, they're able to make a connection between word symbols and adjectives. Knowing this, I wanted to introduce color words sooner rather than later. But teaching these words in isolation wouldn't allow my students to see how color words are used as adjectives.

I needed to find an engaging poem that had just a few color words in it to allow my students to assimilate these special sight words more easily. And I wanted them all to begin with a different letter. But could I find such a poem?

Gathering my collection of children's poetry books, my hunt began! As soon as I saw the title of the poem "Yellow Butter" by Mary Ann Hoberman, I glanced at the color words in the first line and noticed that they began with different letters. I thought, "This poem has potential." Then, after reading it once, I found myself rereading it, trying to say the repetitive lines more quickly with each rereading. Its effective repetition created a cadence that made the words flow. This poem would be fun to read, and I knew I could demonstrate enthusiasm when I presented it. I hoped my enthusiasm for "Yellow Butter" would lure my students to attend to its words.

But how could I maintain their engagement and in the process assess their understanding of colors? I found that response cards had been effective in my last lesson, so perhaps an adaptation might work. For this lesson the students could use different-colored strips and hold the appropriate strip up when that particular color was mentioned as the poem was read. Because the color words are read more quickly as the poem progresses, my students would be more motivated to attend. In addition, I could check their comprehension by asking questions they could answer by holding up their strips.

Materials

The poem "Yellow Butter" by Mary Ann Hoberman, handwritten in large, neat print on manila tag chart paper attached by rings to a wooden chart stand

Two different-colored 2" x 5" construction paper strips per student: yellow, red, purple, or black

Chart paper or a white board and a marker

What This Lesson Looks Like

☀ Gather a yellow, red, purple, and black strip from your construction paper strips. Hold up one strip at a time and ask the class: "What's the color of this strip? What is _____ in color?" As your students respond, write their responses on chart paper or on a white board. Continue this procedure for the remaining colors.

☀ Tell your students, "I chose this poem because it's fun to read, and you'll begin to learn some color words at the same time. This poem mentions these four different colors to describe various items. Listen carefully as I read it aloud to see if you named the same item."

☀ Read the poem aloud with as much enthusiasm as you can bring to it.

❋ Following the reading, ask, "Do you like this poem? Why? Which lines did you like best? Why?" To check your students' listening comprehension, ask them, "Who can name the four foods mentioned in the poem? What was the color of the butter, the jam, the jelly, and the bread?" Then ask, "Did you think of any of these items when we brainstormed together? What kind of jam is red? What kind of jelly is purple?" End with: "What *is* black bread?"

❋ Pass out two different-colored strips to each student. As you hand a colored strip to each student, instruct him or her to name the color.

❋ Explain the purpose of these strips: "I'm going to read 'Yellow Butter' aloud one more time. Be prepared to hold up the appropriate colored strip as I read the color word aloud, and then immediately put it back down on the floor. For example, when I read aloud the title, 'Yellow Butter,' those students who have a yellow strip should hold it up as soon as they hear the word *yellow* and then quickly put it down again." Demonstrate by holding up a yellow strip as you say the words in the title: "Yellow Butter." Then instruct your students: "Now I'd like you to practice." Observe your students as you read the title aloud. "Let's practice the first line." Repeat the practice until your students understand the directions. When your students demonstrate complete understanding, inform them, "As you are aware, the repetitive lines speed up, but for this reading I'm not going to read these lines quickly. If you're able to keep up with me, I'll speed up the pace the next time we read this poem aloud."

❋ Read the poem aloud, emphasizing each color word as it's said. Maintain a steady pace throughout the reading.

❋ Provide positive feedback after the completion of the exercise. Say, "You're such good listeners. Everyone held up the appropriate colored strip on time." If they experienced difficulty, an appropriate response could be, "Nice try! All of you did your best. Holding up the strip will become easier with practice."

❋ To check their comprehension, instruct your students: "If you have the color that describes the color of bread in the poem, please hold it up." Repeat this direction for the other items mentioned in the poem. Mix up the order of the remaining items.

❀ Invite four capable students to participate in the final reading of "Yellow Butter." As you name a student, say, "Please bring up the [name the color] strip with you and stand on the other side of the chart stand." Then explain their role: "I'm going to read the poem again, but this time I'm going to speed up the pace of my reading. Each time you hear your color, hold it up for your classmates to see, and then just as quickly, put it back down. Listen carefully so you hold up the appropriate strip on time. Are there any questions before I begin?" Then read the poem aloud at a lively pace.

❀ As a final activity, read aloud the first line chorally. Then invite a student to read the line independently using the pointer to touch each word as it is said. Ask, "Who can find the same line in a different stanza?" Choose a volunteer to point out the line and read it aloud.

❧ Reflection ❧

This poem was an instant hit with my class. Immediately feeling the strong cadence of the poem, my students swayed their bodies to the rhythm as I read it aloud. Although I planned to do the entire reading by myself, once they heard the first line repeat, some of my students began to chime in every time they heard me say the words *yellow butter*. It didn't annoy me at all. I enjoyed their participation, because their early retention of these lines would make the upcoming lessons easier to implement.

However, their participation in the color-response activity was frustrating to watch. Although everyone enjoyed this activity, a few students still found it difficult to hold up their colors on time, even with me reading at a slow pace. As they familiarize themselves with the poem, it should become easier for them.

I had planned to pick up the pace the next time I did this activity with the whole class. But now I believe inviting four students at a time to perform would be a better idea, because it would allow those who had experienced difficulty more time to learn the words. Providing this gift of time would allow everyone a chance for success.

LESSON NINE

Introduction of Distinctive Features in the Color Words

What I Was Thinking

At the beginning of the year, there are always some children who don't understand the function of letters in words; they are unaware that words are made up of distinct sounds. Since oral blending helps students who have no concept of words or sounds to better understand the alphabetic principle, I was anxious to include this particular exercise as part of our word study. Then my students would be able to hear how sounds are put together to make words. And through my modeling, they would learn how to sound out words independently.

In addition, I recognized that children must not only be able to make the connection between the letters and sounds in a word, but also understand that words consist of individual letters, and that the order of these letters is critical. Although I wanted to jump right in and start our word study by orally blending the phonemes in the color words mentioned in the poem "Yellow Butter," I didn't want to put the cart before the horse. My instincts told me my students needed to work with letters first before they worked with sounds, to help them clarify the concept of a word.

I decided to incorporate a letter activity before trying the oral blending exercise. I found a game called "Letters Line Up" in *40 Sensational Sight Word Games* by Joan Novelli, which I needed to adapt to meet my purposes. The students would be given color-coded letters to use to help spell the color words. Color-coding each letter to match a specific color word would help them know which sight word they would help spell.

Materials

Four different color strips from yesterday's lesson: yellow, red, purple, and black

Four 3" x 5" cards with *yellow, red, purple,* and *black* printed in color-coded large lowercase letters

Yellow, red, purple, and black markers

Twenty pieces of 8½" x 11" white card stock

> ☼ Use a yellow marker to print the letters of the word *yellow* on pieces of white card stock—one letter per card.

✿ Use a red marker to print the letters of the word *red* on white card stock—one letter per card.

✿ Use a purple marker to print the letters of the word *purple* on white card stock—one letter per card.

✿ Use a black marker to print the letters of the word *black* on white card stock—one letter per card.

What This Lesson Looks Like

✿ Review the repetitive lines of the poem. Ask, "Who remembers the words in the first line that begins with the words *yellow butter*?" Invite a volunteer to use the pointer to touch each word as it's said. After the line is read, say, "This line is repeated three more times. Please find the lines and sweep across the line with the pointer as you say the words quickly."

✿ Invite the class to read these repetitive lines chorally.

✿ Discuss the surprise ending with your students. Explain: "This poem's strong rhythm abruptly ends in the last stanza with a reprimand you might have heard from Mom or Dad when you were trying to talk and eat at the same time. Listen as I read the last stanza aloud, and then repeat it when my pointer touches the first word." Point to the words as you read them aloud.

✿ Instruct your students: "I'd like you to read these repetitive stanzas as well as this last stanza aloud." As you give these directions, point to each stanza you want the class to read. "Do you see a pattern created for our reading today?" If no one responds, say, "Listen to the pattern." Point to each stanza as you say: "You read . . . I read . . . You read . . . I read . . . You read . . . I read . . . You read. And then the pattern stops, because you read again! Keep focused on the pointer so you'll be ready to read in one big voice." Then read the poem "Yellow Butter" aloud.

✿ Invite four different students to participate in the color-response activity that ended yesterday's lesson. As you name a student, say, "Please stand on the other side of the chart stand." When all four participants are lined up next to the chart stand, give each student a different colored strip to hold. Then explain their roles: "We're going to read the poem aloud again, and each time you hear your color, hold it up for your classmates to see, and then just as quickly, put it back down. Listen carefully so you hold up the appropriate strip on time. Are there any questions before I begin?" Then invite the audience to chime in as you read the poem aloud.

✻ Explain the focus of the word study: "This poem contains four sight words that are important to learn—*yellow, purple, red,* and *black.* These words are called _____ words." Respond with: "That's right! They're *color* words."

✻ Hold up the card printed with the word *yellow.* Ask, "Who knows this color word?" Invite a volunteer to read it. If the student is correct, instruct him or her: "Name the letters in the word *yellow.*" Then say, "Match this card to the word *yellow* in the poem." When the student does this, tell him or her to cross-check: "Check your accuracy by confirming that the letters on your card are in the exact order as the word in the poem."

✻ Ask the student: "What helped you remember this word?" After the student responds, say, "That's a good strategy, but you can use other strategies, too." Invite your students to look at the word *yellow* for other clues they might use to help them identify the word. "Let's see if we can come up with a variety of strategies. Raise your hand if you notice something that would help you identify the word." Guide the class by telling them to notice the distinctive features of the letters in the word: the initial letter or the final letter, the sound of the beginning letter or blend, the size of the word, the number of letters in the word, and double letters.

✻ Invite six students to stand in front of the class and give each of them a yellow letter card. Hold up the word card printed with *yellow* and tell them, "Rearrange yourselves in order to spell the word *yellow.*" Show them where the first letter should stand.

✻ As a final step, instruct each student in sequential order to hold up his or her letter card and shout, "Give me a [name of letter on card]!" After the letter is cheered, tell the students in the audience: "You'll repeat the letter's name your classmates say." When each student has cheered his or her letter, turn to the students standing at the front of the class and ask, "What word do your letters spell?" Repeat the procedure used in the last two steps for the three remaining color words.

❧ Reflection ❧

My kindergartners had such fun positioning themselves in the correct order to spell the different color words. And how they loved cheering each word! I was glad we were in the downstairs of the school by ourselves, because we would certainly have disrupted other classes. Not only did my students enjoy this activity, they also learned more about letters and their significance in words. When Ella, one of my kindergartners, asked me how the word would read if they didn't rearrange themselves, I knew she had begun to understand the importance of letter order.

Implementing the letter activity benefited me as well as my students. I saw how easily my students could locate and match up words that are the same. This key observation made me realize that I no longer needed to continue the matching procedure in future lessons. From then on, I'd just ask my students to locate the corresponding word in the poem. Although I also observed many students consistently naming the lowercase letters to spell the color words, I still needed to require my students to identify letters during our word study until *everyone* was proficient. Because the learning rate of my kindergartners differs from child to child, I need to consider the needs of all my students so no one gets left behind.

Since most of my students couldn't decode words yet, it was important to show them the visual-cue strategy that would help them commit words to memory. This strategy is especially helpful in learning the many words that can't be sounded out. I was pleased they were able to come up with a variety of visual cues without much guidance from me. I needed to continue to invite students to notice the distinct features of words as they encountered them.

LESSON TEN

Review of Distinctive Features in the Color Words, Oral Blending

What I Was Thinking

Children need to hear words orally blended before they can isolate sounds independently. Since my students had begun to associate some sounds to letters,

I wanted to help them see how sounds are put together to form a word. By my modeling of how to blend sounds into words, my students could then make a connection between the words they put together and what they look like in print. If I introduced this skill by segmenting the sounds in the four color words, I thought many of my students would be able to successfully blend these words, because these particular words contained no more than four phonemes .

Materials

Four 3" x 5" word cards for *yellow, purple, red,* and *black* from the previous lesson

Pocket chart

✢ Insert one word card per pocket, beginning at the top of the pocket chart. Continue until all four cards are displayed in a column.

What This Lesson Looks Like

✢ Reread "Yellow Butter" chorally. Say, "I'd like you to chime in whenever you know the words. If you don't know the words well enough, listen to your classmates and me read the poem aloud. But please keep your eyes focused on the pointer as we read each word aloud."

✢ Reread the poem again with your students. Explain: "Today you're going to supply the words I point to when I stop reading aloud." To maintain a lively pace, use the pointer only to touch words your students will supply. In the second stanza, point to the word *quick.* In the third stanza point to *butter, jelly, jam,* and *bread.* In the fourth stanza, point to *quicker.* In the sixth stanza, point to *eat.* In the last stanza, point to *with your mouth full.*

✢ Review the color words with visual clues. Say, "We're going to play a detective word game to review these color words. I'm going to give you a clue to help you identify the correct word. If you know the word, please raise your hand." After a student has correctly identified the word, instruct him or her: "Please go to the pocket chart and point to the word [name of word]." Turn your attention to the class and say, "Let's spell this word together. When your classmate points to it, say its name."

Examples of visual clues that may be used:

1. This word has three letters. *(red)*

2. This word has double letters. (*yellow*)

3. This word starts with the same letter as Ridgely's name. (*red*)

4. This word has the same number of letters as the word *yellow*. (*purple*)

5. This word starts with a *b*. (*black*)

6. This word starts with the same letter as the word *yes*. (*yellow*)

7. This word has two *p*'s. (*purple*)

8. This word ends with the letter *k*. (*black*)

✸ At the end of the game, remove the word cards from the pocket chart and mix them up. Hold up one card at a time for the class to read aloud. After each word is read, invite one or two students to share a clue that helped them identify the word. After one student shares a clue, ask: "Did anyone use a different strategy?" Invite that student to explain the strategy she or he used.

✸ Explain to your students: "Often readers put sounds of letters together to figure out unfamiliar words. I'm going to show you what readers do when they blend sounds into words. I'm going to say a word very slowly, sound by sound. Then I'll say it a little faster. Finally I'll blend the parts all together and say the word as a whole word. For example, if I say the individual sounds /c/ /?/ /t/, I can blend them together like this: *ca . . . /t/*, and finally say the word *cat*."

✸ Explain the oral blending exercise: "I'm going to say the sounds in some words found in the poem. I want you to listen carefully, and then I want you to say the word when I say, 'Tell me the word.' For example, if I say /?/ /t/ you'd wait until I said, 'Tell me the word,' before you'd say the word *eat*."

✸ Begin with the easiest color word: "/r/ /ĕ/ /d/ . . . tell me the word." Encourage your students with positive feedback after each word has been correctly blended. Say, "You blended the word *red* so easily. Let's try another word. Listen carefully: /bl/ /?/ /k/ . . . tell me the word." Then say: "/p/ /ûr/ /pl/ . . . tell me the word." End the oral blending exercise with yellow. Say: "/y/ /ĕ/ /l/ /ō/ . . . tell me the word."

❧ Reflection ❧

By the time I had isolated the sounds for the word *black*, some children predicted that I had chosen color words for this particular oral blending exercise. Since these special sight words started with different letters, the students only had to hear the beginning sound to determine the word.

At first I was disappointed by my choice of words, but after reflection, I realized that I did accomplish the primary objective of the lesson—to demonstrate how letter sounds can be isolated and put together to identify unknown words. And in the process, my students' self-confidence skyrocketed.

However, I also realized that our work had only just begun because children need a lot of practice with oral blending before they are ready to segment and blend sounds independently. Because the first lesson failed to give them much blending practice, I went back to my drawing board to design a different oral blending exercise using three or four other phoneme words from the poem "Yellow Butter."

LESSON ELEVEN

Oral Blending Continued

What I Was Thinking

Since my students had been exposed to the words in "Yellow Butter" for a few days, using additional words from the poem to implement another oral blending activity would be more meaningful. This particular poem was filled with a sufficient number of three-phoneme words.

Recognizing the short attention span of my students, I'd have to eliminate some words to prevent my students from becoming restless and bored. However, from my own teaching experience, I knew being overly prepared was better than not having enough material. For that reason, I chose eight words whose sounds graduated in difficulty. Although I didn't have to use all eight words if my students exhibited restlessness, I wanted to be ready to extend the activity if the conditions warranted it.

What This Lesson Looks Like

✿ Read "Yellow Butter" chorally. Say, "I know many of you know all the words now, and some of you are still learning the words. I'd like you to read aloud the stanzas in the poem that you can read fluently. If you don't know the words well enough in a particular stanza, listen to your classmates and me as we read that stanza aloud. But please remember to keep your eyes focused on the pointer as we say each word aloud."

✿ Reread the poem with your students. Explain: "Now you're going to read most of the words by yourself. I'll read the first word aloud in each line to help you remember the rest of the line. Then you'll finish reading the line." Point to the first word in the title with the pointer as you say "yellow."

✿ Invite a student to read the poem independently. Say, "You used such a clear, strong voice when you read with your classmates. I was able to hear you say all the words without any problem. I'd like you to use the pointer and read this poem aloud by yourself."

✿ Explain the oral blending exercise: "I'm going to say the sounds in some other words I found in the poem. I want you to listen carefully, and then I want you to say the word when I say, 'Tell me the word.' For example, if I say /s/ /ay/ you'd wait until I said, 'Tell me the word,' before you'd say the word *say*."

✿ Begin with the first word on the following list, and then use the other words in consecutive order. Segment the sounds in the first five words. Continue with the other three words if your class is interested. Encourage your students with positive feedback after each word has been correctly blended. Say, "You blended the word *now* so easily. Let's try another word. Listen carefully."

1. /n/ /ow/ . . . Tell me. (*now*)

2. /j/ /?/ /m/ . . . Tell me. (*jam*)

3. /t/ /ŏ/ /k/ . . . Tell me. (*talk*)

4. /wh/ /?/ /l/ . . . Tell me. (*while*)

5. /th/ /ĭ/ /k/ . . . Tell me. (*thick*)

6. /b/ /ŭ/ /t/ /ûr/ . . . Tell me. (*butter*)

7. /j/ /ĕ/ /l/ /?/ . . . Tell me. (*jelly*)

8. /kw/ /ĭ/ /k/ /ûr/ . . . Tell me. (*quicker*)

Every Child a Reader

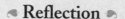

❧ Reflection ❧

My students found this oral blending exercise a bit more challenging than the previous one. When I analyzed the outcome of the lesson, I realized some students weren't able to blend a simple three-phoneme word, and all students had difficulty blending the short *e* sound. I wasn't surprised by these findings, because every year I have kindergartners who can't blend sounds into words. And every year these same students learn how to sound out words in a very short time. How does this happen? By my modeling how to isolate the sounds in unfamiliar words each time they are encountered in the poems we read together, my students get continual practice in blending sounds into words. And as a result, they learn to decode words quickly.

LESSON TWELVE
Introduction of New High-Frequency Words

Autumn Leaves

Fall on me
        autumn leaves,
Fall on my head
        touch me
        autumn leaves,
And I'll never forget you,
I am standing tall
        like a tree
Hoping you will fall
        on me
        autumn leaves
Autumn leaves
        fall on me.

—*Zakiyyah Denton*

What I Was Thinking

When I found "Autumn Leaves" by Zakiyyah Denton in CTL's collection of poetry books, I immediately recognized that this poem offered the perfect opportunity to reinforce the skills I had previously introduced. It contained repetitive words, phrases, and lines; the phonogram -*all*; and numerous high-frequency words. I couldn't allow this one to be passed over!

To prepare for the review lesson, I wanted to allot enough time to thoroughly introduce four new high-frequency words students would need to know to be successful in the review. Since this introduction would be lengthy and involved, I decided to postpone the review lesson for a day in order to maximize the learning of my students.

Materials

The poem "Autumn Leaves" by Zakiyyah Denton, handwritten in large, neat print on manila tag chart paper attached by rings to a wooden chart stand

Four 3" x 5" cards with four new high-frequency words—*me, you, all,* and *on*—printed neatly in large lowercase letters

Word card *my* from the sight-word collection

What This Lesson Looks Like

* Stand in front of the class and recite the poem from memory, with passion. Touch your head as you say the word *head*, and stand at attention when you recite the lines: *I am standing tall like a tree*.

* Check your students' understanding of the poem's meaning by asking the following questions: "What does the word *autumn* mean? What happens in autumn? To whom was the person speaking? Why did she or he want the leaves to fall?" Invite students to share their own experiences by asking, "What do you like to do when the leaves fall from the trees?"

* Introduce the four new high-frequency words by saying, "In this poem, I found four words that you'll encounter a lot in your reading."

  • Hold up the word card printed with *my*. Ask your students, "What does this word say?" Then hold up the new word card, *me*, and place it below the first card. Say, "These two words are often confused. Why would beginning readers mix up these words?" After a correct response is given, confirm the answer: "That's right. Both words begin with the letter *m* and each word has two letters." Then ask: "What could you do to remember this word says *me* [stretch out each sound slowly] and not *my*?" After providing adequate wait time, explain: "In the word *me*, you hear the *e* say its name when you read the word aloud. Listen again as I say the word *me* slowly: /m/ /ē/." To review the reading of the word *me*, hold up the word card, point to the letter *e*, and instruct the class to read this new high-frequency word aloud. Then ask your class to read *my* aloud again. Shuffle the cards. Hold up the top card and ask: "What does *this* word say?" Shuffle again and repeat the procedure one last time.

- Hold up the word card printed with *on*. Explain: "This word card also has two letters. This word can be sounded out. Listen as I stretch out the two sounds: /ŏ/ . . . /n/. What's the word?" After the class correctly blends the sounds, explain how to make the short sound of *o*. "Watch the shape of my mouth as I say the sound of *o*." Then say, "My mouth was shaped just like the letter *o*." Elaborate on your explanation by telling your students, "Every time I make the /ŏ/ sound, I think of my doctor. Whenever he checks my tonsils, he always says, 'Open up wide and say /ŏ/.' I'll pretend to be your doctor. Here is my tongue depressor [hold up a craft stick] that I'll pretend to use to check your tonsils. When I tell you to open up wide, open your mouth and be prepared to say /ŏ/ when I extend my tongue depressor toward you. Ready?" Practice making the /ŏ/ sound together and then say, "Now I'm going to pretend to check each of you. I'll move from student to student, and when I tell you to say /ŏ/, I'll pretend to use my tongue depressor while you make the /ŏ/ sound." Be sure to provide corrective feedback if necessary. When all students have had a turn, return their attention back to the word card. Say, "Listen as I sound out this word: /ŏ/ . . . /n/. Let's sound out the word together [point to each letter as you make its sound]: /ŏ/ . . . /n/. What does this word say?"

- Hold up the word card printed with *all*. Say, "This word says *all*. This word is a sight word because it doesn't make the sounds you'd expect. Listen as I stretch out the sounds." Ask your students, "What sounds did you hear?"

Then say, "Let's spell this word together [point to each letter as it's named]." Invite your students to look at the distinct features of the word. Ask, "How can you remember this word?"

- Hold up the last word card printed with *you*. Say, "This word also can't be sounded out. You have to take a picture of it [pretend to take a picture with a camera] in your mind. Does anyone know what *y . . . o . . . u* [point to each letter as you say its name] spells?" If no one recognizes this word, say, "It spells *you*. Let's spell and cheer this word together" (Cunningham, 1995).

✸ Hold up the word card printed with the word *all*. Say, "This word says [pause to allow your students to supply the word]. Who sees the word *all* in the poem?" Invite a capable student to locate the word. Ask the student, "What do you notice?" If the student doesn't understand the question, be more specific: "Where is *all* located?" Respond with: "It's part of a word that begins with the letter *f*. By blending the */f/* sound and *all*, you'll know the word. What's the */f/* sound?" As soon as the student gives the appropriate sound, say, "*all*." Then ask, "What's the word? Can you locate the word *fall* in other lines of the poem?" When that student has completed the task, give positive feedback about his or her performance: "You understand how to use words you know to figure out new words. Good job!" or "You're so quick at finding words that are the same." Then invite a different student to find the word *all* inside a different word. Say, "This word rhymes with *fall*, because it sounds the same at the end." When the student points to the word *tall*, ask him or her to blend the beginning letter sound and *-all*. Ask, "What's the word?"

✸ Invite different students to locate the other three words in the poem. Hold up a word card and say: "This word says [pause to allow your students to supply the word]. Who sees the word _____ in the poem?" Select a student to point to the word with the pointer and read it aloud each time the word is found in the poem. As the student reads the word aloud, ask him or her to sweep the pointer across the word.

✸ Read the poem aloud with a pointer. Touch each word as you say it.

✸ Point to the words in the title. Ask, "What's the title of this poem?" Then explain to your students, "The words *autumn leaves* [point to each word as it's said] are often repeated in this poem." Instruct your students to silently count the number of times they see these words, including the title. "Show me the number with your fingers." Choose the first student who holds up five fingers to use the pointer to sweep across the line as she or he reads the words *autumn leaves* each time they appear in the poem.

☀ For the final reading, ask your students to chime in each time you touch the words *autumn leaves*.

❧ Reflection ❧

I'm so glad I decided to postpone the review lesson, because the lengthy introduction to the poem exhausted my students. Although I did push them, they remained focused and involved throughout the lesson.

How they loved the doctor act! I'll do anything to facilitate their learning. With this introduction wrapped up, I feel confident that tomorrow's lesson will go well.

LESSON THIRTEEN
Review of Sight Words and Skills and Concepts

What I Was Thinking

It's important to keep in mind that when a new strategy or concept is introduced, the learning needs to be reinforced in order to achieve mastery. Knowing that new skills need to be revisited regularly, I try to capitalize on every opportunity to practice skills previously presented. This poem contains much repetition that would allow a good review of the concept of *word*. My hope was that after the completion of this review activity, my students would view themselves as readers.

In order for the lesson to be successful for all students, I'd need to include a vocabulary review of high-frequency words and have a support system in place for any student who might experience difficulty in locating the repetitive words and phrases. As a scaffold, I'd write the repetitive words and phrases on sentence strips as a visual aid.

Materials

Plastic sheeting to attach over the poem "Autumn Leaves" by Zakiyyah Denton

Two sentence strips (use a black marker to print the phrase *fall on me* on one strip; and *autumn leaves* on the other)

Set of different-colored Vis-à-Vis pens

Collection of sight-word cards previously presented

What This Lesson Looks Like

✤ Reread the poem chorally. Invite a student to use the pointer to touch each word as it is read.

✤ Review all sight words previously learned. Hold up the set of word cards and say, "These are all the sight words you've learned so far. You need plenty of practice reading these words to be able to read them quickly. I'll hold up each one for you to read. Please use a strong reading voice if you know the word. If you don't know the word, please listen to your classmates read the word aloud. The more you see it and hear it, the quicker you'll learn to read it, too."

✤ Explain the review activity to your students: "Since the beginning of the year, you've learned a lot about written language. Today you'll show me what you've learned about words in print. When you find a word you know, you'll read it aloud, and then circle it each time it appears in the poem. By the end of the lesson, you'll be able to see how many words you already know how to read."

✤ Instruct your students to find repetitive lines in the poem. Tell them, "First, raise your hand if you see a line that repeats." Invite a student to point to the line that repeats elsewhere in the poem. If the student has correctly pointed to a repetitive line, ask, "What does this line say? Where else do you see this same line? Please touch and read each word." Then say, "Choose a colored pen and make a big circle around each of these lines." Then put the pen aside so it won't be accidentally used again. Ask, "Who sees a different line that repeats somewhere else in the poem?" Invite a different student to point out another repetitive line. Follow the same procedure you used with the first student.

✿ Your students may have difficulty finding the phrase *fall on me,* which is broken into two lines. If this occurs, ask, "Can you find *fall on me* within these two lines?" Prompt the students by sweeping your hand across the line *Hoping you will fall*, and the next line, *on me.*

✿ Then instruct your students to find words they can read with automaticity. Say, "Please find a word you're able to read. Be ready to circle it each time you see it with the same colored pen you choose to use." If the pen colors run out before all known words are identified, return all pens to the package, and give a new direction: "You know so many words that we've run out of pen colors. Since we don't have any more colors to use, we'll change the shape to enclose your words. From now on, using one of these colored pens, you'll draw a box around the word you know how to read."

✿ After your students can't identify any more words, tell them, "You also have been practicing how to blend sounds to determine an unknown word. Let's practice this skill. After I stretch out the sounds I'll underline each word you're able to blend. If you can't blend the sounds, I'll tell you the word, but I won't be able to underline it. Listen as I sound out the first word." Sound out every word they didn't identify.

✿ Invite a student to read this poem independently. Say, "Please use the pointer to touch each word you say. Read this poem as if you are talking to the leaves on a tree in your yard."

❧ Reflection ❧

Since I had given my students adequate time and support to master these beginning reading skills, I knew they were ready to assume more responsibility for their learning. I wanted them to see for themselves that they were indeed making good progress in becoming independent readers. At first, they had a look of disbelief on their faces when I pointed out how much they were able to do independently. But then, one by one, each sat up straighter and cocked his or her head with an air of self-assurance. This review lesson not only reinforced learning; it also built their confidence. Since my students now viewed themselves as readers, they should be able to work more independently in future lessons.

LESSON FOURTEEN

Beginning, Medial, and Ending Consonant Letter t

What I Was Thinking

Before my students can decode words, they need to know the sounds of consonants and vowels with automaticity. In order to accomplish this goal, I wanted to plan focused experiences around letter-sound associations, along with the incidental learning that occurs during our word study. These lessons would allow my students to attend to the sound of different target letters and words within a meaningful context.

With this objective in mind, I searched "Autumn Leaves" for a suitable target consonant letter. When I noticed that the letter *t* appeared in different positions in several words in the poem, I decided to focus my lesson on this aspect of letter-sound association by using different learning modalities. Using the visual mode, my students would identify the location of *t* in different words in print, and, using the auditory mode, they would identify the position of this letter by listening to the sound of /t/ in these words.

Materials

Plastic sheeting to attach over the poem "Autumn Leaves" by Zakiyyah Denton

Three Vis-à-Vis pens: one green, one yellow, and one red

One green, yellow, and red Unifix cube for each student

A 3" x 5" card printed with a *T*

A 3" x 5" card printed with a *t*

What This Lesson Looks Like

❋ Invite a student to use the pointer to touch each word as you and the class read "Autumn Leaves" aloud.

❋ Then choose a student to come up to the chart stand to read the poem independently. Ask, "Who would like to read the poem aloud to the class?"

✵ Next, hold up the capital *T* letter card and ask, "What's the name of this letter?" Then hold up the lowercase *t* letter card and ask, "What's the name of this letter?" When your students respond that it's a *t*, ask, "Why do they look different?"

✵ Demonstrate how to form a *T* with your two index fingers. Say, "We're going to make a capital *T* using our pointy fingers." Demonstrate each step as you explain. "Put up your pointy finger of one hand. You just made a vertical line. Now put up the pointy finger of your other hand and turn it so it's horizontal. Lay this finger on top of your vertical finger. Make certain your vertical finger's touching the midpoint of your horizontal finger. You just made a *T* with a big line down and a big line across."

✵ Demonstrate how to form a *t*: "To make a lowercase *t*, put up your pointy finger. Now put up your baby finger of your other hand and turn it to a horizontal position. Place your baby finger near the top of your pointy finger. Make sure your pointy finger's touching the midpoint of your baby finger. You just made a *t* with a big line down and a little line across."

✵ Explain the focus of the word study. Tell your students: "You're going on a letter hunt today. Can you guess what letter you're going to hunt?" Respond: "You're right! You're going to hunt for the letter *t* in the poem. When you find this letter, you'll circle the letter with one of these colors." Hold up the appropriate pen as you say each direction. "If the letter *t* is at the beginning of the word, you'll circle it with the green pen. If the letter *t* is inside the word, you'll circle it with the yellow pen, and if it's at the end of the word, you'll use the red pen to circle the letter." Remind them about the traffic-light analogy: "There's a reason I chose the colors *red, yellow,* and *green.* Just as a green light signals a driver to go, a yellow light cautions the driver to slow down, and a red light signals the driver to stop, the reader starts from the first letter, proceeds slowly, and stops at the last letter in a word. Green means go: you're at the beginning of a word. Yellow means slow down: you're inside the word. And red means stop: you're at the end of the word."

✵ Begin the letter hunt by pointing out the letter *t* in the word *autumn.* Ask the class, "Where's the letter *t*?" When you hear a correct response, say,

"The letter is inside this word." Then ask, "Which color should I use to show that the letter is inside the word?" Circle the letter with the yellow pen. Ask your students, "Who knows this word?" If no one answers, segment the sounds for your students to blend. Follow with: "What's the word?"

✳ Invite your students to locate the letter *t* in a word. Ask the following questions each time a different student finds the letter: "Where's the letter located in this word? What color should you use to circle the letter? Do you know what this word says?" If the student doesn't know the word, segment the sounds and ask the student to blend the sounds and tell you the word.

✳ Explain the next activity: "I'm going to slowly move the pointer across the line. I'd like you to say /t/ whenever the pointer is directly under the letter *t*. You must be careful not to get ahead of the pointer. Only say /t/ when the pointer is pointing to the letter *t*." Then begin this exercise.

✳ When the letter-sound activity is completed, give each child an attached tricolor tower of cubes. Hold up a vertical tower and turn it to a horizontal position, with the green cube to the students' left. Say, "Please lay your attached cubes on the floor. The green cube should be the first one in the row, and the red cube should be the last one."

✳ Explain the activity to your students: "Now you're going to listen for the sound of *t*. I'll say one of the *t* words you identified in the poem. Listen carefully as I say the word. If you hear /t/ at the beginning of the word, you'll touch the green cube with your finger. If you hear /t/ inside the word, you'll touch the yellow cube, and if you hear /t/ at the end of the word, you'll touch the red cube." To check their understanding of the directions, ask your students to demonstrate: "Show me what you'll do if you hear /t/ at the beginning of the word, at the end of the word, and inside the word. Let's practice a few times. Where do you hear /t/ in the word *top*? Show me. In the word *top*, /t/ is the beginning sound. Your finger should be touching the green cube. Let's try another word. Where do you hear /t/ in the word *sit*? Show me. You hear /t/ at the end of *sit*, so your finger should be on the red cube. Where do you hear /t/ in the word

Every Child a Reader

until? Show me." Respond with: "This time the /t/ sound was not at the beginning, and it was not at the end, so it had to be inside the word. Your finger should be touching the yellow cube."

☼ When your students indicate that they understand what to do, remind them: "Listen for /t/ and as soon as you hear the /t/, touch the appropriate cube." Use the following words from the poem: *autumn, touch, forget, standing, tall,* and *tree*.

❧ Reflection ❧

This lesson provided me with a few surprises. I never realized that circling letters could be such a fun activity; my students loved it and were disappointed when the activity ended. And who would think that following a pointer across a chart would be so engaging? My students couldn't wait for the pointer to touch the letter *t* so they could say its sound. Sometimes students would say the sound before the pointer reached the letter. These students weren't being silly; they just couldn't contain themselves!

NOVEMBER

LESSON ONE

Review of the -ick Phonogram

The Pickety Fence

The pickety fence
The pickety fence
Give it a lick it's
The pickety fence
Give it a lick it's
A clickety fence
Give it a lick it's
A lickety fence
Give it a lick
Give it a lick
Give it a lick
With a rickety stick
Pickety
Pickety
Pickety
Pick

—David McCord

What I Was Thinking

In my search for another great poem to read, I wanted to find one this time that would reinforce the learning of the *-ick* phonogram. Although I knew the odds were stacked against me, I concentrated my efforts on locating a poem that included primarily *-ick* rhyming words. I couldn't believe my good fortune when I found this one by David McCord.

I was delighted to discover that McCord uses only the *-ick* phonogram and repeats it throughout the poem. I knew my students would be amused by the repeating sound, and as a result they would participate enthusiastically in the reading. In addition, by seeing different words formed from the sound pattern *-ick* and reading these words aloud many times, my students would be able to learn this word family faster and remember it longer.

In order to know how to proceed with this lesson I needed to find out if any of my students would be able to detect this phonogram in the poem without my help. If there were students who were able to recognize the chunk, then they could teach their classmates how to decode by rime analogy. If not, I'd have to reteach this decoding method.

To facilitate my students' learning, I'd use flap cards to emphasize the two rimes: *-ick* and *-ickety*. My students would practice blending the beginning sound and rime printed on each card, and then they'd locate each onset and rime in the poem.

By the end of this word study, it was my hope that my students would be more aware of this particular sound pattern in our written language so that they could decode unknown words more efficiently.

Materials

The poem "The Pickety Fence" by David McCord, handwritten in large, neat print on manila tag chart paper and attached by rings to a wooden chart stand

A 3" x 5" card with *give* printed neatly in large lowercase letters

Seven strips of 3" x 9" manila tag paper:

✻ Fold over about 2 inches of the left side of each paper strip.

✻ Using a red marker, copy the rime *-ick* onto the longer portion of three strips.

- Using a black marker, print an *l* on the back of the folded portion of one of the three strips.

- Using a black marker, print a *p* on the back of the folded portion of the second strip.

- Using a black marker, print *st* on the back of the folded portion of the final strip.

✻ Using a red marker, copy the rime *-ickety* onto the longer portion of the remaining four strips.

- Using a black marker, print a *p* on the back of the folded portion of one of the four strips.

- Using a black marker, print a *cl* on the back of the folded portion of the second strip.

- Using a black marker, print an *l* on the back of the folded portion of the third strip.

- Using a black marker, print an *r* on the back of the folded portion of the fourth and final strip.

What This Lesson Looks Like

☀ Read the title of the poem aloud.

☀ Introduce new vocabulary your students will need to know in order to comprehend the meaning of the poem. Ask, "What does a picket fence look like?" Since the word *picket* most likely won't be part of a kindergartner's vocabulary, sketch this type of fence for the class to see. Explain to them: "The word *picket* means a sharpened post. A picket fence is made up of a series of sharpened posts linked together enclosing an area." Then say, "I want you to listen carefully to the different words the poet used to create the impression of sounds in this poem."

☀ Read the poem aloud using a lively pace. When you've finished reading the poem, ask your students: "Which words imitate sounds? What was used to make the sounds?" Then ask, "How was a stick used to make the noise?"

☀ Begin the word study by telling your students: "The poet, David McCord, uses repeating sounds to imitate a stick being dragged across several wooden posts." Ask them, "Can you identify the repeating sound pattern in these words?" If someone points out the sound pattern *-ick*, ask the student to name this word family. Remind students that they learned about this phonogram in a previous lesson: "You practiced blending the beginning sound and the word part *-ick* together." Invite the student who identified the sound pattern to teach his or her classmates how to blend the two word parts to decode the word by asking: "Would you teach your classmates the steps you use to sound out this word?"

❋ If no one is able to identify the repeating sound pattern, point it out on the chart, naming the letters *i, c,* and *k* each time they appear in words. Remind students that they learned about this phonogram in a previous lesson: "You practiced blending various beginning sounds and the word part *-ick* together to make different words in the pocket chart."

❋ Then use the three flap cards highlighted with the *-ick* sound pattern. Start with words beginning with single consonants before sounding out words with consonant blends. Hold up one flap card. Flip back the beginning sound so that students only see the highlighted word part *-ick*. Ask your students, "What does this say?" Reveal the beginning letter by flipping the flap forward. Say, "Blend this beginning letter sound and *-ick*. What's the word?" After each word is blended, invite a student to locate the word each time it appears in the poem and read it aloud.

❋ Hold up the four flap cards highlighted with the *-ickety* rime. Flip back the beginning sound so only the word part *-ickety* is exposed. Explain to your students: "When you look at a word, you should look for word parts you recognize within the word." Ask your students, "Do you see a sound pattern you recognize?" Invite a volunteer to come up and point it out. Ask the student, "What did you see?" Affirm his correct response: "That's right! The letters *i-c-k* spell *-ick*." Explain how this sound pattern helps a reader decode more efficiently: "Since I recognize this sound pattern, I can just say /ick/ and sound out the remaining letters. Listen: /ĭk/ /ĕ/ /t/ /?/ *-ickety*." Tell your students: "Read this word part with me." Reveal the beginning letter by flipping the flap forward. Ask, "What's this letter?" Invite your students to say the letter's sound. Then say: "Let's blend the two word parts together. What's the word?" Invite a volunteer to locate the word and read it aloud each time it appears in the poem. Follow this procedure with the remaining word cards.

❋ Review all the words in the poem with the *-ick* phonogram. Direct your students: "I want you to read each word I point to with my pointer. Look carefully at the sound pattern. It might say *-ick* or it might say *-ickety*." Begin at the top and sweep across each line with the pointer. Stop at every word with this particular phonogram so that your class can read it aloud.

* Introduce the new high-frequency word: *give*. Explain to your students: "Once you know these words, you'll be able to read this poem all by yourselves."

  * Hold up the word card printed with *give*. Tell your students the word. Ask them: "How many letters are there?" Then say, "Listen as I sound out this sight word: /g/ /ĭ/ /v/. How many sounds did you hear?" Respond with: "You're right. You heard three sounds, but there are four letters. One letter in the word *give* doesn't make a sound." Then ask: "Which letter is silent?" Read, spell, and cheer the word (Cunningham, 1995).

* Shuffle the word card collection a few times. Tell the class: "Let's see how quickly you can read these sight words. As soon as you read the word aloud, I'll put it at the back of the pack. As soon as you see another word, read it aloud." Hold up the pack of sight words. Ask, "Are you ready? Let's read!" When you come to a word that causes a problem, ask a student who read it confidently, "What helped you remember the word?"

* Invite your students to read the poem chorally. Choose a student to use the pointer to demonstrate one-to-one matching (i.e., voice-print matching) as the poem is read aloud.

Reflection

Since most of my students were at the emergent stage of their reading development, it didn't surprise me that only a few students had remembered learning about the *-ick* phonogram. I sampled the understanding of the group by calling on Carter, who was already reading predictable texts. If he couldn't locate the repetitive sound pattern, it was highly unlikely that another student could. Although he recognized the sound pattern and read the word aloud without hesitation, I was surprised that he was completely baffled when I asked him to teach his classmates how he figured out the word. He just kept repeating, "I didn't figure it out. I just knew it." As I thought more about Carter's response, I realized that he was right. He had seen that word pattern enough to be able to recognize the word by sight.

Recognizing that my students would benefit from step-by-step guidance in learning to blend the two word parts, I guided Carter as he modeled the blending of sounds. Using the flap cards helped my students to better visualize the two parts of the word.

Every Child a Reader

By the end of the lesson, my students had a better understanding of decoding by analogy. However, I know they need much more work in analyzing words before they'll be able to independently recognize common spelling patterns in unfamiliar words. When they can competently analyze words sound by sound, they'll be more prepared to study phonograms. To enhance my students' knowledge of sound-spelling relationships, I must find meaningful poems that contain many CVC (consonant-vowel-consonant) words.

LESSON TWO
Figurative Language

Brooms

When the wind is high

Tall trees are brooms
Sweeping the sky.

They swish their branches

In buckets of rain

And swash and sweep it,
Blue again.

—Dorothy Aldis

What I Was Thinking

When I discovered the poem "Brooms" by Dorothy Aldis, I knew this would be a perfect poem to use in the month of November because it vividly describes the dreary weather in Maine we endure during this month. However, I also realized it would present a challenge to most of my students because of the poet's use of figurative language. I'd need to wait for a storm to hit before I presented the poem to my class so that my students would have specific weather-related images, such as bare-limbed trees swaying in the wind, fresh in their memory. In addition, I'd have a broom handy to use as a visual aid to make imagery come alive for those students who couldn't comprehend the figurative language.

Materials

The poem "Brooms" by Dorothy Aldis, handwritten in large, neat print on manila tag chart paper and attached by rings to a wooden chart stand

A broom

What This Lesson Looks Like

❉ Introduce the poem by saying: "This poem vividly describes the weather that we just had. Listen carefully as I read it aloud to you, so you'll be able to see how the poet's choice of words helps to create a picture in your mind."

❉ Read the poem aloud to your students. Emphasize the sounds of language in the poem.

❉ After reading the poem, ask your students, "What picture was created in your mind as I read this poem aloud?" Then ask: "Were there any words that struck you and helped you create that picture in your mind?" If your students can't remember the specific language used by the poet, reread the poem to them. Say, "I'm going to read the poem again. This time, pay attention to the poet's choice of words. As I read, ask yourself, 'Which words do I especially like, and why?' Remember these special words or lines so you can share them during our discussion." Then reread the poem aloud to your class.

❉ Begin the discussion by asking, "Which words struck you?" Most likely some student will suggest the word *swish* or *swash*. Explain to your students: "These words are sensory words because they help us hear the sound of the branches. Hearing is one of our senses." Then say, "Another sense is seeing. Dorothy Aldis helps the reader to visualize the tree better by comparing it to what object?"

❉ Hold up a broom for your students to see. Ask them, "What do you do with a broom?" If someone responds, "You sweep the floor with it," ask, "Why do you sweep a floor?" Invite a volunteer to demonstrate the sweeping movement of the broom. Then ask your students, "Who can use this broom to show how a tree could be like broom?" As a student demonstrates, ask: "What is this 'tree' cleaning?" If the student says the tree is cleaning the sky, prompt him to elaborate on his answer with these questions: "What would the sky look like on a stormy day? What color would the sky be on a rainy day? And then what happens when the rain stops? What would be the sky's color when sunny weather returns?"

✹ Invite your students to chime in during the final reading of the poem: "I'm going to read this poem again, but this time I want you to help me read some of the words aloud. Whenever I pause after I touch a word with the pointer, I want all of you to read it aloud in one big voice." Pause at these words in the poem: *brooms, sky, branches, rain,* and *blue.* If your students can't identify the word *blue,* try using contextual clues to help your students make sense of the word. Reread the last stanza and skip the word *blue.* When a student correctly supplies the missing word, invite your class to read the last stanza aloud with you.

❧ Reflection ❧

Phew! I'm so glad I had the broom handy, because most of my students couldn't understand the metaphor that Aldis used. Without this crucial understanding, my students wouldn't have been able to make sense of the poem. And as a result, they wouldn't have been able to enjoy the poet's choice of words.

Could it be that kindergartners are so literal in their thinking that they aren't able to comprehend a tree being like a broom, or could it be that they haven't been exposed to figurative language in their literary experiences? Even with my use of the visual aid (i.e., the broom), I observed puzzled expressions on the faces of many of my students. So I asked one of my kindergartners, Ridgely, to point out what each part of the broom represented as he held it upside down. After his demonstration, everyone appeared to understand the comparison of a tree to a broom. But to be certain, before ending Poetry Time, I decided to reinforce the meaning of the poem by asking my students to act it out as I read the stanzas aloud again. I knew they understood the metaphor when some children exclaimed, "Look! The ceiling's whiter now!"

LESSON THREE

Introduction of New Sight Words and the Consonant Digraphs <u>th</u>, <u>ch</u>, and <u>sh</u>

What I Was Thinking

When I looked for possible word-study lessons, I noticed the common consonant digraphs and various consonant blends scattered throughout the poem. Although I was anxious to teach my students how to stretch out sounds in unfamiliar words, I realized that these special sounds needed to be learned first in order to help them decode words successfully and quickly. Since emergent readers often sound out the first letter they see in the word, it would be better to introduce the common digraphs (e.g., *th, sh,* and *ch*) prior to the introduction of consonant blends to alleviate future confusion between the two. My students needed to learn that each digraph makes its own special sound totally unlike either of the consonant letters. Teaching the digraphs now would serve as a bridge to learning about consonant blends such as *tr, sw,* and *bl.*

Materials

Plastic sheeting to attach over the poem "Brooms"

Two 3" x 5" cards with *they* and *of* printed neatly in large lowercase letters

Vis-à-Vis colored pens

Chart paper

A red marker

A black marker

What This Lesson Looks Like

☼ Introduce the new sight words.

- Hold up the word card printed with *they*. Ask your students, "What's this word?" By this time of year, there will be a few students who can recognize many high-frequency words, so I want to involve these students as much as I can. However, if no one can identify it, tell the class the word: "This word says *they*." Explain to your class: "It's another word that can't be sounded out. You have to memorize it by remembering its special characteristic." Ask your students, "Do you see a word inside of *they* which you already know?" When a student points out the word *the*, provide him or her with specific feedback: "Wow! You really know the word *the* because now you can even recognize it when it's inside a word." Then say to the class, "When I want to remember a sight word, I try to picture it in my mind." Continue by thinking aloud, "I know the word *the* is spelled *t-h-e*, so to remember the word *they*, all I have to remember is when I see a word with *t-h-e* at the beginning and the letter *y* at the end, the word is *they*." Instruct your class: "Please close your eyes and try to picture the letters as I say them: *t-h-e*. Now add a *y*. What's the word? *They*." Then say, "Now I want you to spell the word *they* aloud as we spell and cheer this new sight word" (Cunningham, 1995). To maintain a whole-group response, instruct your class: "Please name the letter when I point to it. Watch my finger so you can recite together in one big voice." When they've finished the cheer, tell them: "Let's practice picturing the word *they* in our minds. What word's at the beginning of the word *they*? And what letter's at the end of the word? So how do you spell *they*?" After your students spell *they*, hold up the word card and say, "Let's check your accuracy: *t-h-e-y* spells *they*!"

- Hold up the word card *of*. Ask your students, "What does this word say?" If none of your students correctly reads it aloud, tell your class the word: "The word *of* [print it on the chart paper] is often confused with this word [print *off* under *of*]." Pointing to the word *off*, tell them, "This word is *off*." Invite students to use their visual and auditory discrimination skills by asking, "Why do you think these words are so easily confused?" Students' responses may include: "They look similar except there's one more *f* in *off*," "The word *of* is at the beginning of the word *off*," and "If you didn't know that the word *of* was a sight word and tried to sound it out, it would sound like the word *off*." Then ask them to look at the sight word *of*. Generate ideas for remembering this new sight word by asking: "What's going to help you remember this word?" After students have offered their suggestions, spell and cheer the word *of* together (Cunningham, 1995).

- Invite your students to locate the new sight words in the poem by asking, "Who sees the word *they* in the poem? If you find it, raise your hand and keep your eyes focused on the word. Most of the time I can tell if you've located the correct word by looking at where you focus your eyes. Let's see if I'm right this time." Choose a volunteer whose eyes appear to be focused on the word *they*. If the student has correctly located the word, instruct him or her: "Sweep the pointer across the word as you read the word." After the student reads it aloud, invite him or her: "Please point to each letter as you spell the word *they*." Follow the same procedure for locating the word *of*.

- Invite your students to point out other sight words they've previously studied.

✿ Choose a student to use the pointer to track the print as the class reads the poem aloud with you. Remind the class: "You must say the word that your classmate touches. Keep your eyes focused on the pointer so you don't get ahead of it."

✿ Explain the purpose of the word study: "There are three special sounds in this poem called consonant digraphs that you need to learn." Use a red marker to print *th, sh,* and *ch* on the chart paper. Say the letters as you write them.

✿ Ask your students, "What do each of these letter combinations have in common?" When a student responds that the letter *h* follows the first consonant letter in each digraph, point to each digraph and emphasize the *h* as you name each letter of the digraph. Say, "*t*-**h**, *s*-**h**, *c*-**h**."

✿ Continue your explanation by saying, "They're special because each of these digraphs is a combination of two consonant letters that make a special sound entirely different from either of the letters that creates it. You don't say /t/ /h/; you say /th/. You don't say /s/ /h/; you say /sh/. And you don't say /c/ /h/; you say /ch/."

✿ Explain how to make the /th/ sound: "To make the /th/ sound, place the tip of your tongue between your teeth. Blow air out through the front of your tongue." Then say, "Let's practice making the /th/ sound together." Hold up your thumb as you say: "The word *thumb* starts with *th*. We'll use the word *thumb* to help us remember /th/. Say /th/ as you tap your thumb on your index finger."

✸ Invite your students to locate all *th* words. Say, "Two of them are words you already know how to read. Can you find and read these words aloud?" After a student locates and reads one of the sight words aloud, tell the student to circle the *th* digraph: "Choose a colored pen to circle the *th* digraph in the word you found." After the student chooses a color, tell the class, "You'll use this color each time you find a *th* word." After another student has completed circling the *th* in the second word, tell your class, "I'll help you read the last *th* word if you don't know it. Your job is to locate this word, circle the *th*, and say the special sound that the *th* makes."

✸ Reread the *th* words chorally in consecutive order. Sweep across the word with the pointer as you read each word aloud.

✸ Explain how to make the /sh/ sound: "This is my favorite sound. To make the /sh/ sound, round out your lips and stick them out. Keep your teeth together and blow out air in a steady stream." Demonstrate how to make the /sh/ sound. Ask your students, "Do you know why the *sh* is my favorite sound?" Respond by saying, "I call it 'the quiet sound,' and you know I like quiet workshops." Then say, "Let's practice the /sh/ sound together." Touch your index finger to your lips and say, "This quiet signal will help us remember the /sh/ sound."

✸ Invite your students to search the poem for the only word with the *sh* digraph. Choose a student to point to the word: "Where is the *sh* located in this word?" Then guide the student to isolate the individual sounds in this word. After the student isolates the sounds, repeat the blending of the sounds so she or he is able to determine the word. Then, instruct the student to circle the *sh* digraph by saying, "Choose a different pen color to circle the *sh* digraph in the word *swish*."

✸ Demonstrate how to make the /ch/ sound: "This sound is made almost the same way you make the /sh/ sound. The only difference is that your tongue hits the roof of your mouth as you produce the sound. Watch me as I make this sound." Invite your class to practice the /ch/ sound with you. Then ask, "Does this sound remind you of something?" Respond to the posed question if no one answers: "It makes me think of the word that describes the sound of a train chugging down a railroad track—a *choo-choo* train! *Choo-choo* and *chugging* both begin with the */ch/* sound." As you enunciate the */ch/* sound, make circular motions with your clenched hands to simulate the wheels of a train moving down a track. Tell your students, "This will be the special signal for */ch/*."

✦ Invite your students to search the poem for the only word containing the *ch* digraph. Choose a student to point to the word. Ask, "Where's the *ch* located in this word?" Blend the sounds of the word *branches* for the student. Then ask, "What does this word say?" Invite the student to circle the *ch* digraph by saying, "Choose a different pen color to circle the *ch* digraph in the word *branches*."

✦ Say, "Today we learned about three consonant digraphs." Point to each digraph as you name it—*th*, *sh*, and *ch*. To check students' understanding of digraphs, invite them to participate in the review by saying, "I'd like you to share one piece of information you learned about these digraphs."

Note: Your students most likely will remember that each digraph makes a unique sound and that some digraphs are a combination of two consonant letters with the letter *h* following the first consonant. However, it's unlikely they'll remember the specific sound for each of them.

✦ Review the key words for each digraph and practice the signal cue associated with each of them: *thumb, choo-choo,* and *SH-H-H!* As you review a key word, sketch a pictorial clue beside the appropriate digraph, and practice making the digraph's sound. Sketch a thumb for *th*, a train for *ch*, and an ear crossed out for *sh*. Explain to your students: "I'm going to sketch an ear beside the *sh* to help you remember this digraph's special sound. But I'm going to cross out it out with a big *X*." Ask your students: "Why did I cross out the ear with an *X*?" When a student correctly responds say: "That's right! It's the quiet sound." Then put your finger to your lips. Tell your students, "This is the signal for *sh*." Choose someone to demonstrate the sound for the *sh* digraph. Ask the student, "Can you show me the signal for the */sh/* sound?" Then invite the class to practice the sound together.

Every Child a Reader

✤ After the digraphs have been reviewed, generate a short list of three or four words containing the /th/ sound in the initial position. Begin the brainstorming by saying, "I can think of a word that starts with /th/. Our new sight word begins with th." On chart paper, print the word they under the th column. Say the name of the letter as you write it: "T-h-e-y." Ask, "What's the word?" If nobody responds, say, "It's the word they." Explain to your students: "Today you'll begin a list of words that begin with /th/, /sh/, and /ch/. When you've given me two or three more /th/ words, we'll brainstorm a few /sh/ words, and then end the activity by thinking of some /ch/ words for me to write. Our list will gradually grow longer, because I'll add new words that begin with these common digraphs as we encounter them in the poems we read." Then begin the exercise by asking your students: "Can you think of some words that begin with /th/?" As you enunciate the sound, tap your thumb on your index finger. Follow this procedure for each digraph.

❧ Reflection ❧

Since other kindergarten groups have learned the sh digraph with relative ease, I expected similar results with this class. And once again, these students had no difficulty generating /sh/ words. However, they were stumped by the /th/ digraph. To help them produce some /th/ words, I gave them word riddles to solve, such as, "What number comes after 12?" They enjoyed solving the riddles, and it also helped them become more aware of words that begin with the /th/ sound.

Since I realize they'll need support from me for some time to help them remember digraph sounds, I need to review the actions associated with the key words for each digraph because I'll be using those actions to help them remember the appropriate digraph sound. In addition, I must remember to take time to point out different digraphs in words my students encounter during the day. Eventually, they'll learn the distinctive features of these special sounds—just like all my former classes have.

I've often wondered why kindergartners learn the sounds of different digraphs with relative ease. Is it because young children are intrigued by each digraph's unique sound, or does the memory device of associating actions and key words with these digraphs help children remember them?

LESSON FOUR
Review of the Consonant Digraphs
<u>th</u>, <u>ch</u>, and <u>sh</u> and Consonant Blends

What I Was Thinking

As I thought about the progression of skills for my next lesson, I knew I had to answer one question that nagged at me: should I introduce blends now or wait until my students strengthen their understanding of digraphs? The answer was made clear when I noticed the abundance of consonant blends in this poem, especially s-blends and r-blends. I knew then that I definitely needed to take advantage of this ideal opportunity to explore consonant blends, which this poem offered.

In order for this lesson to work effectively, I'd need to depart from my normal teaching routine. First, when Poetry Time began, I'd review the digraphs before reading the poem aloud as we usually do. Then, during the reading, my students would utilize their knowledge to identify different digraphs contained in various words in the poem. Since my students aren't able to recognize some of these words yet, I'd have them listen as I read the poem aloud, so they could focus on the sounds in the words rather than the recognition of the words. After the warm-up activities are completed, my students should be ready for the introduction of consonant blends.

Materials

Six 3" x 3" cards printed with *st, sw, sk, br, tr,* and *bl*—one consonant blend per card

Pocket chart

Sticky notes
   ☼ Before class, use sticky note tabs to cover the *sh* in *swish*, the *th* in *the*, the *th* in *they*, the *th* in *their*, the *ch* in *branches*, and the *sh* in *swash* in the poem "Brooms."

Chart paper labeled with *th, eh,* and the drawn symbols of a thumb, train, and a crossed out ear.,

What This Lesson Looks Like

   ☼ Explain why some letters in different words are covered in the poem "Brooms,"

Say, "I covered digraphs for you to identify when I read these particular words aloud. But first, let's review the different sounds of these common digraphs."

☀ Point to the different headings on the chart paper labeled with *th, sh,* and *ch.* Say, "Let's name each digraph as I point to it." Ask, "What's the common letter in each of these digraphs?" Then ask, "Why is there a picture of a thumb next to the *th*?" Confirm a student's response by saying, "That's right. **Thumb** [emphasize the */th/* sound as you say the word] starts with */th/.*" Invite your students to practice this sound with you. Continue the same procedure for the *sh* and *ch* digraphs.

☀ Check your students' understanding of the sounds of the common digraphs. Ask them, "What's the sound for *sh* . . . for *th* . . . for *ch*?"

☀ Review the actions associated with each key word. After you demonstrate the signal for */th/* invite your students to perform the action. Tell them, "Tap your thumb on your index finger each time you say */th/.*" Continue with the demonstration by saying, "I bet you don't need my help giving me the */sh/* signal. Show me the */sh/* signal." Then ask, "Why is there a train next to the *ch* digraph?" Respond to a student's correct answer by saying, "It is a *choo-choo* train chugging down the track." Demonstrate the action that will be used as a signal for the *ch* digraph. Then invite your students to practice the signal with you: "Let's get the train's wheels moving."

☀ Check your students' understanding by asking them to demonstrate the action of the specific digraph named by you, "Show me the signal for */sh/* . . . for */th/* . . . for */ch/.*"

☀ Introduce the warm-up activity to your students: "I'm going to say a word that begins with *th, sh,* or *ch.* Please listen carefully as I say the word because when I say, 'Show me,' you're going to perform the action associated with that particular digraph's key word. Don't perform the action until you hear me say these two words: 'Show me.' " Use the following words: *shoe, thermometer, chain, chart, thirteen, shark, thimble, change, shell,* and *shawl.*

☀ Emphasize the digraph's sound as you say the word. After your students signal their responses, demonstrate the appropriate action: "*Shoe* begins with */sh/.* And the signal for */sh/* is this [put your index finger to your lips]. What letter combination makes this special sound?" Respond by naming the appropriate digraph. Follow this procedure for each word.

☼ After the warm-up exercise, turn your students' attention to the poem. Explain: "Now that you're warmed up, you're ready to be a sound detective. Please listen as I read the poem aloud. I'll stop at every word containing a digraph. If you can identify the sound, please signal me with the appropriate action. Remember: touch your lips for *sh*; move your fists around and around in a circle for *ch*; and tap your thumb on your index finger for *th*. Now listen carefully." Begin reading the poem aloud. Stop after you read the word *the*. Ask your students, "What sound do you hear at the beginning of *the*?" Then say, "Show me." Ask a student who responds with the correct signal: "Which digraph says /*th*/?" Tell the student, "Let's see if you're right." As you remove the sticky note, say, "The digraph that says /*th*/ is [remove the sticky note] *t-h*." Follow the same procedure for the remaining covered digraphs.

☼ Read the poem again chorally. Invite a student to use the pointer to touch each word as the class reads the poem aloud.

☼ Explain the purpose of the new word study: "There's another combination of two or three consonants that can appear together at the beginning, in the middle, and at the end of the word. But each sound is heard as they're blended together. Now that you can recognize a digraph, you'll be able to distinguish a consonant blend from a digraph." Ask, "What's the common letter in digraphs?" Reiterate a student's correct response by saying, "Yes, the letter *h* always follows the first consonant letter. So if there is no *h* in a group of consonants, then you know each sound will be heard."

☼ Explain to your students that the alphabet is made up of consonants and vowels: "There are many more consonant letters than vowel letters. If you know the vowel letters, then it's easy to figure out which letters are consonants. Let's see if this is true." Invite your students to take turns naming different vowels: "Raise your hand if you can name a vowel." Draw a box on the chart paper. When a student correctly responds, write the vowel letter in the box. Continue this process until all of the vowels have been identified. Ask your students to say the names of the vowels aloud with you. If a student names the letter *y*, explain to the class: "The letter *y* can be both a consonant and a vowel. The letter *y* is a consonant if it's at the beginning of the word. If the letter *y* is at the end of the word, then it's a vowel. Since you'll be looking for consonant blends at the beginning of words, I'm not

Every Child a Reader

going to list the *y* as a vowel." Then ask them: "How many vowels are in the alphabet?" When someone responds with the number five, say, "Yes, there are five vowels listed, and now we know that *y* sometimes is a vowel, too. So how many vowels are there in all?" Tell them: "The alphabet's composed of 26 letters. If we know there are six vowels, how many more letters are there in the alphabet?" These 20 letters are called consonants.

Note: I like to pose a challenging math question whenever an opportunity arises because there usually are one or two students who are mathematically adept. However, since I don't expect my students to be able to solve this problem at this time of year, I tell them the answer if nobody can solve it.

✿ Fold under the bottom half of the chart paper containing the vowels so you can write the consonants on a clean page, but your students will still be able to refer to the list of vowels to help them identify consonant letters. Number the new piece of chart paper from one to 20. As you begin numbering, tell them, "There are 20 consonants in the alphabet. If you know these letters are the vowels [point to the box of letters], what are the names of the consonants?" Choose each student in turn to name a consonant until the list is complete.

✿ Instruct your students to look for words in the poem that begin with consonant blends. Begin the exercise by finding a consonant blend. Say, "The word *brooms* begins with two different consonants: *b* and *r*." State the sounds that each consonant makes and then blend them together. Ask, "Do you see other words that start with two different consonants a consonant blend?" As a student points out a consonant blend in a word, insert the corresponding consonant blend card into the pocket chart. When all have been identified, turn your students' attention to the pocket chart. Point to the first consonant blend and say, "Name the consonant letters that makes up this blend. Say the sounds of these letters. Now blend them together." Follow the same procedure for the remaining blends.

❧ Reflection ❧

Introducing digraphs prior to consonant blends proved to be the better approach. Because my students remembered the letter *h* was part of every digraph, they didn't confuse the digraphs and consonant blends when they were asked to locate different consonant blends. Without this prior knowledge, my students most likely would have insisted that *th, sh,* and *ch* were consonant blends because they, too, are made up of consonant letters.

I believe the success of this lesson was primarily due to the visual aid we produced together. Having the consonants listed on the chart paper helped all students identify the different consonant blends, especially those students who didn't have much experience with letters before entering kindergarten.

However, one more quick review of these particular blends is needed before I introduce another poem. Although I could have attempted to squeeze it into this lesson, I knew I'd be pushing my luck. I'd rather end our learning on a happy note. We'll continue to explore consonant blends during our next word study. Besides, I don't have to create a new lesson—it's already done!

LESSON FIVE
Review of Consonant Blends

What I Was Thinking

Since I didn't have time during yesterday's lesson to review the specific words in the poem that begin with consonant blends, I knew that spending another day focused on this poem would serve to enhance my students' reading skills. In addition, by rereading this poem, my students would be able to remember more of its words. I also hoped they'd be able to associate the consonant blends, which were displayed in the pocket chart with specific words from the poem.

To actively involve all students, I'd put them in pairs to sort the consonant blends, practice blending the sounds of each consonant cluster, and identify the words in the poem that begin with each blend. Then we'd come together as a whole group to share their findings.

Materials

One set of 3" x 3" cards for each pair of students printed with *st, sw, sk, br, tr,* and *bl*

One set of 3" x 3" cards for each student with *s-blends, r-blends,* and *l-blends* printed in red

A list of my students, grouped into pairs—capable students paired with less-skilled students

One copy of the poem "Brooms" for each pair of students

What This Lesson Looks Like

☀ Invite a student to lead the class in the rereading of the poem: "Who would like to lead the class in rereading the poem 'Brooms'? You need to read clearly, and use the pointer to touch each word as you read it aloud."

☀ After the poem is read chorally, direct the students' attention to the consonant blend cards in the pocket chart. Say, "Yesterday you identified these six blends in the poem. Let's name them together: *st, sk, sw, br, tr,* and *bl*." Then say, "Now let's make the sound of the *st* blend. Remember that each sound is heard in a consonant blend. *St* says /*st*/." Follow this procedure for the remaining five blends.

☀ Explain the sorting activity. Tell your students, "There are three groups of blends: *s*-blends, *r*-blends, and *l*-blends." As you say a type of blend, hold up the card labeled with it. "You'll work with a partner today. First, you'll work together to sort the six blends into their appropriate groups. Then, you and your partner will practice saying the blended sound of each consonant cluster chorally and individually. Finally, you'll work together to identify the words from the poem that begin with each of these consonant blends. When you come together as a whole group, I'll ask each pair to identify at least one word that begins with a particular consonant blend." Ask your students, "What will you and your partner do with these cards?" When your students respond, "Sort them," continue your questioning: "After you sort the cards into their appropriate groups, what should you and your partner practice?" After your students respond, say: "First, sort them." Then, say to them, "Last, look for them." Remind them: "When you and your partner return to the large group, be prepared to tell me a word from the poem that begins with each of these blends. You need to be prepared for all six blends because you don't know which blend I'll choose for you and your partner. If you have any questions or concerns, please raise your hand." Before dismissing your student pairs, say, "I expect you to work well together. Use soft voices, take turns, and allow your partner time to think before helping."

✿ As you name a pair of students, hand the blend cards and labels for sorting to one of the students in each pair. Tell each pair: "Find your own personal space to work where you won't be distracted by another pair of students."

✿ Stop at each group to listen and watch. Check to see if they are working cooperatively and are on task. If some students have difficulty remembering specific words from the poem, give them a copy of the poem to help them identify the words. Observe how they identify these words. During your observation, keep in mind the following questions: Do they reread each line from the beginning to the word containing the specific blend? Do they attempt to sound out the word? Do they immediately recognize a word or words?

✿ When the majority of students appear to be almost finished, announce: "You need to return to the large group when the big black hand of the clock is on the [name the number]."

✿ When your students have returned to the large group, review what they practiced with their partners. Call on a student to sort the six blends by types.

✿ After they've been sorted, say, "Let's blend the sounds for each s-blend." Then choose a student to blend the sounds for each s-blend independently. Follow the same procedure for the r-blends and the l-blend; but choose different students to blend the sounds independently.

✿ Review the words that start with each of the blends. Explain to your students: "There are 10 words in this poem that begin with a blend. Let's start with the s-blend words." Ask your students: "There are four different words in the poem that begin with sw. Can you name one of the words that starts with /sw/?" When someone identifies the word sweep, explain to your students: "There's another word in the poem that begins with the word sweep and ends with ing. Does anyone know this word?" If no one knows, blend the two parts and ask, "What's the word?" Then ask, "How's the word sweeping different from the word sweep?" If your students can't remember all four words, direct their attention to the poem and ask, "Where do you see the *sw* blend?" When a student points to a word, help him or her stretch the sounds and blend them together. Then ask, "What's the word?" After all four words are identified, repeat these words back to the class, emphasizing the beginning blend. Say, "*Swish, swash, sweep,* and *sweeping* all begin with /sw/. Let's name some other words that begin with /sw/." As a student contributes a word, repeat the growing list of *sw* words. When two or three words have been suggested, point to the next heading. Say, "I know I'm stopping you before your supply of *sw* words has been exhausted, but we have two more kinds of blends to discuss. I'll make sure everyone has a chance to contribute other words." Then continue the same procedure for the *r*-blend and *l*-blend words.

✺ Explain to the students: "We've read this poem several times together and studied many of its words in depth. I believe you can read this poem all by yourselves. We'll read it together first so I can hear you say the words aloud one last time. Then I'll choose one of you to stand in front of the class and read it aloud to your classmates." Begin reading chorally.

✺ Call on a student who demonstrated fluency during the choral reading to read independently. Give the pointer to the student to practice voice-print matching.

❧ Reflection ❧

I was pleased that my students worked so well in pairs, sharing responsibility for completing the activity and staying on task throughout. Since I knew my students' strengths and weaknesses, I was able to couple up those who I knew would work well together. They were accepting of their assigned partners because they knew the difference between a learning partner and a play partner. As I often tell my students, "Our learning partners may be different from our play partners."

Although they've been in kindergarten for only two months, I'm already noticing a positive change in their behaviors. They've become such a cohesive group—caring more about their classmates and less about themselves. Even though it's difficult for young children to be patient, they did their best to give their partners time to think. It was a noticeable difference from the beginning of the year.

Making Predictions and Using Multiple Strategies to Figure Out New Words

---

I'm Small

The wind is
shaking every tree.
The wind is strong
But trees are tall.

The wind is
pounding every wall.
But walls are strong
And they won't fall.

I think
I'll hold on
tight today.
I'm small.

—Lilian Moore

What I Was Thinking

This poem made me recall an incident that had happened earlier in the month. On a blustery November day, I gazed out a back window of the school to watch my kindergartners walk down the hill to the "barn" with their gym teacher, Pam. There they were—attempting to move forward in a straight line and trying to stand upright. But the strong wind kept pushing them back—and even down to the ground. Pam stopped the line and instructed each of my students to tightly hold hands with his or her classmates. Walking against the strong gusts of wind, they looked so small as they valiantly battled the wind.

Because this image was still so vivid for me, I was hoping one of my kindergartners would remember the same experience after I shared this poem with the class. Since they had personally felt the strength of the wind that day, I believed this poem would be especially meaningful and perhaps be instilled in their hearts as well as in their minds.

Materials

The poem "I'm Small" by Lilian Moore, handwritten on manila tag chart paper in large, neat print and attached by rings to a wooden chart stand

What This Lesson Looks Like

☀ Read the title aloud. Invite children to share their ideas about when it would be useful to be small and when it would be difficult. Then ask them to make predictions about the poem: "How many of you think this poem will describe a situation that would make it difficult to be small? How many think it will describe a situation that would make it helpful to be small?"

☀ Read the poem aloud in a conversational tone. Then ask your students, "What did this poem describe?" Discuss the action words in the poem. Ask, "What word did Lilian Moore choose to use to let the reader hear the force of the wind against the wall?" If necessary, give this hint: "What's the wind doing to the tree?" Continue the discussion by asking, "What do you think the child is holding?" After each idea is shared, ask, "Why?" Invite the children to share their own experiences of windy weather.

☀ Invite your students to share their knowledge of words. Tell your students, "Before you help me read the poem, I'd like each of you to point to a word you already know how to read. It may be a sight word you've learned or it may be a new word that you'd like to teach your classmates. When you're ready, put your hand on your head." When most students have signaled that they've found a word, whip around the class.

Note: Accept duplicate words at this time. Your immediate goal is to instill self-confidence in your students. You'll find that as the year progresses, your students will develop the necessary skills to figure out new words to share.

☀ When everyone has pointed out a word that they know, reread those words to your students. Praise them by saying, "Wow! You know many words in this poem. Soon you won't need me to read the poem aloud to you. You'll be able to do it by yourselves! Keep up the good work!"

❀ Before you reread the poem, explain to your students that this poem contains words that rhyme with *small*. Point to the word *small* in the title and ask, "What little word do you see in the word *small*?" When a student correctly responds, sweep the pointer across the word *all* as you say the word. Then invite your class to spell the word *all* with you as you point to each letter. Tell your students, "You know that words rhyme when they sound the same at the end. If this poem contains words that rhyme with *small*, what will each rhyming word sound like at the end?" Then say, "That's right! They'll say *all* at the end."

❀ Explain to your students how they'll participate during the final rereading of the poem. Inform your students: "Please listen to the poem as I read it aloud. When I come to a rhyming word, I'll pause for you to say it aloud. Be sure to focus on the pointer as I touch each word that I say. And be ready to read the rhyming word aloud each time I pause."

❀ Reread the poem aloud, pausing at *tall*, *wall*, *fall*, and *small*.

❧ Reflection ❧

Allowing my students to share words they knew proved to be a good, quick assessment of their reading progress. Not only was I delighted to see the variety of words they pointed out, I was particularly pleased with the risks some students took to share unfamiliar words.

When students pointed out new words, I took time to ask them how they had figured them out. I wanted their classmates to see the variety of strategies they could use to determine an unknown word. In addition, it gave me valuable information about these particular students as readers. For example, Carissa, a sight reader, recognized the word *trees* because she remembered seeing it in the poem "Brooms"; Josie used rime analogy to share the word *tall*; and Ridgely, a phonetic reader, sounded out the word *wind*. Each of these students utilized a different strategy to figure out unfamiliar words because they chose a technique with which they were most comfortable. In future lessons, I'd help them become more comfortable using other methods as well.

LESSON SEVEN

Review of Digraphs, Blends, and Sight Words

What I Was Thinking

This poem contains both digraphs and consonant blends, and I knew it wouldn't hurt to review both types of sounds with my students because this continual exposure would help reinforce their recognition of the unique sounds of the digraphs. They had already practiced several two-letter *s*-blends in the poem "Brooms," but they needed to understand that blends also could be a combination of three consonant letters. This poem contained a three-letter *s*-blend, *str*, which I wanted my students to discover by themselves. To accomplish this, I'd cover all the blends in the poem in order for them to determine the beginning consonant sounds aurally as I read the word aloud. Then they'd choose the appropriate letter cards to build the blend in a pocket holder.

Materials

Construction paper strips attached with tape to cover each of the following blends: the *sm* in *small*, the *sh* in *shaking*, the *str* in *strong*, the *tr* in *tree*, and the *th* in *think*

Two 3" x 5" cards with *is* and *are* printed neatly in large lowercase letters

One pocket holder per student

   ✿ Place an 8½" x 11" piece of white card stock in landscape position.

   ✿ Fold up the bottom edge to make a 3-inch pocket; tape the sides with filament tape.

   ✿ Put a smiley-face sticker on the upper left corner of the pocket holder to help students understand directionality.

   ✿ After the pocket holder has been laminated, cut the top edge of the pocket to open it up.

One set of five 1" x 5.5" letter cards per student

   ✿ At the top of each of the five cards neatly print one of these lowercase letters: *s, t, r, m, h*.

   ✿ Wrap a rubber band around each set of letter strips, which includes one of each of the five letters.

What This Lesson Looks Like

✿ Explain why parts of some words have been covered with strips of paper: "Today you're going to use your knowledge of letter sounds to figure out the letters I've covered in some words in the poem."

✿ Before you begin this activity, review what your students have learned about digraphs. Begin by asking, "What's a digraph?" When someone responds that a digraph makes a special sound, ask your students, "Can you remember one of the digraphs and the special sound it makes?" As each digraph is identified, write its name on the white board with a sketch of the key word associated with that particular digraph. If your students can't remember a certain digraph, prompt them by giving the action associated with that digraph. When *th, sh,* and *ch* have been printed on the white board, ask your students, "What letter do digraphs have in common?" When someone states the letter *h* is the common letter, ask that student to elaborate on his or her answer, "Where is the *h* located in each digraph?"

✿ Point to each digraph and ask your students, "What's the special sound for *th*? For *sh*? For *ch*?"

✿ Then ask your students, "What's a blend?" Follow with: "How is it different from a digraph?"

✿ Remind your students: "You've learned about three kinds of blends: *s*-blends, *r*-blends, and *l*-blends." Print each type of blend on the white board. Then say, "Who can remember one word from the poem 'Brooms' that begins with an *s*-blend?" If no one is able to recall a word, ask: "What do you do with a broom?" When your students call out the word *sweep*, instruct your students to listen for the consonant blend as you slowly repeat the word. Ask them, "What two consonants make up the blend at the beginning of *sweep*?" Repeat the same procedure for the other two kinds of blends.

Note: Your students should easily recall the words *brooms* and *blue*. If they have difficulty recalling the words, prompt their memories by providing them with clues.

✿ Pass out a set of letter cards and a pocket holder to each student. Direct them: "Please place your pocket holder on the floor in front of you. Remove the rubber band from your letter cards and place it in the pocket of your pocket holder for safekeeping. Then arrange each letter card in a line above your pocket holder. When you've completed these three steps, focus your eyes on me so I know that you're ready to begin the activity."

* Explain your behavioral expectations and directions for this lesson. Begin to draw a face. As you draw the eyes, say, "During this lesson, your eyes should be focused on your own work." Then draw a zippered mouth and say, "Your lips should remain zipped throughout the entire activity. I should be the only one speaking." Then draw big ears. Add wavy lines outside the outline of the ears to represent sounds. Explain to your students: "You should listen carefully to the beginning sounds that I've covered because you'll place the appropriate letter cards from this pack [hold up a set of letter cards] into a pocket holder [hold up a pocket holder] to display the blend you heard in the word I read aloud."

* To check their understanding of what they'll be doing during the activity, invite your students to practice with you: "Let's practice what this activity should sound like and look like. When I say a word you'll choose the letter cards that make up the consonant blend or digraph you hear at the beginning of the word and put them into your pocket holder. Remember: it's important to display the letters in the correct order." Ask them, "In which direction do we read?" After your students respond correctly, repeat with: "Yes, we read from left to right, so place the letter sound you heard at the beginning in the packet first. Then place the second letter *after* the first letter." Instruct them to point to the smiley-face sticker: "The smiley-face is on the left. I'll help you remember where to begin building the consonant blend." Begin with a practice word such as *treat*. "Listen as I say the word *treat*: **treat**. What blend do you hear at the beginning of *treat*? Choose the two consonant letters you hear at the beginning of the word and place them in the pocket holder. Remember to place the letters in the correct position—from left to right. When you've finished, look at me to signal me you're ready to check your accuracy." Remind them: "I shouldn't hear a sound. Everyone should work quietly."

* Observe your students as they work on the task, but do *not* correct them if errors are made. Instead, when everyone has finished, call on someone who has correctly built the blend in his or her pocket holder to identify the appropriate blend. After the student responds, say, "You heard the *tr* blend?

Let's see if you're right." Say the word slowly, emphasizing the consonant blend: "/tr/ /e/ /t/." Ask the class, "What sound do you hear at the beginning of *tree*?" When the letter *t* is identified, place the *t* letter card in the pocket, saying, "Since it's the first sound, I need to put it on the left side of the pocket holder. Notice how the smiley-face helps me know where to begin." Continue building the consonant blend by repeating the word *treat*. Ask, "What's the next consonant sound you hear in the word *treat*?" Insert the *r* next to the *t* and sound out the blend: /tr/. Praise the student for correctly identifying the blend at the beginning of the word *treat*. Say to the class, "If you made a mistake, please fix it now." When everyone has *tr* displayed in the pocket holders, ask them, "What blend starts the word *treat*? Let's make the sound of /tr/ together." Continue with more practice words if you observed many of your students hesitate before selecting letter cards as they worked independently.

✿ When your students demonstrate complete understanding of the directions, read the title of the poem aloud. After reading the word *small* aloud, say, "Listen carefully to the beginning blend as I say *small* once again." Emphasize the /sm/ sound as you repeat the word: "*Small*." Then ask, "What blend do you hear at the beginning of *small*?" Instruct your students: "Place the consonant letters you hear at the beginning of *small* beside each other in the pocket holder." Remind them: "We read from left to right. The smiley-face sticker is on the left side to help you remember where the first letter needs to be inserted."

✿ Follow the same procedure you used during the practice round to verify the correct blend. Choose a student who correctly identified the blend to name the consonant blend. Then say the word slowly to isolate the sounds. As you isolate each sound in the word, stop to identify each consonant letter sound. Insert the corresponding letter in the pocket holder. After the consonant blend has been identified, invite your students to name the blend and make the sound of the blend with you.

✿ After you read the word *shaking* aloud, say, "Listen as I say the word *shaking* again." Emphasize the /sh/ sound as you repeat the word. "*Shaking* begins with a special sound—my favorite sound. Show me this digraph's name by placing the two letters that form this sound in your pocket holder." If most students have correctly identified the digraph, ask the class, "Tell me this digraph's name." Otherwise, ask a student who has displayed the correct letters in his or her pocket holder. After the correct response is given, put your finger to your lips as you make the /sh/ sound. Say, "You hear the /sh/ sound [put your index finger to your lips] when the s and h are next to each other." Then follow this procedure when you come to the word *think* at the end of the poem.

☼ After all the words are uncovered, introduce the new sight words *is* and *are*.

- By this time of year, some students will know the word *is* by sight. Hold up the word card printed with *is* and ask, "Who knows this word?" Choose a volunteer to read the word aloud. After the word has been identified, ask the class, "Why is this word a sight word?" If no one knows, slowly stretch out the sounds. Then continue the analysis of this word by asking these questions: "What sound did you hear at the end? What letter is at the end of the word? Does s usually say /z/? What letter says /z/?" Summarize your findings by saying: "So the letter s at the end of the word sounds like a [pause to allow students to supply the letter]. It's a sight word because you can't sound it out. If you tried to sound it out, it would sound like this: /i/ /s/." Invite your students to spell and cheer the word chorally. Tell them: "Let's name the letters to spell the word *is*. Then we'll cheer the word by reading it aloud loudly and raising a fist above our heads" (Cunningham, 1995).

- Tell your students: "This word is located in three different lines in the poem. Put your hands on your head when you've found all three." Call on a student who appears to know all three locations to identify the sight word in each location. Then say, "Sweep the pointer across the word in each line as you read it aloud."

- Hold up the word card printed with *are*. Since someone in the group may also know this word, ask the class, "Who knows this word?" If no one is able to read it, identify the word. Then ask, "How many letters are there in this word?" After the class answers, invite them to name each letter as you touch it. Then explain: "This word is a sight word because you can't sound it out. But it's an easy sight word to remember. Listen as I say the word: *are*. The word *are* sounds like you're saying the letter r. That's because it begins with an r-controlled vowel—*ar*. Seeing the letter r in the word may help you remember this sight word because the word *are* sounds just like the name of the second letter."

- Tell your students: "The sight word *are* is located in two different lines in the poem. Put your hands on your head when you've found them." Call on a student who appears to know the two locations to identify each location by pointing to the word with the pointer. Then ask the student to sweep the pointer across the word as she or he reads it aloud.

✿ Invite your students to reread the poem with you. Tell them, "I'll be listening for strong, clear reading voices. When we finish reading the poem together, I'll choose one of you to read it aloud to the class."

✿ Call on a student to read the poem independently: "You read this poem so fluently. It sounded just like you were talking to me about the wind. I'd like you to read this poem aloud to the class so your classmates will have an opportunity to enjoy your reading of this poem, too."

❧ Reflection ❧

As I passed out the pocket holders, I noticed an increased level of anxiety emanating from all of my students regardless of their skill abilities. For example, Abram, who was progressing well in his literacy development, needed reassurance that he would be successful. And Avery, who was just beginning to learn her letter sounds, feared that this task would be too difficult for her. To alleviate any unnecessary concerns, I explained to them that it didn't matter if they made mistakes because they'd be allowed to fix them. I told them it was okay to make mistakes because everyone makes mistakes—I do, too. I stressed that the best learning takes place when you do make a mistake, because you can learn from your mistakes.

Always mindful of my students' self-esteem, I never want to demean them in any way. If I pointed out mistakes made by students in front of their classmates, those students most likely wouldn't develop confidence in their abilities. Besides, there was no need to publicly announce their errors. They could see for themselves what needed to be fixed. And they fixed their mistakes before I continued reading. I just made note of common mistakes I observed so that these misunderstandings could be addressed in future lessons.

One common error I did observe regarded directionality. During the practice round I noticed some students inserted the letter cards from right to left, which impacted the correct reading of the blends. It took a few practice words before these students understood where to place their letters—even with the smiley-face to help them. However, by the end of the activity, all but Abram enjoyed this hands-on activity. A perfectionist with a capital *P*, he didn't like to make errors. Since I believe his anxiety caused him to make mistakes, I'm sure I'll win him over as he becomes more comfortable with this particular procedure. It's far too valuable an activity to abandon.

LESSON EIGHT

Making Predictions, Learning to Decode, and Savoring Alliteration

Gray Squirrel

Hurry, hurry, scamper, scurry,
Little squirrel all gray and furry.
Find an acorn; crack it, crunch it,
Nibble, nibble, munch, munch, munch it.
Find another, fat and round,
To bury quickly in the ground.
Gather nuts—don't stop to play!
For winter winds are on the way.

—*Joan Horton*

What I Was Thinking

Since most of my students had a solid understanding of basic letter-sound association skills and they could easily blend the sounds in words I had segmented, I believed they were ready to sound out words by themselves. Although I knew exactly what I wanted to do for a word study, it took me a long time to find an appropriate poem. I was looking for a seasonal poem that I liked and could use for the word study. It was important that I liked the poem so I could enthusiastically share it with the class. However, ones I liked contained unsuitable vocabulary for learning to decode. The just-right poem needed to contain a sufficient number of simple three- or four-phoneme words to make the lesson worthwhile. As luck would have it, whenever I found a poem I liked, it didn't contain suitable vocabulary to begin the process of sounding out words.

After days of scouring through a multitude of poetry anthologies, I finally found the ideal poem: "Gray Squirrel" by Joan Horton. When I read the last line of the poem, "For winter winds are on the way," I believed it would present a perfect transition into December poetry. In addition, the playful sounds of language throughout the poem were enticing to me because I could reinforce concepts that had been previously introduced, such as alliteration and word families. And more importantly, a sufficient number of words were in the poem for my students to decode.

Materials

The poem "Gray Squirrel" by Joan Horton, handwritten on manila tag chart paper in large, neat print and attached by rings to a wooden chart stand

Two construction paper strips attached with tape to cover the word *squirrel* in the title and in the second line of the poem

What This Lesson Looks Like

* Stand next to the poem and tell your students, "As you can see, two words have been covered with paper strips. The covered word in the title is the same word I've covered in the second line. Why do you think I've covered these two words in the poem?" After students have exhausted their ideas, explain: "This poem is about a woodland animal. By covering its name, I've made a riddle for you to solve. The poem contains clues to help you identify this particular animal."

* Read the poem aloud using a lively pace. When you've finished reading, ask your students, "Who thinks they can identify the animal?" Call on a student to give his or her prediction. Ask, "What makes you think it's a [name the

animal the student identified]?" Then say, "Let's see if you're right." Ask the student, "What's the beginning letter in [name the animal the student identified]?" Emphasize the beginning sound as you say the animal's name. After the student states the first letter of the animal's name, reveal only the beginning letter of the covered word in the title. Invite the class to name the revealed letter. If the animal identified by the student doesn't begin with the revealed letter *s*, call on another student whose prediction does begin with an *s*.

✴ After the student names an animal that starts with the letter *s*, say to the class, "Let's slowly stretch out the beginning of the word [name the animal the student identified] to hear each of the sounds in the word. Pretend you're holding each end of a rubber band. Begin to stretch it out as you say the first sound: /s/. Now stretch it a little more and say the next sound with me." Ask, "What letter makes this sound?" Then, as you reveal the second letter of the covered word, ask your students, "Is this a [name the letter the student stated]?" After the *q* has been identified, reveal the *u*. Explain: "The letters *q* and *u* are always side by side. The *u* always follows the *q*. Together they say /kwa/."

✴ Invite your students to say the *squ* blend together.

Note: If the correct animal was not previously identified, your students will most likely call out the word *squirrel* after the consonant blend *squ* has been identified.

✴ As you announce the animal's name, remove the paper strip. Say, "It *is* a squirrel." Before you remove the second paper strip, tell your students, "I want you to name each letter as I slowly remove the paper strip." Then remove the paper strip one letter at a time.

✴ Remind your students: "You know that poets like to play with language to make it sound musical and pleasant. Sometimes they use *alliteration* to strengthen the sound. Does anyone remember the term alliteration?" If no one remembers the term, explain its meaning by saying, "Alliteration is the repetition of the beginning sound in two or more words of a phrase." Inform your students: "The poet, Joan Horton, uses alliteration to enhance her poem 'Gray Squirrel.' "

✴ Explain the purpose of the rereading, "I'm going to read the poem again. I want you to listen for words with repeating beginning sounds. Be ready to share a pair of words that start with the same sound." Then read the poem aloud.

* After you've finished reading the poem aloud, ask your students, "Which words begin with the same beginning sound? What's the sound you hear at the beginning of both words?" After the sound is given, point to the letter combination in both words. If your class is unable to identify the pairs of words, prompt them by saying, "I'll read a line in which the poet uses alliteration. After I finish reading the line, please raise your hand if you heard two words beginning with the same sound." Read only the lines your students need to hear again: line one to identify *scamper* and *scurry*, line three to identify *crack* and *crunch*, and/or the last line to identify *winter* and *winds*.

* Explain to your students, "The poet also repeats words in her poem. Who remembers a word that repeats?" As different students recall a particular word, invite your students to read it aloud each time it appears in the line as you touch it with the pointer. If your students are unable to recall all the repeating words, tell them, "You missed [state the number] words. Listen carefully as I read the poem aloud one more time. Be ready to tell me the repeating word[s] you didn't remember. And then we'll read the repeating words together."

* Explain to your students how they'll participate during the final rereading of the poem: "Please listen to the poem as I read it aloud. When I come to a rhyming word, I'll pause for you to say it aloud. Be sure to focus on the pointer as I touch each word that I say. And be ready to read the rhyming word aloud each time I pause." Pause at the words *furry, ground,* and *way.*

* When you've finished reading the poem, explain to your students: "The repeating sounds at the end of the rhyming words produce a musical quality to the poem." Then invite your students to recall the rhyming words by saying: "*Scurry* rhymes with [pause to invite your students to supply the word or words]." Point to each rhyming word in the poem as it's named. Sweep across the repeating ending sound in each word and read it aloud. Follow the same procedure for *crunch, round,* and *play.*

❧ Reflection ❧

I knew the cadence of this poem would be appealing, but I was amazed by how quickly many of my students learned the words. Since I didn't expect them to know all the words to the poem immediately after this introductory lesson, I was stunned when several students asked if they could read the poem aloud independently. And they read with such fluency!

After they had finished reading, I stood before these readers in disbelief—staring at the printed words on the chart paper and wondering how they were able to remember vocabulary words such as *scamper* and *scurry*. What strategies did they put to use? Did they rely on context and graphic cues to solve these unfamiliar words? Or was it primarily due to the enticing sounds of the language? My students couldn't explain to me how they were able to read this poem so easily, but they were beaming with pride.

The positive reaction to this poem proved to me that it was definitely worth the time to find a poem I liked and one I hoped my students would also enjoy. Witnessing 5- and 6-year-old children enthusiastically reading poetry aloud motivates me to keep searching for "keepers" like "Gray Squirrel." I'm determined to enhance every child's opportunity to learn to read and, in the process, yearn to learn.

LESSON NINE

Review of Sight Words, Meeting New Sight Words, Preparing for Sounding Out Words

What I Was Thinking

My main objective for this poem's word study was to allow my students an opportunity to practice isolating sounds in some words contained in "Gray Squirrel." However, since some of the words I planned to cover might be too difficult for some of my students to predict, I knew more reading practice was needed to ensure success for every student before I could execute the primary word study. I didn't want to take too much time just to figure out the correct words; I'd rather use the time to practice stretching out the words. That meant my students needed to become more familiar with the poem's words for the lesson to flow smoothly. Otherwise, they'd definitely tire from this mental exercise and lose their perseverance—and I certainly didn't want that to happen. So I decided to spend this day reinforcing the words of the poem, knowing it would be time well spent.

Materials

A package of Vis-à-Vis pens

Plastic sheeting to attach over the poem "Gray Squirrel"

Two 3" x 5" cards printed with the sight words *little* and *find*

What This Lesson Looks Like

❋ Explain to your students: "We're going to prepare for the word study by becoming more familiar with the words in the poem 'Gray Squirrel.' Let's begin by highlighting the sight words you already know." Ask, "Who sees a sight word?" Call on a student whose hand is raised to identify one by locating it in the poem and reading it aloud. If the student is correct, invite him or her to choose a pen color from the package. Say, "Please draw a circle around [name the identified sight word] each time you see it in the poem." When the child is finished, hold on to the pen; do not return it to the package. Different sight words should be circled with different colors. Continue this procedure until *all, and, it, to, in, the, are,* and *on* have been circled.

❋ Invite your students to analyze the circled words by saying, "Now I want you to be a word detective. Look at the circled words and find the word that was circled the most. When you find it, put your hand on your head." When most of your students have signaled they know the word, call on a student and say, "Tell me the word." If the student is correct, ask him or her, "Please come up to the chart and count the number of times [name the identified word] appears in the poem."

❋ Invite your students to point to specific words in the poem. Instruct them: "Find and read a word that begins with a digraph. Find and read two different words that begin with the same letter. Find four two-letter words. Find four three-letter words."

✻ Introduce the new sight words by saying, "I chose two new sight words from this poem for you to learn."

- Hold up the card printed with *little*. Ask, "Who can read this word?" If no one volunteers, tell the class the word. Ask the class, "Do you see a two-letter word you already know inside the word *little*?" After the word is named or if your students don't see the word *it* in the sight word *little*, cover all the letters on the word card except for *i* and *t*. Ask, "What's this word?" Continue the word analysis by saying, "What else do you notice about the word *little*?" You may hear a variety of responses such as the following: "There are two *t*'s in the middle of the word." "*Little* begins with an *l*." "You can't hear the *e* at the end of the word." "There are six letters in the word *little*." Then invite the class to clap out the syllables with you. Clap as you say *lit*; clap again as you say *tle*. Tell your students, "You can remember how to spell this word with a syllable cheer." Instruct your students: "Please watch as I cheer this word. Then you can cheer *little* with me." Demonstrate the cheer for your students. Clap your hands to the left as you name the letters in the first syllable. Clap and cheer, "*l* [clap] *i* [clap] *t* [clap]." Then clap your hands to the right as you name the letters in the second syllable. Clap and cheer: "*t* [clap] *l* [clap] *e* [clap]." Invite your students to clap and cheer the letters in *little*.

- Hold up the word card printed with *find*. Ask, "Who already knows this word?" Call on a volunteer to read the word aloud, or if no one knows the word, identify it. Ask your students, "What sound does the *i* say in *find*?" Say the word *find* slowly and emphasize the /?/ sound as you stretch the word. Call on a student to answer. When the correct sound is given, say: "Yes, you hear the *i* say its own name: *i*." Then explain to your students, "If you tried to sound out this word, you would say /f/ /ĭ/ /n/ /d/ because there is no *e* at the end to make the *i* say its name." Spell and cheer this word with the class (Cunningham, 1995).

- Conclude the word study by asking your students to find the new sight words *little* and *find*. Ask the class, "Who can find and read the word *little* each time it appears in the poem?" Follow with: "Who sees the word *find*? Please point to it and read it aloud each time it appears in the poem."

✻ Invite your students to listen as you read the poem aloud. Say, "You've done a lot of word work today. Take a few minutes to sit back and listen to me read 'Gray Squirrel' aloud to you. After I've read it aloud, I'm going to ask you to join me in the final reading, so listen carefully and keep your eyes focused on the pointer as I touch and read."

✺ After you finish reading, invite your students to read the poem aloud as you point to each word. Say, "I'd like you to read this poem using clear, strong reading voices. I'll touch each word with my pointer as you read it aloud. Your job will be to read the words; my job will be to point to the words." Listen carefully as they read. If your students are not yet familiar with most of the words, reread the poem with them before ending Poetry Time.

◆ Reflection ◆

Although several students had already demonstrated their proficiency in reading this poem, to ensure success for *every* student, practice was a necessity and a routine welcomed by my students. Since they understand they must be able to locate a specific word without hesitation, finding and circling the sight words went smoothly and quickly. They always enjoy using the Vis-à-Vis markers to circle the sight words. This procedure not only reinforced their sight-recognition skills and kept them engaged, it also illustrated the frequency of sight words in reading material.

By the time this poetry session had ended, my students' oral reading was clear, strong, and expressive. They were more than ready for the final word study.

LESSON TEN
Sounding Out Words

What I Was Thinking

Now that I knew my students were quite familiar with the words in this poem, I believed they were ready to tackle decoding it. With the prep work behind us, I hoped this lesson would flow smoothly so that my students would be more likely to stay on task. More importantly, I hoped my students would experience some success in segmenting sounds.

Every Child a Reader

Materials

The poem "Gray Squirrel" on chart paper

Five construction paper strips attached with tape

☼ Cover the phonogram -*unch* in the word *crunch*.

☼ Cover the phonogram -*at* in the word *fat*, and snip off the end of the strip if it's too long.

☼ Cover the word *nuts*, and snip off the end of the strip if it's too long.

☼ Cover the phonogram -*op* in the word *stop*, and snip off the end of the strip if it's too long.

☼ Cover the word *way*, and snip off the end of the strip if it's too long.

What This Lesson Looks Like

☼ Explain the purpose of the strips: "I didn't cover these words so you could make predictions. Instead, they're covered because I want you to practice stretching out words. Since you know the poem 'Gray Squirrel' so well, I know you'll say the covered word automatically. Then we'll stop and use our pretend rubber bands to stretch out the sounds in the word."

☼ Begin reading the poem chorally. When you come to the word *crunch*, pause to allow your students to supply the word. Then face your group and say, "Let's get our rubber bands ready so we can stretch the word *crunch*. Pretend you're holding each end of a rubber band. Since the consonant blend isn't covered, we can say the first two sounds without stretching our rubber bands." Invite your students to say the /cr/ sound by asking, "What does the consonant blend *cr* say?" Confirm their response by saying, "You're right! It says /cr/. Now let's slowly stretch our rubber bands until we hear the next sound. Ready?" Begin to stretch the imaginary rubber band as you say the consonant blend /cr/ and stop stretching when you say /ŭ/. Ask your students, "What sound did we just make?" Follow with: "What letter makes the /ŭ/ sound?" Call on a student to answer. When the appropriate letter is stated, print it at the beginning of the strip. Instruct your students: "Now stretch your rubber band a little more and stop when you say the next sound." Elicit the sounds /cr/ /ŭ/ /n/. Stop and ask, "What was the last sound you made?" Follow with: "What letter makes the /n/ sound?" Call on a different student to answer. When the letter *n* is mentioned, print it next to the letter *u* on the paper strip. Tell your students, "We're almost to the end of the word. Listen as I stretch out the sounds we've heard so far: /cr/ /ŭ/ /n/." Then say, "Stretch it with me. Remember to use your rubber band as you stretch out the word. Ready?" Sound out the word *crunch*. Say, "//cr/ /ŭ/ /n/ /ch/. What sound did you hear at the end of this word?" Follow with: "This is a special sound. Who remembers the name of this digraph?" If prompting is needed, act out the motion of a train's wheels. When a student correctly responds with *ch*, add the *ch* at the end of the strip. Explain to your students: "Now I'm going to remove this paper strip to reveal the printed word. If these letters [point to the phonogram *-unch* printed on the strip] match the printed word in the poem, then you know you've heard every sound in the word *crunch*." Remove the paper strip to reveal the word *crunch*. Then match up the phonogram on the paper strip to the printed word in the poem. Exclaim: "It's a match! Good job!"

☀ Continue reading chorally until you arrive to the covered word *fat*. Give the sound for *f* and then pause to see if someone remembers the word. If no one recites the word, suggest to your students: "Let's skip it and read the remainder of the line. Then we'll return to the beginning of the line to repeat it, skipping the covered word to see if you can make sense of it." Reread the line and skip the covered word. When the word *fat* is supplied, follow the steps described in the last bullet to stretch out the word.

☀ Continue to read, pausing at each covered word to allow your students to identify it. Follow the same procedure each time: read the word chorally, segment each sound with your students, record the corresponding letter on the paper strip, and check their accuracy in isolating individual sounds.

☀ After all the words have been revealed, invite your students to reread the poem chorally. Say, "Let's read this poem in a lively pace to convey a sense of urgency. The squirrel shouldn't dawdle; he needs to get ready for winter. Read aloud as if you're giving orders to the squirrel."

☀ Invite a student who read with great expression to read the poem aloud independently. Ask the student to use the pointer to touch each word as it is read.

Every Child a Reader

❧ Reflection ❧

This lesson proceeded smoothly for two reasons: my students' instant recall of the covered words and their collaboration in identifying the isolated sounds of each covered word. What my students enjoyed most was checking their accuracy when I removed the paper strip to reveal the correct spelling of the word printed on the chart paper. They applauded their success each time a spelling was checked. By the end of the lesson, they believed they were the world's best spellers.

DECEMBER

LESSON ONE

Prediction, Visualization, and Sensory Imagery

Prediction

Yesterday,
It was not there,
This pointed flavor
In the air.

Yesterday,
We gathered leaves
To wear like emblems
On our sleeves.

But now there is
A different feel:
The silver sky
Has rims of steel.
And in the night,
(I know! I know!)
The snow will fly!
The snow! The snow!

—Barbara Juster Esbensen

What I Was Thinking

In Maine, snow arrives long before the official start of winter. Sometimes the first snow falls as early as Thanksgiving, but it usually starts near the beginning of December. The weather gods seem to know when the ground has been tidied of fall's remnants and readied for winter's arrival. No sooner has the last leaf been raked than snow covers the barren earth.

Every Child a Reader

Snowy weather is easy to predict in Maine. Because you often hear people exclaim, "Looks like snow's coming!" as soon as the sky darkens and the air becomes brisk, I believed my students would be able to describe the ominous signs of snow and visualize Esbensen's sensory images in their minds without any difficulty. I also loved the title Esbensen chose for this particular poem—"Prediction"—because my students often hear me use this vocabulary term throughout the school day, during reading, math, and science. By discussing the definition of the title prior to the reading of the poem, I thought it might enrich the dialogue after the poem was read aloud. At the end of this conversation, I'd inform my students to be prepared to offer their thoughts regarding Esbensen's choice of words. I hoped this directive would motivate my students to listen more attentively to my oral reading.

Materials

The poem "Prediction" by Barbara Juster Esbensen, handwritten on manila tag chart paper in large, neat print and attached by rings to a wooden chart stand

A calendar

What This Lesson Looks Like

❋ Read the title aloud. Say: "Hmm. You've heard me use the word *prediction* at Story Time, when I've covered words in a big book, and when we've done different math activities. What's a prediction?" When a student says, "It's a guess," elaborate on the student's answer by saying, "Yes, it *is* a guess based on some evident clues. For instance, when I ask you to predict what you think is going to happen next in the story, context clues or picture clues may help you make a prediction." Then inform your students: "This poem is about the weather." Initiate a conversation with your class by saying, "Have you ever heard someone make a weather prediction, like 'Looks like rain'?" When your class responds affirmatively, ask, "Does Mother Nature give us clues that it's about to rain? What are the telltale signs of impending rain?" Then invite your students to share their own weather prediction stories.

❋ Before reading the poem aloud, state the purpose of this reading: "Barbara Juster Esbensen's choice of words will create a vivid picture in your mind. Listen carefully as I read this poem aloud, and be ready to tell me why the title 'Prediction' is a good choice for this poem."

❄ Read the poem "Prediction" aloud with feeling.

❄ After reading it aloud, ask, "Why is the word *prediction* a good title for this poem?" Then follow with: "How does she know it's going to snow? What signs does she see and feel?"

❄ Inform them, "Esbensen supplies the reader with three clues before she reveals her prediction. Raise your hand if you can recall one of them." Because the children may not necessarily remember Esbensen's choice of words and may reword them instead, point to the appropriate phrase and reread it aloud after each response. If your class doesn't remember all three clues, point to each forgotten phrase and reread it.

❄ Discuss Esbensen's choice of words in this poem. Ask the following questions:

  • Why do you think Esbensen refers to snow as a *pointed flavor*?

  • What's an emblem? Why does Esbensen compare a leaf to an emblem?

  • Why does Esbensen say the sky has rims of steel when we know the sky is not made of steel? (Prompt them by saying, "When you touch steel, does it feel hot or cold?")

❄ Invite your students to listen to you read the poem aloud again. Tell them, "After I finish reading this poem, I want you to tell me which season Esbensen describes. Listen carefully to the words. Don't be tricked. One stanza supplies the answer."

❄ After you finish reading it aloud, ask, "Who knows the season?" Then, after a student correctly responds, ask, "How did you know it's fall?" When students repeat some words from the poem such as *gathered leaves*, respond: "Yes, gathering leaves *is* a sign of fall. Leaves *fall* off the trees in the *fall*." Point out the words *gathered leaves* in the second stanza and then reread the second stanza aloud, emphasizing the words *yesterday* and *gathered leaves*.

❄ To clarify the concept of seasons, explain to students, "Winter officially arrives on December 21." Show your students the month of December on a calendar. Invite a student to point to the appropriate date by repeating the date: "Point to the twenty-first day of December. Does winter arrive at the beginning or near the end of December? How do you know?" Follow with: "People usually gather leaves in October or November." Hold up the calendar as you turn back the calendar to October. Ask, "Do October and November come *before* or *after* December? When students reply, "Before," follow with, "That's right. So which season comes *before* winter?" Repeat the correct answer given by a student, or tell students the answer if no one responds. Explain: "The season that comes *before* winter is fall."

☀ For the final reading, invite the class to supply some words when you pause. Explain to your students: "Please listen to the poem as I read it aloud. There's one word in each stanza I want you to read aloud. When I come to that particular word, I'll pause for you to say it aloud. Be sure to focus on each word I say as I touch it with the pointer. And be ready to read the word aloud each time I pause." Pause at *flavor, emblems,* and *steel.*

❧ Reflection ❧

When I found this poem, I was concerned the sophisticated vocabulary would hinder my students' ability to grasp the meaning and appreciate the poet's word choices. I knew I had to anticipate these trouble spots and allow the time needed for a discussion of each stanza. Although I realized this poem probably wouldn't immediately appeal to most of my students, I still wanted them to experience the richness of the language.

Through the years I've learned to trust my "teaching instinct," and once more it was on target. By thoroughly preparing the presentation, I alleviated my students' confusion about the order of the seasons and helped them appreciate and understand Esbensen's rich, poetic language. I heard many confident voices read the words *flavor, emblems,* and *steel* correctly whenever I paused at these particular words. More importantly, allowing sufficient time for discussion before and after the reading was instrumental to the successful outcome of this lesson.

LESSON TWO

Introduction of New Sight Words and the Digraphs <u>ee</u> and <u>ea</u>

What I Was Thinking

Although my students were able to decode CVC (consonant-vowel-consonant) words easily, they continued to be stymied by unfamiliar words that contained vowel combinations. I decided to begin with the *ee* and *ea* combinations, because this poem contained a sufficient number of *ee* words to make the lesson worthwhile. By using the high-frequency word *see* they had previously learned as a key word, I thought my students would be able to grasp the *ee* sound quickly. Although I wasn't so sure what would happen when they encountered the word *wear*, I knew this literacy activity would provide me with some valuable information about my students' reading skills.

Materials

Three 3" x 5" cards printed with the words *in, to,* and *was* in large lowercase letters—one word per card

Two 3" x 5" cards printed with *ee* and *ea* in large lowercase letters—one vowel digraph per card

A card printed with the high-frequency word *see*

Plastic sheeting to attach over the poem "Prediction"

A red Vis-à-Vis marker

What This Lesson Looks Like

✵ Point to the title as you ask, "Who remembers the title of the poem I shared with you yesterday?" If no one responds, prompt your students by sweeping across the first few letters with the pointer as you say the start of the word. Enunciate the sounds as you say, "Predi . . ." When someone accurately responds, ask, "What's this poem about?" Most likely, your students won't give a detailed response. Accept a generalized statement if it's correct.

Every Child a Reader

✲ Inform your students, "The poet, Barbara Juster Esbensen, uses rich, descriptive words to help the reader vividly visualize the scene and feel the change in the weather." Then instruct them: "Listen carefully to the words in this poem and see how many different mind-pictures you can create as I read the poem aloud."

✲ Read the poem aloud to your class.

✲ As soon as you finish reading the poem aloud, remind the class, "Yesterday we practiced reading some words that could cause some problems for you. Let's see if you remember them." Direct your students, "When I point to a word, please read it aloud if you can." Confirm an accurate response by saying, "Yes, it is [word]. Follow with: "Let's all read it aloud now." Then sweep the pointer across the word. Follow this procedure for the words *flavor* and *emblems*.

✲ Invite a capable student to share a mind-picture with the class. Then ask the student, "Can you locate and read aloud the words in the poem that helped to create this mind-picture?" If the student has difficulty locating the appropriate words, support him or her with a clue. Begin with a general clue and become more specific if necessary. For example, a progression of support might begin with a general clue: "Look in the last stanza." If the student requires additional support, say, "Look near the middle of the last stanza." If the student is unable to identify the line or phrase, instruct the class: "If you see the line that matches your classmate's mind-picture, raise your hand." Call on a student to come up to the chart. Help the child by sweeping your finger across the appropriate line. Then allow the first student to read it aloud. Follow with: "Who has a *different* mind-picture they'd like to share?" Use the same procedure to identify the words that match the student's mind-picture. If no one else shares a different mind-picture, describe one that could be generated from the poem. For example, say, "Well, in my mind I saw children with an armful of leaves they had gathered from a pile of leaves. When they throw them into the air, some of the leaves cling to the sleeves of the children's sweaters." Then ask, "Who can find and read the stanza that matches my mind-picture?" Continue describing different mind-pictures until each stanza has been reviewed.

❁ Introduce the new sight words. Explain to your students: "Before we read the poem aloud together, I'd like to introduce three new sight words."

- Hold up the card printed with *in*. Explain: "This word isn't really a *sight word*, because it *can* be sounded out. Let's say each letter sound together: /ĭ/ /n/. Because you'll encounter the word *in* frequently in your reading, it will be helpful if you can read this word quickly." Then snap your fingers and say, "Just like that!" Direct your students' attention to the poem. Hold up the card printed with *in* as you inform the class: "The word *in* is located in two different lines in this poem." Invite your students to search for the word by saying, "Hunt for the word *in* and raise your hand as soon as you see the word." Call on the first student who raises his or her hand. Instruct the student: "Use the pointer to sweep across the word as you say it aloud." If the student doesn't automatically identify the second location, ask, "Who sees the word *in* elsewhere in the poem?" Call on another student, who appears to know, and follow the same procedure with this student. Before moving on to the next sight word, focus your students' attention back to the word card and say, "Let's spell and cheer *in*." Accompany your class in naming each letter you touch with your finger. Then announce, "Cheer it!" At this moment, your students should extend one of their arms toward the ceiling with a fist and cheer the word—*in*! (Cunningham, 1995).

- Hold up the card printed with *to*. Explain: "This *is* a sight word, because you can't sound it out. You'll see this word printed on many gift tags attached to your birthday presents." Then ask your students, "Who knows this word?" As soon as you see at least one hand raised, instruct your class: "If you know this word, tell me what it says." When you hear a correct response, confirm the reader's accuracy by saying, "Yes, it's the word *to*." However, if no one correctly identifies the word, read the word aloud to your class. Then invite everyone to read it aloud together. Next, explain: "There are two other words that sound like this word, but they are spelled differently and have different meanings." Hold up two fingers as you say: "The number word *two*, which is spelled *t-w-o*, and *t-o-o*, which means also." Hold up the card printed with *to* as you say, "But for now, let's focus on just this word. Where is the word *to* located in the

Every Child a Reader

poem? When you find it, focus your eyes on the word. I'll call on someone who seems to know where it's located." As soon as you see someone staring at the second stanza, call on that student: "Come up and show us the word *to*." If the student correctly identifies the word, invite the student: "Now I'd like you to spell the word. Point to each letter from left to right and identify it by name." After the student finishes spelling the word, say, "Let's spell and cheer this word together." Accompany your class in spelling the word. Explain: "Please name each letter I touch with my finger." As soon as you complete the spelling, extend your arm toward the ceiling with a fist and cheer the word—*to*! (Cunningham, 1995)

- Hold up the card printed with *was*. Inform the class: "This is another sight word. Although it *looks* like a word that can be easily sounded out, your knowledge of letters and sounds is not going to help you attack this word. Let's see what happens when you try to sound it out. Make the letter sound as I point to the printed letter on the card. Ready?" When the class finishes isolating the sounds, accompany the students as they blend the sounds together. Announce the nonsensical word: */w/ /ă/ /s/*." Follow with: "Is this a real word? Of course it isn't; it's gibberish. Does anyone know what this word really says? Raise your hand if you know this word." Then call on a capable student whose hand is raised to read the word aloud. Confirm the student's accuracy by saying, "You're right! The word is *was*." Invite the class to say the word with you as you sweep you finger across the printed word on the card. Then instruct your students: "Close your eyes and take a picture of this word in your mind. As I slowly spell this word, I want you to try to see each letter as I say it. Ready?" After you've completed the spelling, put the word card face down and direct your students: "Spell the word *was*." Direct your students' attention to the poem and say, "I see the word *was* in the first stanza. I'm going to sweep the pointer slowly across each word in the first stanza. When the pointer touches the word *was*, I want you to read it aloud. Stay focused so you'll be able to identify it accurately."

☼ Reinforce your students' sight-word vocabulary: "Before we read the poem aloud together, let's review all the sight words in this poem that you should now know. I'll start at the beginning of the poem and slowly sweep across each line with my pointer until I arrive at the last word in the poem. I'll stop the pointer on any sight word you've already learned. When I stop at a particular word, your job is to read it aloud in one big voice. Keep focused, so you'll be ready to read the word whenever I stop."

✸ After the sight-word practice is completed, read the poem aloud with your class. Say, "You've practiced reading many of the words in this poem. Would you please join me now to read it aloud? Let's try reading this poem with feeling."

✸ Explain the focus of today's word study: "Today we're going to learn about two vowel combinations." Hold up the cards printed with *ee* and *ea* as you name the two letters on each card.

✸ Hold up the card printed with the high-frequency word *see*. Ask your students, "What does this word say?" When you hear the word accurately read, say, "You're right! It does say *see*. Now look closely at the letters in the word *see*. What do you see?"

✸ After someone responds that there are two letter *e*'s in the word *see*, invite your students: "Say the word slowly with me so you can hear the two distinct sounds in this word." Then ask, "What vowel sound do you hear?" After you hear the correct answer, confirm the answer. Say, "The two *e*'s in the word *see* do say /?/." Explain to your students: "When there are two vowels side by side in a word, you usually hear the first one. The second vowel doesn't make a sound; it remains silent." Then, as you hold up the card printed with *ea*, ask, "So what would this vowel combination say if it follows the rule?" After a student gives the correct sound, repeat the rule pointing to each letter as you speak: "Usually the first vowel—for example, *e*—says its letter name, and the second vowel—for example, *a*—is silent."

✸ Invite your students to be word detectives: "In this poem there are several words that contain either *ee* or *ea*. I'd like you to be word detectives and search for these words." Hold up the *ee* and *ea* cards and ask, "Who sees a word containing *ee* or *ea*?" Call on someone whose hand is raised to point out a word in the poem. If the student is correct, hand him or her the red Vis-à-Vis marker and say, "Please circle one of these vowel combinations and tell us the sound it usually makes."

Every Child a Reader

✿ Then invite your students to sound out the word their classmate found. Explain: "Since the rule usually works, you should first apply the rule when you sound out an unfamiliar word. If the rule doesn't work, the word will be gibberish when you blend the sounds together." Invite the class: "Let's see if it follows the rule in this word. Let's stretch out this word together." Then ask, "What's the word? Does the word make sense?" Follow this procedure for the remaining *ee* and *ea* words.

Note: When your students discover that the rule can't be applied to the word *wear*, invite the class to use context clues to determine the word. Invite them to read aloud the line that contains the word *wear*. Tell your students to skip the word *wear* and read the remainder of the line to see if they can figure it out.

❧ Reflection ❧

When I designed the lesson, I wondered how my students would transition from one word activity to another. But to my relief, they remained engaged throughout the lesson. I think the variety of activities helped to alleviate any restlessness that might have occurred due to the intensity of the word practice in this lesson.

In addition, I learned so much about my students' reading progress. Their automaticity with sight words has become amazing. Each time I stopped at a word, I heard many voices speak as one voice. And just as I had predicted, my students had no difficulty finding and sounding out the *ee* words. However, when they sounded out the word *wear* as /wɛr/, they thought it was a real word until I wrote the word *we're* on the board for them to see. Although my students will need to encounter many more words that contain *ea* before they can automatically decode them, I'm confident that automaticity will come, because there are many school days remaining before the end of the year and many more poems to read.

LESSON THREE

Visualization and Prediction

> **The Snowstorm**
> Heave-ho,
> Buckets of snow,
> The giant is combing his beard,
> The snow is as high
> As the top of the sky,
> And the world has disappeared.
> —*Dennis Lee*

What I Was Thinking

Since Esbensen uses more sophisticated words in her poem "Prediction," I knew I'd need to return to this poem each day for more reading practice until my students demonstrated proficiency. Because of this, I wanted the next poem to be not only engaging, but also an easy one to learn.

When I discovered Dennis Lee's poem "The Snowstorm," I immediately knew this poem would be a perfect choice. My students would easily relate to it because we had just had a major snowstorm, which had dumped almost two feet of snow. Snow banks looked like mountains along the sides of roads, driveways, and sidewalks.

In addition, this poem had all the ingredients for success. Not only was it short, but its strong rhythm and rhyme would help my students learn the words quickly, and it would attract the attention of the boys because of their interests in pirates and giants. This poem was going to be a fun one to read aloud.

Materials

The poem "The Snowstorm" by Dennis Lee, handwritten on manila tag chart paper in large, neat print and attached by rings to a wooden chart stand

Every Child a Reader

What This Lesson Looks Like

❈ Introduce the poem by saying, "From the many poems we've read, we know poets create pictures in our minds with their wonderful choice of words. We also know poets pay particular attention to the rhythm of the words they use. In this poem, 'The Snowstorm,' the strong rhythm of the words mimics the rhythm of shoveling snow—one shovel at a time. Be ready to describe what this poem made you picture in your mind."

❈ Explain to your students, "As I read the poem aloud, I'll keep my hands positioned as if I'm holding a shovel, and I'll move them back and forth as if I'm shoveling snow." Then read the poem aloud, demonstrating the rhythm of the words.

❈ Pause for a moment after you've finished reading the poem to allow students time to reflect on it. Invite students to share their mind-pictures by asking, "If I asked you to illustrate this poem, what would you include in your picture?" As students describe the scene, prompt them to elaborate by asking the following questions: "Is it snowing or has the snow ended? How much snow has already fallen?"

❈ To check your students' understanding, discuss the poet's choice of words by asking, "What does the line 'the giant is combing his beard' suggest?" Prompt your students by saying, "We know there aren't really giants. The poet is comparing the size of a giant to the size of the snowstorm." Then ask, "Do you think it was a major snowstorm? What makes you think so?" Follow with: "Dennis Lee exaggerates when he says, 'And the world has disappeared.' What's he telling us?"

❈ Explain the purpose for the second reading: "I'm going to read this poem again, and I'd like you to listen carefully as I read. Please focus on the words Dennis Lee uses to create this gigantic snowstorm, because I'll ask you to locate specific lines in the poem we've discussed."

❈ Read the poem again. After you've finished reading, direct the class: "Raise your hand if you can find and read the three lines that tell us how much snow has fallen. I'll choose someone who is showing me with his or her eyes where the lines are located." Call on a volunteer whose eyes are focused on these particular lines to come to the chart with the pointer in hand to read the lines aloud. Then ask, "Which two lines describe someone shoveling deep snow?" End this segment by asking: "Can you find the line that gives you an idea about how much it's snowing?"

✺ Read the poem chorally. Say, "You've proven to me how well you know the different lines in this poem, so let's read the poem together from beginning to end."

✺ For the final reading, invite a volunteer to read it aloud with appropriate pacing.

❧ Reflection ❧

This poem instantly appealed to my students. Immediately after I had finished reading the poem aloud, my students began chanting the first two lines again and again. It took a few minutes for the chanting to subside and for me to refocus them for my final reading.

After they had finished reading the poem with me, all my students wanted a chance to read this poem aloud independently. To my surprise, even Nolan, a boy who often felt intimidated by his classmates' reading prowess, was ready to read. And of course, I chose him. I wanted him to experience success so that he would begin to relax and savor poetry as much as his classmates did. And succeed he did. His spirited reading left his classmates and me speechless.

If only I could find more poems with such magnetic appeal, perhaps children like Nolan would be lured into participating more often during these group experiences. This text, although seemingly beyond Nolan's current reading level, was within his control, and he eagerly read it aloud to his classmates. Watching Nolan as he read confirmed for me the importance of choosing poems that would stimulate my students' interest, so their reading skills could develop naturally and with enthusiasm.

Every Child a Reader

LESSON FOUR

Review of Sight Words and the Vowel Digraph ea

What I Was Thinking

Although most of my students remembered the *ee* sound, they continued to be perplexed by the *ea* combination whenever they encountered unknown words with this specific vowel digraph in their other reading. Since this poem contained a few *ea* words, I wanted to take advantage of this opportunity to reinforce this special vowel sound. Even though the lesson would be brief, I believed it would be a beneficial word study.

Materials

The poem "The Snowstorm" by Dennis Lee, handwritten on manila tag chart paper in large, neat print and attached by rings to a wooden chart stand

One 3" x 5" card printed with the vowel digraph *ea*

One 3" x 5" card printed with *as*

What This Lesson Looks Like

✿ Invite your students to share their knowledge of words: "Who sees a sight word you know in this poem, or a new word you'd like to share with your classmates?" Then hand the pointer to a student to sweep across the word as he or she reads it aloud. Continue calling on other students to share different words they can read until no more words can be recognized.

✿ Introduce the sight word *as*. Hold up the word card and ask, "Who knows this word?" Call on a capable student to read it aloud. (This word may seem easy to recognize, but you don't want to risk a mispronunciation.) When the word is identified, say the word aloud, emphasizing the final sound. Then point to the last letter and invite your students to complete the sentence you start: "The letter *s* sounds like a _____." When your students call out the letter *z*, confirm their accuracy by saying, "That's right! Even though it looks like it would be easy to sound out, it's a tricky word." Direct your students' attention to the poem and say, "The word *as* is located in two different lines in this poem. As soon as you see them, raise your hand and show me with your eyes that you know where the word *as* is located."

☀ Explain the procedure for reading the poem aloud: "Let's take turns reading different lines of this poem." Point to the first line with the pointer as you speak: "I'd like the boys to read the first line." Then point to the second line and say, "Then the girls will read the second line." As you move the pointer to the third line, announce, "We'll read the third line all together in one big voice. We'll continue with this pattern for the remaining lines of the poem. Any questions?"

☀ Invite the class to read the poem aloud.

☀ As soon as the class reads the last line aloud, point to the appropriate line as you speak: "Now let's read the poem again, but this time the girls will read the first line, the boys will read the next line, and then all of us will read the third line together. We'll keep repeating this pattern until we finish reading the poem." Then reread the poem.

☀ Direct your students' attention to the words in the poem: "This poem contains a special vowel combination we just studied. What is it?" As soon as you hear the correct answer, exclaim: "It is *ea*!" Hold up the card printed with the vowel combination *ea*. Remind them: "We discovered in a recent word study that both *ea* and *ee* can make the same sound. Who remembers what *ea* can say?"

☀ When someone accurately responds, explain: "In this poem, there are a few words containing the *ea* vowel combination. And in each of these words *ea* says /ē/." Then ask, "Who sees a word with this vowel combination that they recognize?" Call on a student to identify the word. Say, "Use the pointer to show the class where the *ea* vowel combination is located." Then invite the student to read the word aloud. Repeat the word slowly so your class can hear the *ea* sound. Follow this procedure for the remaining two words. After the three words have been identified and discussed, invite the

class to read the three words aloud chorally, "Let's read these words again together. When I point to one of these words with my pointer, please read it aloud in one big voice."

✹ Invite the class to read the poem aloud, "Before we end this poetry session, I'd love to listen to you read this poem aloud to me. Read it aloud with feeling. I'll do the pointing, and you'll do the reading. Ready? Eyes focused, please." When your class complies, quickly point to each word to maintain the rhythm of the poem.

❧ Reflection ❧

Although this lesson went smoothly and effortlessly, I knew my students still needed more instruction to internalize this particular vowel digraph. To accommodate their different learning styles, I compiled a list of different approaches to reinforce their learning, such as introducing a key word to help them remember this sound, including more *ea* words in our daily class message, pointing out instances in which we encountered words containing the *ea* combination in our poems, and creating a game. I knew if I wanted all my students to find success, I had to employ a variety of modalities to make it happen.

LESSON FIVE

Introduction of New Sight Words

> ### I Heard a Bird Sing
>
> I heard a bird sing
> > In the dark of December
> A magical thing
> > And sweet to remember.
> "We are nearer to Spring
> > Than we were in September,"
> I heard a bird sing
> > In the dark of December.
>
> > *—Oliver Herford*

What I Was Thinking

For people like me who don't enjoy winter sports, not to mention freezing weather and slippery roads, winter in Maine can be long and arduous. After witnessing the beauty of the first pristine snowfall of the season, my positive attitude about snow quickly sours. Whenever I express my contempt for snow to my kindergartners, they stare at me in disbelief. Although no words are spoken, their expressive faces convey their bewilderment. How could she not love winter's wonderland? So when I discovered this poem, I immediately knew I wanted to share it with them. They would understand its message because of my constant whining about the lengthy winter season in Maine. I knew I'd be able to deliver its message convincingly and enthusiastically because it expressed exactly how I feel. Through this poem, my puzzled students would come to understand I'm not the only one who can't wait for winter to end.

Materials

The poem "I Heard a Bird Sing" by Oliver Herford, handwritten on manila tag chart paper in large, neat print and attached by rings to a wooden chart stand

A red marker

The *previous* year's calendar with December 21 circled

A current year's calendar with March 21 circled

Two 3" x 5" cards printed with the words *than* and *were* in large lowercase letters, with one word per card

A 3" x 5" card printed with the word *then* in large lowercase letters

A 3" x 5" card printed with the word *where* in large lowercase letters

What This Lesson Looks Like

* Introduce the poem "I Heard a Bird Sing" by saying, "Today we're going to read a poem that allows the reader to look at winter from a different perspective. Listen as I read [point to the title] 'I Heard a Bird Sing.' "

* Read the poem aloud to the class.

* After pausing a moment, ask, "What message did the bird express through its song?" Follow with: "When does spring arrive?" If no one knows, tell the class: "Spring arrives on March 21." Turn to the month of March in a current calendar, then ask, "When did the bird sing its song?"

* Summarize what has been answered through questioning: "The bird, who sang its song in December, said spring was near. Let's count the months to see how near we are to spring." Turn back to January on a current calendar and say, "December ends a year, so we begin a new year with January. [Show the month of January.] Let's begin our counting with January and continue to count as I turn to a different month. I'll stop when I come to March. Ready?" Begin counting. When March is revealed, close the calendar and ask, "How many months to spring if it's December right now?" Write the number three on the white board or chart paper.

* Point to the words *we are nearer to Spring than we were in September* and read them aloud. Instruct your students: "Let's count from September to March to see if this is an accurate statement." Hold up last year's calendar and turn to September: "Let's check to see if we are indeed closer to spring than we were in September. We'll begin to count from September on and continue to count as I turn to a different month. I'll pause to pick up this

year's calendar, but we won't stop counting until we reach March. Ready? Begin counting." When March is revealed, write the number six below the number three. Ask, "Which wait is longer: three months or six months?"

✤ Ask, "Why would this poem appeal to a person who dislikes winter?"

✤ Explain the poet's choice of words: *in the dark of December.* Turn to the month of December on last year's calendar and hold it up for all to see. Point to the circled number and say, "December 22 is the winter solstice. On this day there aren't many hours of daylight; it gets dark very early. Oliver Herford's poetic phrase *in the dark of December* refers to this special day in December."

✤ Introduce the new high-frequency word *than.*

- Instruct the class: "I chose two tricky words from this poem to add to our collection. If you know this word, read it aloud." Then hold up the card printed with the word *than* for students to see and read.

- If some students say *then* instead of *than,* direct them to listen to you read the word. As you read the word, stress the vowel sound while you point to the letter *a:* "Than." Then instruct the class: "Listen as I say the word *then* slowly: /th/ /ĕ/ /n/. What vowel sound did you hear?" When someone responds correctly, hold up the word card printed with *then.* Place the word card *than* directly below the word card *then* to compare the letters. Say, "No wonder this word was incorrectly read. Most of the letters are the same." Direct the class: "Name the letter I point to in each word." Point to the letter *t* in *then* and then point to the letter *t* in *than.* Continue pointing out the same letters found in the same position in both words. Ask, "What did you notice?" Then reiterate what a student said by saying, "Yes, these words have the same letters in the same order except for one letter— the vowel."

- Explain the meaning of the word: "The dictionary defines the word *than* as 'if, or when compared with something else.' " Then use the word *than* in a sentence, emphasizing the word *than.* Say, "I like the steamy days of summer more *than* the frosty days of winter."

- To facilitate the learning of this word, ask, "What little word do you see inside the word *than*?" When someone correctly answers, circle the little word *an* with a red marker.

- Invite the class to say, spell, and cheer the word with you (Cunningham, 1995).

- Continue to hold up the word card for students to see, and ask, "Who can locate this word in the poem?" Call on a student and say, "Sweep the pointer across the word as you read it aloud."

✿ Introduce the new sight word *were*.

- Explain to the class: "This word tricks many beginning readers, because it's so much like another high-frequency word you'll come across in your reading. Be sure to look carefully at this word before you read it aloud."

- Remind the class: "If you know this word, read it aloud. If you don't or aren't certain, please listen." Then ask the class, "What's this word?" Hold up the card printed with the word *were* for capable students to see and read aloud.

- Hold up the card printed with the word *where*. Ask, "Who knows this word?" Call on a capable student to read it aloud.

- Place the word *where* below the word *were*. Explain: "These two words also can cause confusion because they have several letters in common." Then ask, "What makes them different?" Validate a student's correct response by saying, "That's an excellent observation. The only letter that's different is the letter *h* [point to it] in the word *where*. So if there is no *h* after the letter *w*, it's the word *were*. [Hold up the word card.] If it begins with the *wh* digraph, it's *where*." Hold up the word card.

- Invite the class to say, spell, and cheer the word *were* with you (Cunningham, 1995). Then hold up the word *where* and ask, "What is this word?" Follow with: "Which letter helps you know?"

- Begin to shuffle the word cards *were* and *where*. Instruct the class: "I'm going to give you each a turn to read one of these word cards.

When you say, 'Stop!' I'll show you the top card to read aloud." Keep shuffling the cards as you speak. "Remember, the word *where* begins with *wh*. The letter *h* is not found in the word *were*." Whip around the class to give everybody a turn.

- Hold up the word card *were* for your students to see, and ask, "What's this word? Who can locate this word in the poem?" Call on a student and say, "Sweep the pointer across the word as you read it aloud."

❋ Ask, "Do you see other words you can read? They may be class words we've learned together or new words you learned from your own reading." Call on volunteers to point to words they know.

❋ Review the words identified by individual students. Inform the class, "When I point to a word, I'd like all of you to read it aloud in one big voice."

❋ Say, "Herford repeats the title [point to the words in the title] 'I Heard a Bird Sing' elsewhere in the poem. Who can point out these lines to the class?" Hand the pointer to a student who appears to know the location of these repetitive lines.

❋ Then ask, "Do you see another line that repeats elsewhere in the poem?" If no one notices this repetition, point to the second line of the poem and read it aloud. Ask, "Where is this line repeated?" Call on a volunteer to respond. Then invite the student to read each word as she or he sweeps across the last line with the pointer.

❋ Explain the procedure for the choral reading: "I'd like you to read the first two lines and the last two lines of the poem. I'll read the remaining lines by myself." As you give the directions, point out the lines your students will read. Then point out the lines you'll read.

❋ For the final reading, explain to your students their reading roles: "In addition to reading the repetitive lines, I'll pause at the last word in each line I read. When I pause, please supply the correct word." Pause at *thing, remember, Spring,* and *September.*

❧ Reflection ❧

To my surprise, the children liked this poem as much as I did, but the reason for this lies more in the poem's simplicity than in its message. The repetitive lines helped my children quickly learn to read it. In addition, they had previously encountered many of the same words in other reading activities. For example, many students recognized the words *September* and *December* because of our daily calendar work. And other students already knew the sight words I had selected from this poem because they had come across these words many times in their Just Right books and in the daily class message.

LESSON SIX
Introduction of the -<u>ing</u> Chunk

What I Was Thinking

Although most kindergartners have great difficulty working successfully with phonograms, for some reason they are able to grasp the *-ing* phonogram easily. Perhaps success comes more easily because they happen upon this particular phonogram frequently in rhyming text and predictable readers as well as in their own writing.

Since this poem includes only three words from the *-ing* word family, and I knew that wasn't a sufficient number to familiarize my students with this phonogram, I decided to introduce the lesson with these three words. To extend my students' thinking, I'd invite them to create additional *–ing* words with both an oral exercise and a hands-on activity.

Materials

The poem "I Heard a Bird Sing" by Oliver Herford, handwritten on manila tag chart paper in large, neat print and attached by rings to a wooden chart stand

Collection of sight-word cards

Chart paper

A red marker

A black marker

A pocket holder for each student

Highlighting tape

Three 3" x 5" white cards printed with the words *September*, *December*, and *remember* in large lowercase letters—one word per card

　☼ Use a black marker to print the beginning letters until the rime *-ember*.

　☼ Use a red marker to print the rime *-ember*.

Three 3" x 5" white cards printed with the words *sing*, *thing*, and *spring* in large lowercase letters—one word per card

　☼ Use a black marker to print the beginning consonant, digraph, and blend.

　☼ Use a red marker to print the rime *-ing*.

1" x 6" paper strips printed with the consonants *d, p, r, s,* and *w* in large lowercase letters—one set of five strips per student, which includes one of each of the five letters

　☼ Use a black marker to print each consonant at the top of each strip.

　☼ Wrap a rubber band around each set.

1" x 6" paper strips printed with the consonant blends *br, cl, fl, sl, st,* and *sw* in large lowercase letters—one set of six strips per student, which includes one of each of the six blends

　☼ Use a black marker to print each blend at the top of each strip.

　☼ Wrap a rubber band around each set.

3" x 6" cards printed with the *-ing* phonogram—one card per student

　☼ Use a red marker to print the phonogram at the top of the card.

Class set of craft sticks, one for each child printed with the student's name

What This Lesson Looks Like

　☼ Review all previously learned sight words. Hold up the sight-word collection and say, "Look at all the sight words we've covered so far. Let's see how many of them you can read without hesitation. When I show you a card, I'd like you to read it aloud in one big voice. I'll place the word cards I hear read by everyone on the floor beside me; the cards that aren't read quickly in one big voice will remain in my hand." Then ask, "How many of you predict there'll be more cards on the floor than in my hand when we finish?" If some children don't raise their hands, ask, "How many think I'll have more in my hand than on the floor?" For the remaining children, ask, "If you don't think either of these predictions will result, what do you think *will* happen?" Someone will probably predict that there will be an equal number of cards on the floor and in your hand. After your students finish with their predictions, then go through all the word cards at a steady pace.

✿ Direct your students' attention to the two packs of cards. Gather the cards on the floor and hold up the pack for all to see. Comment on the number of cards by saying, "Look at how many you know well!" Then hold up the remaining cards in your other hand and ask, "Are these packs equal? Why or why not?" Then say, "Let's count the cards to find out how many sight words you can read quickly as a group." Count the cards aloud with your class.

✿ Before reading the poem aloud with your class, review the words *September, December,* and *remember*. Start with the words *September* and *December*: "These words are names of months you've seen many times during our calendar activities. Read them aloud with me." As you read each word, sweep slowly across it. Then invite your class to listen as you say these words aloud. Stress the rime as you say each word. Ask, "What did you hear? What kind of words are these?" When your students tell you that the words *September* and *December* are rhyming words, ask, "How do you know they rhyme?" After someone explains they sound the same at the end of both words, focus your students' attention on the letters in *September* and *December* by saying, "Let's take a closer look at the letters in these words." Call on a student to identify each letter as you point to it. Then ask the class, "Which group of letters is the same in both words?" When someone correctly answers, say, "Yes, they contain the same spelling pattern." Then tape the two word cards printed with *September* and

December on the board to provide a visual for the students. Say, "There's another word in the poem that rhymes with *September* and *December*. Look for another word in the poem that has the same spelling pattern as *September* and *December*. In other words, it ends with the same group of letters. Raise your hand when you see it." Call on a student who appears to know its location to point out the word to the class. Instruct the student: "Compare the last five letters in your word with the last five letters in *December* to prove that these letters are the same as those in *September* and *December*." Sweep across the rime *-ember* in the word *December* printed on the chart paper as you give the direction. After the student has demonstrated his or her accuracy, place the cards in a pocket holder with *December* directly below *September*. Invite the student to read the word *remember* aloud. Guide the student if necessary by saying, "*September . . . December*." Say the beginning of the word to prompt the student: "*Re . . .*" If the student needs more support, add the next letter sound by saying, "*Re . . . m . . .*" As soon as the student says the word, place the word card printed with *remember* in the pocket chart below the word *December*.

❖ Before reading the poem aloud with your students, reassure them by saying, "There may be words in this poem you don't know yet, but don't let that stop you from trying. If you give it your best, you'll be able to read this poem fluently in no time." Then read the poem aloud chorally.

❖ Call on a capable student to read the poem independently.

❖ After the student finishes reading the poem aloud, provide him or her with positive feedback. Then say, "I heard three other words that rhyme in this poem. Who can name these other rhyming words?" If no one recalls them, instruct your students: "Please listen carefully as I recite the poem. Listen for other words that rhyme in this poem besides *September, December,* and *remember*." Then recite the poem at a deliberate pace. Immediately following your recitation, ask, "What other words rhyme in this poem?" As soon as one of the words is identified, place the corresponding word card in the pocket holder. When someone recalls another *-ing* word, place it directly below the first one. Place the third card printed with the last rhyming *-ing* word below the second one. Point to the *-ing* phonogram as you ask, "How do we know these words rhyme?" If a student states that they all end with the same letters, affirm this response by saying, "Yes, these letters are the same: *i-n-g*. Since the letters are the same, they sound the same." Then inform your students: "Sometimes, though, there are words that don't have the same letters at the end, but they still rhyme. For example, *bait* rhymes with *Kate*." As you say each word, write each one on the chart paper. Pause a moment and then say slowly with emphasis: "Words that rhyme always *sound* the same at the end."

❄ Direct your students' attention to the word cards printed with *sing, thing,* and *spring*. Say, "All three words end with the same spelling pattern, *i-n-g*." Sweep across the phonogram on one of the cards as you say: "*I-n-g* says *-ing*." Invite your students: "Let's read these three words together." Point to each card as you read it aloud with your class.

❄ Invite your students to brainstorm other words that rhyme with *sing, thing,* and *spring*. As each rhyming word is mentioned, write it on the chart paper, highlighting the *-ing* phonogram with highlighting tape.

❄ When your students are unable to think of any other *-ing* words, say, "Let's read the list of rhyming words you generated."

❄ Pass out an individual pocket holder, a set of consonant letters, a set of blends, and a card printed with *-ing* to each student.

❄ Provide procedural directions for the hands-on activity. Instruct your students: "Please put the card printed with *i-n-g* in your pocket holder." Review the *-ing* rime by asking, "What does *i-n-g* say?" After hearing the correct response, say, "Let's all read this chunk together." Then continue with the procedural directions by explaining: "Since this activity will begin with the consonants, please remove the rubber band and line up the consonant cards above your pocket holder. Put the elastic inside the pocket of your pocket holder for safekeeping. Do *not* touch the set of blends; set it on the floor next to you, please."

❄ Explain the directions of the activity: "I'll name a letter for you to put into your pocket holder *before* the card printed with *-ing*." Hold up a pocket holder that contains the card printed with *-ing* in one hand and hold up the letter card printed with *d* in your other hand. Demonstrate where the letter should be placed: "*Before* means 'ahead of.' Watch where I put the letter *d* so it's *before -ing*." As you position it, say, "It's the beginning sound of the word." Invite your students to practice inserting a letter strip before the phonogram: "I'd like you to take a letter strip and place it in your pocket holder *before* the *-ing* phonogram card." Check your students' pocket holders and give support to those students who need help. Then say, "Please remove your letter strip and return it to the line of letter cards above your pocket holder." Next, explain the second component of the activity by saying, "After I've checked your pocket holders to see if you've followed my direction, I'll ask you to read the word you made. For example, if you put the letter *d* in your pocket holder, I'd ask, 'What does *d-i-n-g* say?' And you would say aloud in a strong, clear voice, 'Ding.' " Before beginning the exercise, ask, "Do you have any questions before we start?"

* Begin the rhyming activity with beginning consonants. Instruct your students: "Take the [name of letter] and place it before *-ing*. Then ask, "What does it say?" After your students read it aloud, add it to the list your students started if it's a new rhyming word. Direct your students: "Take the [name of letter] out of your pocket holder and replace it with [name of a different letter]. Now what does it say?" Add the word to the list if it's a new rhyming word. Continue this procedure for the remaining consonants.

* Provide procedural directions for the second part of the rhyming activity. Direct your students: "Before we make more words with the other set of letter strips, I'd like you to gather all five consonant strips and wrap your rubber band around them. I'll come around and collect them from you when I see your hand up holding the set of letter strips." As soon as all sets have been collected, say: "Now remove the elastic from the set of blends and place them *above* your pocket holder—just like we did with the first set of letter cards. Remember to put the elastic in your pocket holder. As soon as you've finished lining up your letter strips, we'll begin. Signal me by focusing your eyes on me."

* Implement the rhyming activity with beginning consonant blends. Instruct your students: "Take the [name of consonant blend] and place it before *-ing*. What does it say?" After your students read it aloud, add it to the list

Every Child a Reader

your students started if it's a new rhyming word. Direct your students: "Take the [name of consonant blend] out of your pocket holder and replace it with [name of a different consonant blend]. Now what does it say?" Add the word to the list if it's a new rhyming word. Continue this procedure for the remaining consonant blends.

✿ Direct your students' attention to the completed list of rhyming words: "Let's read the list of rhyming words we created today. I'll point, and you'll read. Who would like to read this list independently?"

Note: A fair method to use for choosing a student—one that's accepted as fair by all students—is to blindly select a student by using craft sticks with the names of students written on them (i.e., one name per stick). From the class set, pull out the craft sticks with the names of those students who raise their hands. Hold these sticks with the students' names covered by your hand. Invite a student to pull out one stick and read the student's name aloud.

❦ Reflection ❧

Before this lesson was introduced, I thought my students thoroughly understood the concept of rime because of their regular practice in supplying rhyming words I'd purposely omit when I read aloud to them. When I initially developed the lesson, the brainstorming activity was intended to be a quick lead-in to the spelling activity. I didn't anticipate any problem rearing its ugly head.

To my surprise, it took a lot of hard work and more time than I had predicted to produce a short list. By the end of the activity, I was mentally exhausted. To help probe my students' thinking, I had to read the list of words they had created each time a new word was suggested, but that didn't seem to help that much. When the room fell silent for a few moments, I decided to move on to the spelling activity to maintain the momentum of the lesson. I knew I'd be adding more words to the list, so my students would still be able to practice reading and seeing more words containing the -ing chunk. I'm thankful I made this teaching decision because it saved my lesson from disaster. By the end, my students had gained more knowledge about rhyme. More importantly, they experienced success and their self-confidence remained intact—all because I paid attention and shifted course.

LESSON SEVEN

Discussion of Family Traditions, Predictions, Word Identification

---

Day Before Christmas

We have been helping with the cake
And licking out the pan,
And wrapping up our packages
As neatly as we can,
And we have hung our stockings up
Beside the open grate,
And now there's nothing more to do
Except
to
Wait!

—*Marchette Chute*

What I Was Thinking

Since all my students celebrated Christmas last year, I thought they'd enjoy reading about a holiday that held such meaning for them. But I also think teachers should have on hand holiday poems that represent their class's makeup, so that all students' customs can be acknowledged and discussed. Although there are many Christmas poems for young children, I selected "Day Before Christmas" because the vocabulary was appropriate, and Chute's message was obvious. I also thought it would be a perfect opportunity to introduce the term *tradition*.

When I asked the children what makes December special, they announced, "Christmas!" With each passing day, they became more excited about Christmas, and since they still hadn't a concept of time, waiting for Christmas Day was very difficult for them. Prior to the holiday, many families plan special activities to help expend their children's energies. And because many families have their own unique traditions at this special time of year, I predicted a lively discussion would ensue.

Materials

The poem "Day Before Christmas" by Marchette Chute, handwritten on manila tag chart paper in large, neat print and attached by rings to a wooden chart stand

Chart paper

A red marker

A green marker

What This Lesson Looks Like

❋ Introduce the poem "Day Before Christmas." Point to the title as you say, "The title of this poem is 'Day Before Christmas.' " Then turn over the chart so the words cannot be seen. Say, "The title gives the reader an idea of what the story is about." Invite your students: "I'd like you to predict what the poet describes in her poem. As you know, a prediction is a guess. We won't know for sure until I read the poem to you." Prompt your students by saying, "We do know poets write about things they know and care about. What do you think the poet experiences the day before Christmas?" After your students have shared their predictions, reveal the words of the poem and say, "Listen as I read 'Day Before Christmas.' You shared some great ideas. Now let's find out what the day before Christmas means to the speaker of the poem."

❋ Read the poem aloud, paying attention to pacing. Pause after reading each of these words to emphasize the slow passage of time: *except, to,* and *wait.*

❋ Explain to your students: "Christmas is an exciting time of year. For me, the holiday goes by too quickly. This poem suggests that when there is nothing left to do, time goes by especially slowly on Christmas Eve. How many of you agree with her feelings?" Begin the discussion by saying, "Parents try to involve their children in different activities, in part to keep them occupied. When these special activities occur year after year, we refer to them as *traditions*." Tell your students, "In this poem, the children participate in different activities on the day before Christmas. Who can remember what they did?" If your students can't remember all four activities, refer to the poem. Begin to read the appropriate lines and pause at the item to be identified (i.e., *cake*, *pan*, *packages*, or *stockings*) by your students.

❋ Suggest to your students, "Let's list the four Christmas activities that are mentioned in the poem. Again, name something they did." Use a red marker to write a student's response. After the activity is listed, ask, "What else did they do?" Then use a green marker to write a different activity. Continue to alternate colors for the remaining two activities. Using two different colors helps students differentiate the various responses.

❋ Ask your students, "In this poem, where did they hang their stockings?" If no one remembers, refer to the poem and read the line "beside the open grate." Ask, "What's a grate?" Explain its meaning to your students: "It's a frame made of iron bars that you put inside the opening of your fireplace to hold logs you burn."

❋ Invite your students to share different customs in which they are involved. Ask, "What special traditions does your family have?" If they differ from the activities already recorded, add them to the list.

❋ Turn your students' attention back to the poem: "Let's read this poem again, but this time I'd like you to supply the last word in each line. And when we come to the last three words [point to these words], I want you to read them with me. Let's practice the correct pacing. The white space lets us know to slow down [point to the white space]. Ready?" Practice reading the last three lines together: "Except to wait." Then remind your students: "I'll read most of the poem. You'll supply the last word in each line, and then you'll join me in reading the last three words."

Every Child a Reader

DECEMBER

∞ Reflection ∞

In retrospect, "Day Before Christmas" was the perfect poem to use just before the winter vacation. It not only captured the children's state of mind at this special time, but it also provided a stimulus for a wonderful, enlightening discussion about their family traditions. Many students eagerly and enthusiastically recounted traditional Christmas preparations, such as finding the perfect tree and trimming it with favorite handmade ornaments. Although some of their preparations were completed long before Christmas Eve, students also shared similar activities mentioned in the poem, but with a slightly different twist, such as baking special Christmas cookies, making gingerbread houses, and hanging their stockings on bedposts. However, Jacob's tale reminded me of a TV program from my past: Art Linkletter's *Kids Say the Darndest Things*. He told the class his dad had his own special holiday tradition—waiting until the day before Christmas to buy presents for Jacob's mommy. Now I know why we see so many men in the malls on the day before Christmas: this tradition must be passed down from one generation of males to the next!

JANUARY

LESSON ONE
Exploring Verbs Through Movement

Wide Awake

I have to jump up
       out of bed
       and stretch my hands
       and rub my head
       and curl my toes
       and yawn
       and shake
       myself
       all wide-awake!

—*Myra Cohn Livingston*

What I Was Thinking

Returning from a two-week hiatus from school for winter break is always a difficult transition for my students *and* for me. Added to this reality is the fact that I don't sleep soundly the night before I return to work from a school break, which makes it impossible for me to feel refreshed and wide-awake. If *I* had trouble sleeping, some of my students probably didn't sleep at all!

As soon as I read the poem "Wide Awake," I knew it would be an ideal one to introduce on the first day back from vacation. It would be easy to learn, and I could involve the children by asking them to act out each line as they read the poem aloud. Incorporating this modality would not only keep them engaged, it would also help students learn the words more easily.

Materials

The poem "Wide Awake" by Myra Cohn Livingston, handwritten on manila tag chart paper in large, neat print and attached by rings to a wooden chart stand

Chart paper

A marker

What This Lesson Looks Like

☀ Introduce the poem by pointing to the title and reading it aloud. Ask your class, "When you first wake up in the morning, do you feel wide-awake right away? I know it takes me a few minutes before I'm ready to start my day—especially after a leisurely weekend or after a vacation break. In this poem, the poet describes what the poet does just after waking up in the morning. When I finish reading this poem, we'll talk about what you do before and after you get out of bed in the morning."

☀ As you read the poem aloud, imitate the actions of the verbs. Invite your students to join you in the various movements.

☀ After you've finished reading the poem, inform your class: "The poet describes six actions she does upon awakening." Then ask your class, "Who can tell me one thing the poet does when she first wakes up?" Call on a student to recall one action, and write the student's response on chart paper or on the white board. Continue this procedure until all actions have been identified.

☀ Invite the class to read the list with you. Point to each word as you read.

☀ Identify and read each action phrase in the poem. Point to the first action on the list that was generated by your students, and read it aloud. Then ask your students, "Who can locate these words in the poem? Show me by raising your hand and keeping your eyes focused on these words as you raise your hand." Invite a student to identify and read the appropriate line in the poem aloud to the class. Follow this procedure until all actions in the poem have been identified and read aloud.

☀ Explain to the class: "I'm going to imitate one of these actions. If you know what I'm doing and can locate the action word on this list, please raise your hand, keeping your eyes focused on the appropriate words." Imitate one of the action words at random, and look for a student whose eyes appear to be focused on the correct line. Invite the student to identify the action. "

✤ Survey your students regarding their morning rituals. Say, "Let's see how many of you do the same things when you first wake up. After I read an action, please raise your hand if you do it." Make a tally of your students' responses for each listed action. At the end of this list, draw a line to separate these actions from the next list they'll compile. After you have tallied the last action word, ask your students, "Do you do something that's not listed when you first wake up?" After a student responds, ask, "Raise your hand if you [name the suggested action]." Continue to list the various responses, and tally these additional actions until your students are unable to think of any more.

✤ Discuss the tally results regarding the speaker's actions. Instruct your class: "Please look at our tally. I'd like to begin with the speaker's actions. Which action has the most tally marks?" Call on a student to come up and read that action. Then invite the student: "Please count the tally marks next to that action. Then record the total next to the tally marks." Provide specific positive feedback about the student's counting and number-writing skills. For example, you could say, "You did a great job counting first by fives and then knowing how to count by ones. And you formed your numerals perfectly. You made them so carefully and neatly. What impressed me the most was that you noticed a reversal and corrected it without a reminder from me. Good job!" Continue analyzing the tally results to reinforce counting and number-writing.

✤ Discuss the tally results of other actions performed by different students when they wake up. Instruct the class: "Now let's look at other actions you do." Point to the list of actions printed below the drawn line you made: "Which action on this list has the most tallies?" Call on a third student to come up to the white board or chart paper to identify the appropriate action. Tell the student, "Please point to each word as you read." If the student is correct, invite him or her to count and record the total number of tally marks.

✤ To build a sense of community, invite your students to provide positive feedback to their classmate. After the student has finished, ask your class, "Who noticed something that [name of student] did well?" When students raise their hands, call on one of them to comment. If the student performed other skills proficiently, ask, "Did any of you notice anything else?" If no one responds, mention to the student what you noticed.

- Summarize the tally results. Sweep your finger from the top to the bottom of the entire list. Say, "Now let's look at all the different actions people do when they wake up. What action is used the most?" After a student correctly identifies the action, ask, "What action is used the least?"
- Invite your students to act out each line of the poem as they read it aloud with you, "Let's perform the actions in this poem as we read it aloud: Everyone, please stand. Let's begin . . ."
- Call on a capable student to read the poem aloud independently.

Reflection

During the first reading, I had planned for the class to watch me as I acted out each line I read aloud. However, they began acting it out as soon as I had read the second line of the poem. I'm sure they were thinking, "This poem suggests movement, so why not move!" They were completely engaged and calmly moving their bodies as they attended to every word I said, so I decided to forgo my lesson plan and invite them to join me in this kinesthetic activity. At that moment, the strong bond I had developed with my students became even stronger. We were a family—a community of learners. The best ideas always seem to come from my kindergartners!

Through movement, the children were comprehending. Not only did they learn each line of the poem easily, but the movement also helped to kindle a delight in the language. Because they thoroughly enjoyed this kinesthetic experience, my students asked if we could begin each day by reciting and acting out this poem. Tomorrow their wish will come true.

LESSON TWO
Silent e

What I Was Thinking

Since my students consistently demonstrated they could decode simple CVC (consonant-vowel-consonant) words and read most of them with automaticity, I knew it was time to introduce CVCe (consonant-vowel-consonant-silent e) words. When I looked at this poem's title, "Wide Awake," and noticed that both words contained the CVCe spelling pattern, I thought, "There's no time like the present!"

However, because this particular spelling pattern appeared only three times in the poem, I knew I needed a supplemental activity to reinforce the concept. I wondered whether creating a visual aid to use during the exercise would facilitate my students' understanding. I decided to give it a try, because I had to live by our kindergarten motto: You don't know what you can do until you try.

Materials

The poem "Wide Awake" by Myra Cohn Livingston, handwritten on manila tag chart paper in large neat print and attached by rings to a wooden chart stand

Eight 4" x 6" cards printed with the words *bite, cute, dime, hope, huge, mate, note,* and *plane* in large lowercase letters—one word per card

* Use a red marker to print the two vowel letters in each word.
* Use a black marker to print all other letters.

Eight 2" x 4" strips of card stock

* Cover the letter *e* at the end of each CVCe word with a 2" x 4" strip
* Attach the top of the strip to the 4" x 6" card with transparent tape.

What This Lesson Looks Like

* Read the poem aloud with your class. Explain: "We'll read this poem two times. The first time we read, I just want you only to *read*—no movement allowed—because I want you to concentrate on the words. And then, we'll read it again with actions. Okay?"

✸ Invite your students to read the poem aloud again: "Now let's perform the actions in this poem as we read it aloud. Make sure you still focus on the words so you won't lose your place. I want to hear strong reading voices throughout."

✸ When your class has finished acting out the poem, call on two capable students—a boy and a girl—to take turns reading the poem aloud independently.

✸ Begin the word study. Say, "Today I'll teach you about a different spelling pattern called CVC*e* words. You already know that CVC means consonant-vowel-consonant. The *e* stands for the letter *e* at the end of a one-syllable word." Then say, "Before I show you some CVC*e* words, let's practice reading some easy CVC words." Hold up the set of flip cards and show the top card to your students. Ask, "What does this word say?" Continue through the remainder of CVC words at a comfortable reading pace.

✸ Use a flip card to introduce the CVC*e* spelling pattern.

- Hold up the flip card with the word *not*. Keep the last letter covered with the attached piece of card stock.

- Ask your students, "What does this word say?" When they read it aloud, say, "You're right. It says *not*." Then ask, "What sound does the letter *o* make in this word?" After your students say /ŏ/ confirm their accuracy by reiterating: "It does say /ŏ/."

- Direct your students: "Watch this." Lift the piece of card stock to reveal the letter *e*. Then immediately say, "Now it says *note*." Then cover it with the flap and say, "Now it says *not*." Quickly uncover and cover the letter *e* a few more times, reading aloud the word that is exposed: "*Note . . . not . . . note.*"

- Say, "It's like magic. Let's take a closer look at these words. Are these words the same?" First lift the flap to show the word *note*, and then cover the letter *e* with the flap. Call on a student to answer. If the response is incorrect, allow the student to see both words again. Then ask, "How is the word *note* different from *not*?" Confirm the student's response, and then elaborate: "Yes, there's an *e* at the end of the word *note*. If you don't look carefully at all the letters, you could mistake it for the word *not*. But we know that for words to be the same, they must have the same letters in the same order."

- Direct your students: "Listen as I slowly say the sounds in the word *note*: /n/ /?/ /t/. What does the vowel *o* say?" Call on a student to respond. After the student gives an accurate response, say, "You're right! It does say /?/." Point to letter *e* as you say, "I'm going to tell you a story about this letter. It's called the *magic e*, because it gives all of its power to the other vowel. The letter *e* is silent, because it has no power left to say its name."

- Hold up a different flip card with the flap in place. Invite your class to read the CVC word aloud. Then lift up the flap to reveal the letter *e*. Say, "This is the magic letter *e*. It gives all its power to the other vowel in this word, so the other vowel is able to say its own name." Ask, "What's the name of the other vowel in this word?" Follow with: "What sound does the vowel make? What happens to the letter *e* when it gives all its power to the other vowel?" If no one responds, explain: "The letter *e* is silent; it doesn't make a sound." Invite your students: "Let's blend this word." Remind your students: "Remember: the first vowel says its own name." After your students finish blending the sounds, ask them: "What's the word?" Repeat the sequence of questions for a few more flip cards or until you sense they are ready to read the CVC*e* word cards without your support.

✿ Direct your students' attention to the poem. Explain: "This poem contains three silent *e* words. Can you find them?" Follow with: "As soon as you see one, raise your hand and keep your eyes focused on it, so you can identify it quickly."

✿ Call on a student who appears to know the location of a CVC*e* word and say: "Sweep across the word you found." After she or he points to a word, comment: "This word *does* end with the letter *e*." Then invite the student: "Would you please blend the sounds of this word for us?" Provide support as necessary. Follow this procedure for the remaining two words. Invite your class to read the words *wide, awake,* and *shake* in unison.

❧ Reflection ❧

This lesson proved to me that my students needed more practice with CVC*e* words before they would be comfortable reading them. Although some students grasped the silent *e* concept quickly, other students remained perplexed during the lesson. I continually had to remind them about the vowel change before they blended the sounds of words I showed them on the flip cards. And when I invited them to read the silent *e* words independently, they continued to give the short vowel sound and forgot that the letter *e* was silent.

If I didn't reinforce this new concept quickly, my students most likely would forget I had even mentioned it. But I wondered if I could find another great poem containing at least a few CVC*e* words for my next lesson. Even if it took hours of searching, I was determined to persevere. Reviewing this fundamental concept was essential.

LESSON THREE

Personal Connections, Predictions, and New Sight Words

January

January is
when your sled hurries
to the park after school
and flurries you
down
the
hill
again
and
again
until your nose is a dull cold pain
and your big toe starts to complain
about the hole in your sock
and you begin to wish
your sled would stop
whispering
"one more time"
and once—
just once—
pull
you
back
up
that
hill!

—*Bobbi Katz*

Every Child a Reader

What I Was Thinking

Bobbi Katz's poem "January" evoked memories of my own childhood. Needless to say, I immediately connected with this one. Although I haven't gone sledding for years, I still remember that torturous climb back up the hill. At first, I'd scramble up the steep hill because I couldn't wait to take another thrilling run. But after a few climbs, my quick ascent dramatically slowed down. I'd s-l-o-w-l-y trudge up the hill—my legs burning with each step—wishing someone would carry me up the rest of the way.

Since many of my kindergartners choose to sled down a steep hill at recess whenever there is enough snow, I hoped they, too, would identify with this poem. In addition, I believed my students no longer needed the support of a rhyming pattern to read a poem successfully, so I wanted them to experience a free-verse poem.

Using context clues to determine unknown words is one skill many of my students need reinforced. I hoped they'd be able to identify the word *sled* if I covered it. More importantly, I wanted them to be able to support their prediction by recalling appropriate lines in the poem.

Materials

The poem "January" by Bobbi Katz, handwritten on manila tag chart paper in large, neat print and attached by rings to a wooden chart stand

Highlighting tape

Two strips of construction paper to cover the word *sled* each time it appears in the poem

Four 3" x 5" cards printed with *again*, *begin*, *once*, and *pull* in large lowercase letters

What This Lesson Looks Like

☀ Discuss the reason why a word is covered in the poem. Say, "As you can see, I've covered two words in this poem." Point to the first covered word in the second line as you say, "This word and this word [point to the other covered word] are the same." Then ask your students: "Why do you think

I've covered these words?" When your students call out the correct answer, validate their response by saying, "That's right. You're going to guess the word that makes sense."

✦ Explain the directions for the initial reading: "I'd like you to listen carefully as I read this poem aloud. Be ready to tell me your guess for the covered word." Support them by supplying them with a clue: "I'll give you one clue: the covered word is an object."

✦ Read the poem aloud using appropriate pacing and tone.

✦ When you finish reading the poem aloud, ask, "Who has a prediction?" Call on a student to give his or her prediction, then ask, "What makes you think it's [predicted word]?" If no one responds, prompt the class by referring to the lines in the poem. Read aloud the words *and flurries you down the hill*. Then ask, "Do you know what the poet's suggesting by using the action word *flurries*?" If no one responds, define the word, "The word *flurries* suggests the object takes you down the hill very quickly." Then ask, "What object could you use to race down a hill?" If they need further support, point to the title and ask, "What's the title of this poem?" When the word *January* is read aloud, ask, "January is in what season?" Follow with: "What falls from the sky in winter?" When your students call out the answer—snow—rephrase the question by asking, "What object would you use to take you quickly down a snow-covered hill?"

✦ Check the accuracy of your students' response by saying, "Let's check the beginning letter of the covered word to see if it begins with the same letter as your prediction. If it does, then it's likely you've guessed the correct word." Reveal the first letter. If it matches the first letter of the predicted word, call on a capable speller to encode the predicted word. Print each letter the student names on the paper strip. Provide support as needed. Then remove the paper strip and compare the two words to see if they're the same. If your students' prediction doesn't begin with the same letter as the covered word, ask the class, "Can you think of an object that begins with an *s* you would use in winter to fly down a hill?" If someone identifies an object, follow the same steps as in the first scenario.

Every Child a Reader

✤ Tell your students, "Sometimes poets use a technique called *personification* to give human qualities to nonliving things." Then ask your class: "What's the poetic device that makes nonliving objects sound like people?" Support your students by saying *personification* with them. Print the word *personification* on the board. Ask your students, "Do you see the word *person* inside of the word *personification*?" If someone sees it, invite the student to highlight the word *person* with highlighting tape. If not, highlight the word for them to see. Explain, "Bobbi Katz uses personification in this poem. She makes the sled sound and act like a person."

✤ Invite your students to find some lines in the poem in which the poet employs personification. Direct your class: "I want you to listen closely as I read this poem again. Be ready to point out examples of personification after I finish reading it aloud." To clarify the direction, say, "Pay particular attention to the lines in which the sled acts or sounds like a person."

✤ Read the poem again using a slow, deliberate pace. Slowly sweep the pointer across each line you read.

✤ After you finish reading the poem aloud, explain: "Bobbi Katz personifies the sled in two lines of this poem. There's an example of personification on this page, and there's also another example on the second page." Then say, "Let's begin with the first page. Can you find an example of personification on this page? What words make the sled *act* like a person?" Instruct your students: "Focus your eyes on a line that illustrates this special poetic device." Call on someone whose eyes are looking upward and say, "Point to the line that shows what would usually be used to describe the action of a person. But instead of a person, Bobbi Katz is talking about the sled." If the student correctly identifies the line, request: "Please read the line aloud for us." Continue to find the second example of personification by turning to the second page of the poem. Say, "There are also lines on this page in which the poet's choice of words makes the sled *sound* like a person. If you know the specific line, focus your eyes on it." Call on a different volunteer whose eyes are focused near the end of the poem to identify the two lines. If the student is correct, invite him or her to read the lines aloud.

✳ Introduce four new sight words: *again, begin, once,* and *pull*. Review your behavioral expectations during the sight-word exercise by asking various students to answer your questions. Ask, "[Name of student], when I hold up a word, who should answer?" If that particular student doesn't give the correct answer, continue to call on different students until you hear the correct response. Confirm the student's accuracy by saying, "That's right. Only those who know the word should say it aloud. Otherwise, it will cause confusion if different words are said." Follow with: "[Name of student], what should the others do?" When you hear the student's correct response, say, "You're right! Students who *don't* know the word should keep their lips zipped and their eyes focused on the word as it's read. Hearing the word *and* seeing the word will help you learn it more quickly."

• Hold up the card printed with *again*. Say, "This word may be unfamiliar to many of you. Raise your hand if you know it." Call on a capable student who raises his or her hand to read it aloud. After the student reads it aloud, invite the class: "Let's say it aloud together." Then direct your students: "Let's say it again, but this time let's clap out the parts in the word as we say it. Clap as you say each syllable: "*a-gain*." Then point to the first letter, *a*, and ask, "What sound do you hear at the beginning of this word?" When someone responds, "/a/," explain to your students, "In a word with more than one syllable, if the letter *a* is the only letter in the first syllable, it almost always says /?/. Listen as I say some words with more than one syllable that begin with the letter *a*. You'll hear only one sound in the first syllable." Clap your hands together as you say each syllable. Say, "A-bout, a-maze, a-ston-ish, a-wake." Invite the class to say the word *again* in unison. Ask, "What's this word?" If your class enjoys jokes and can maintain self-control, spice up the exercise by adding a bit of humor to their answer: "Okay, if you want me to ask you again, I will. What's this word?" By this time, someone will notice the joke, and respond, "We were just reading the *word*. We weren't telling you to ask us the question again." Redirect their attention back to the word study by saying, "Let's see if you can find the word *again* in two different lines of the poem. It's an easy word to find because it's the only word in the line." When someone raises his or her hand, direct that student: "Come up and show the class where the word *again* is located." After he or she identifies the word, instruct the student: "Clap the two parts of the word *again* for us." Then explain: "Now I want you to say the two parts once more, but this time, I'd like you to use the pointer to sweep across the first part slowly and stop before you begin the second part of the word. Then, as you begin to say the second part of the word, sweep across to the end of the word." Inform your students: "Just knowing the first two sounds of this word will enable you to make a good guess." Most likely, the student will be able to locate the word *again* without difficulty. However, if he or she doesn't identify it instantly, invite a different student to locate the word.

- Hold up the card printed with *begin*. Say, "This word is also a sight word, but I'm going to show you a fast way to figure it out." Expose only the first syllable by covering the second syllable, *-gin*, with your hand. Point to each letter as you ask your students: "What does *b-e* say?" When someone says the word *be*, cover up all but the last two letters of the word. Then ask, "What does *i-n* say?" As soon as someone says the word *in*, reveal the letter *g* and say, "If the *g* followed the rule, it would say /j/ since it's next to the letter *i*." Demonstrate both sounds for the letter *g* by saying, "It would sound like the letter *j*: /j/. But in this word, it makes the hard sound of *g*: /g/." Ask your students, "If you put the hard sound of /g/ before *in*, what would it say?" When someone gives a correct response, inform the class: "Now you have the information you need to figure out the word." Cover up the second syllable of *begin*, revealing only *be*, and ask: "What does this say?" Upon hearing a correct response, say the first syllable again, cover it up, and reveal the second syllable. Encourage your class to finish the word by pausing after you say the word *be*. Say, "Be . . ." Follow with: "What's the word?" Then invite your class: "Find the line in which the word *begin* is located. When you find it, read the whole line to yourself so you'll be ready to read it aloud to the class if you are invited. Signal me that you've followed both directions by putting your hands on your head." Observe your students' reading behaviors as they attempt to locate the word and as they silently read the sentence. When most students have completed the task, call on a student who you believe is able to correctly read the line.

Note: It's easy for me to determine a student's accuracy at this point in the year, because when children begin to read independently, they'll whisper the words as they read silently.

- Supply a clue to help identify the sight word *once*: "This sight word almost always begins a fairy tale." Then hold up the card printed with *once* and warn them: "Don't be tricked by the beginning letter. It won't help you figure out this word." Ask, "If you know the word, read it to us." After someone reads it aloud correctly, say, "It *is* the word *once*." Then invite your students: "Let's spell and cheer this word aloud together" (Cunningham, 1995).

- Supply a clue to help identify the word *pull*. On chart paper or on the board, write the word *push*. Directly below it, write the word *pull*. Then say, "You've seen these words on store doors to help you know how to open the door." Invite your students to compare the letters in the words by asking, "Let's look closely at the letters in these words. What do you notice?" If any student needs more information, follow with: "How are the letters the same? How are they different?" When it's mentioned that the *p* and *u* are in both words in the same sequence, use a marker to connect each *p* and each *u* by a line. And when it's mentioned that the last two letters in the words are different, draw a big circle around them in each word. Draw your students' attention to the vowel: "How many vowels do you see in this word?" Call on a student to answer. When the student correctly responds, follow with: "What's the name of the vowel?" Then explain to your students: "Both words are CVC words. The vowel says /oo/ in both words." Invite your students to blend the sounds in the word *push*. Just before they blend the last sound, remind them: "The *sh* sound is my favorite sound." After they finish blending the sounds, ask, "What's the word?" To help them identify the word *pull*, prompt them by saying, "On one door is the word *push*, and on the other door is the word . . ." Hold up the card printed with *pull* as some students say the word. Then turn to the second page of the poem and invite your class to locate the word *pull*. Say, "You'll be able to find this lickety-split, because it's the only word in the line." Call on a student to identify it.

✻ Explain to your students: "This poem's format is perfect for a whip-around reading. You'll take turns reading one line in consecutive order from the beginning of the poem to the end." Use your pointer to demonstrate a zigzag motion. Point to the student sitting at the end of the front row on the left side and say, "[Name of student] will read the title and the first line of the poem." Then sweep your pointer across each row, making a zigzag line to identify the order in which each student will read a line.

✻ Next, sweep across the second line of the poem and say, "Then the next person will take a turn to read this line." Continue to sweep across each line until you reach the last line of the poem. Emphasize: "You need to focus and be ready to read the next line as soon as the classmate sitting next to you finishes reading his or her line. It's important to try to maintain the flow and rhythm of the poem. If you don't know a word in the line you read, I'll help you."

✻ After your students have finished reading the poem aloud, invite them to share their own sledding experiences: "Think of a time you went sledding. Tell us something you really enjoyed about your experience, and something you didn't enjoy at all." Discuss whether or not they shared feelings similar to those of the poet.

✻ Finally, invite the class to read the poem aloud with you. Remind them: "Remember to whisper the words *one more time* when we come to that line. And read with feeling. Use your voice to make the poem come alive."

❧ Reflection ❧

A line from Robert Burns's poem "To a Mouse" aptly summarizes this particular lesson: "The best laid plans go oft awry." During the process of designing lessons, I try to consider potential trouble spots. Often a lesson will proceed exactly as I've planned it, but this particular lesson didn't turn out as I expected. I didn't take into account how literally kindergarten students think.

Although I had given my students clues to help them determine the correct word, they were stymied. Only one student offered a guess. Because of the grammatical structure of the sentence, Kate realized her prediction, *feet*, didn't make sense when she reread the sentence. Even with an excessive wait time, nobody else ventured a guess.

When I revealed the covered word and announced it to the class, a magical teachable moment occurred—all because of a little boy's wonderings. Nicco couldn't understand how a sled could hurry to a park or whisper. Emphatically he exclaimed, "Only people can do that!" And that's when I knew this moment was a perfect opportunity to introduce personification. I didn't expect many students to remember this word, but I knew some children, like Nicco, would benefit from this spontaneous discussion. And indeed they did! The next day, when I asked if anybody remembered the device poets use to give human qualities to nonliving objects, a few children—one being Nicco—raised their hands. When I chose Nicco to answer, he confidently responded, "Person-ification"! Although he mispronounced the word, I knew from his spoken version of it that he clearly understood its meaning.

This "teachable moment" helped Nicco gain more knowledge about figurative language, and for me, it provided an opportunity to mention a poetic device that usually is introduced in first grade or later. What was a good lesson turned into a better one—all because of one student's curiosity.

Note: This lesson plan reflects the necessary revisions I made after implementing my original.

LESSON FOUR

Introduction of New Sight Words

My Book!

I did it!
I did it!
Come and look
At what I've done!
I read a book!
When someone wrote it
Long ago
For me to read,
How did he know
That this was the book
I'd take from the shelf
And lie on the floor
And read by myself?
I really read it!
Just like that!
Word by word,
From first to last!
I'm sleeping with
This book in bed,
This first, FIRST book
I've ever read!

—*David Harrison*

What I Was Thinking

As a kindergarten teacher, I *love* the month of January! It's because there's always an explosion of learning during these four weeks. The children who had previously demonstrated slow progress in their reading development suddenly take off, and everything begins to click for them.

I especially love to watch my students during independent reading time. There they are, in their personal spaces—some on their tummies while others are on their backs—immersed in their reading of stories, completely unaware that I'm watching them. I savor the wondrous scene of readers "in the zone," as Nancie (Atwell, 2007) defines it. At this time of year, my students begin to read their books independently for a sustained period of time. Although their reading time is only 5 to 10 minutes at first, it's still sustained. For the first time, silence permeates the room during independent reading. Aah! A just reward for our efforts.

After winter break, several children abandon the predictable, leveled readers for more complex reading: simple chapter books! Even those students who continue to read the predictable, leveled readers are now able to use many reading strategies to determine unknown words. Reading has begun to click for all my students, and they can't wait to read their books.

Although I had found the poem "My Book!" several months before, I wanted to wait until all my students had read their first books so they could identify with the feelings expressed in this particular poem. My wait was over.

Materials

The poem "My Book" by David Harrison, handwritten on manila tag chart paper in large, neat print and attached by rings to a wooden chart stand

Four 3" x 5" cards printed with the words *come, done, know,* and *word*

What This Lesson Looks Like

- ❋ Introduce the poem "My Book!" by David Harrison: "When I discovered this poem several months ago, I thought it would be a great one to use in the second half of the school year, so I filed it away and waited until everyone would be able to relate to it. Ta-da! Now is the perfect time!"

- ❋ Explain the new procedure for reading poems. Summarize your students' progress: "You're doing such a wonderful job with your reading. After you returned from the holiday break, I noticed a huge difference. When you read now, you immediately recognize a lot of words, so your reading is becoming smoother. And when you come to an unfamiliar word, you're able to use different strategies by yourself to figure it out." Then announce: "I'm not going to introduce this poem by reading it to you. You're going to read the poem all by yourselves! First, I'll give you a few minutes to read it to yourselves. And then we'll read it aloud together."

☀ Introduce four new sight words: *come, done, know,* and *word*: "Before you read, I'd like to review four sight words that may be tricky for some of you." Remind them: "Say it if you know it. Listen if you don't."

• Hold up the card printed with the word *come*. Say, "I know many of you have come across this sight word in your leveled readers. If you know it, say it." After the word has been read aloud, ask, "If you didn't know the word was *come*, how would you sound it out?" When someone pronounces it as *comb*, say, "You're right, you probably would think it was *comb*, because it *looks* like a CVCe word pattern. And you'd say to yourself, '*Comb* is a real word.' " Use the word *comb* in a sentence, "I comb my hair in the morning." Then ask, "When would you discover your mistake?" Repeat someone's correct response. Say, "You'd know it was wrong, because when you read the line, it won't make sense. But it might help you to figure out the correct word!" Direct your students' attention to the third line in the poem. Invite your students: "Let's read this line using the word *comb* to see if it makes sense." After reading it, say, "Although it didn't make sense, using the sounded-out version would help you to correct your mistake." Then invite your students: "Let's read the line again correctly." Remind them: "Sometimes words don't follow the rules. You need to use other strategies for figuring out sight words. Sometimes you can try to make sense of them like we just did. And memorizing these words will help your reading flow more smoothly." Invite your students: "Let's read aloud the word *come* in one big voice. Try to picture it in your mind as you say it."

• Hold up the card printed with *done*. Say, "Another sight word with a silent *e* at the end of it. And since I called it a *sight* word, it tells you that it can't be sounded out." Then instruct your students: "Read this word if you know it." After it's correctly read aloud, cover the last two letters in the word with your fingers and say, "Inside this word is a little word you already know. What's this word?" When your students read the word *do* aloud, explain: "You can use the word *do* to help you remember the word *done*." Keep the letters covered as you say, "After you *do* something . . ." Then reveal the whole word as you say, ". . . it's *done*." Direct your students' attention to the poem and ask, "Who sees the word *done* near the beginning of the poem?" Call on a student whose hand is raised to point it out. Then sweep the pointer across the preceding line and say, "I'd like you to read from this line." Then sweep the pointer across the next line and say, "Continue until you come to the word *done*." Allow the student sufficient wait time to solve any unfamiliar words. Give support only when necessary.

- Hold up the card printed with the word *know*. Say, "This word can be tricky. You *can* sound out this word, but you need to know the *k-n* sound and the other sound for *o-w* to sound it out correctly." Then ask, "Who knows this word?" Call on a capable student to read it aloud. If nobody knows it, tell the class the word. Point to the first two letters and say, "The letters *kn* say /n/." Then point to the last two letters and say, "The letters *ow* make the /?/ sound." Next, remind your students: "You already know a word that sounds exactly like this word. How is that word spelled?" After the class spells it aloud, say, "I see the little word *no* inside of this word *know*." Call on a student to point it out to the class. After the student points to *no* inside of the sight word, say, "Seeing the little word *no* might help you remember that this word sounds just like it. But they don't have the same meaning. What does the little word *no* mean?" If someone says it's the opposite of yes, elaborate by saying, "Yes, it means *not so*." Sweep across the word *know* printed on the card and say, "Listen as I read the line in the poem that contains this word and see if you can think of a word that means the same thing." If no one suggests an appropriate word, say, "In the line, 'How did he know,' the word *know* means 'to understand.' " Read the line again, but this time use the word *understand* in place of the word know, "How did he *understand*?"

Every Child a Reader

Follow with: "*K-n-o-w* can also mean 'be acquainted with.' I'll give you an example by using it in a sentence. 'I *know* you.' " Before introducing the last new sight word, review the two words *no* and *know*. Cover up the letters *k* and *w* with your fingers. Ask, "What's this word?" After they read it aloud, remove your fingers and direct your students: "Now read this word."

- Instruct your students: "Read this word aloud if you know it. Just listen if you don't know it." Then hold up the card printed with *word*. If no one can identify it, read it aloud. After it's read aloud, ask, "Do you know why this word's a *sight* word?" If no one's accurate, say, "If you could sound it out you would say /w/ /ôr/ /d/. But the vowel in *word* says /ûr/, not /ôr/." Then invite your students: "Let's read this sight word aloud together." Direct your students' attention to the poem and ask, "Who can locate and read the line that begins and ends with this word?" Hold up the card printed with *word*. Call on a student to identify the word in the poem. If the student is accurate, say, "Please read the line aloud."

☀ Invite your students to read the poem silently: "Now I want you to take a few minutes to read this poem to yourselves, so when we read it aloud together, you'll be able to read it more fluently." Then explain: "This poem is rather long. I had to use two pieces of chart paper to copy all of it. When you reach the end of the first page, please signal me by putting your hands on your head. When most of you have given me the signal, I'll turn the chart paper over so you'll be able to read the remainder of the poem that I wrote on another piece of chart paper."

Note: While your students are reading silently, observe their reading behaviors and jot down relevant information (e.g., names of students who subvocalized, students who read quickly or very slowly, students who became distracted or didn't persevere, and so on).

☀ When most of your students have finished reading the poem silently, ask, "What was this poem about?" Call on a student to answer.

☀ Invite your students to share their personal stories about reading a book for the first time: "Do you remember the first time you read a book all by yourself? Tell us all about this special event in your life." Encourage your students to elaborate by asking, "What book did you read all by yourself? How did it make you feel to be able to read a book all by yourself? Did you read it to anyone else?"

✿ Draw your students' attention to the words in the poem: "I'd like each of you to share a word you can read with your classmates—one that you figured out by yourself or one you already know but believe others may not know yet."

✿ Use the whip-around procedure to read the poem aloud for the first time. Invite your children: "Let's take turns reading the lines of this poem. You'll read a line in the poem, and then your neighbor will read the next line until the poem is completed. Since there are 22 lines including the title, everyone will get at least one turn to read. [Name of student] will begin by reading the title and the first line of the poem. [Name of student] will be last to read a line. If there are more lines left to read, we'll start whipping around again until the poem has been read from beginning to end." Remind them: "Be sure to look ahead at the punctuation marks, so you know when you should sound excited or when you should make your voice go higher. To get the most out of this poem, it needs to be read with a lot of feeling."

✿ After your students have finished reading the poem aloud, provide positive feedback regarding their oral reading: "What a great job! You read with such feeling. You made the poem come alive."

✿ Read the poem aloud again, chorally. Invite your students: "Let's read it again from beginning to end with feeling."

❧ Reflection ❧

Since my students previously had encountered most of the words in this poem, I knew in my heart they were ready to take a few moments to read this poem silently before I shared it with them. I wasn't sure how seriously they would carry out this new routine, but my confidence in their success grew as I watched their eyes move across the chart paper and saw their lips whisper the words. Some

Every Child a Reader

children read quickly, while others stopped to figure out words. When many students smiled as they read the last line, I recognized they had been able to read with understanding.

After a few minutes had elapsed, I knew it was time to move on, so I asked Joe, who had finished reading and was grinning from ear to ear, to express in his own words the meaning of this poem. I'll never forget his simple but honest description: "It's about how excited you feel when you're able to read a book by yourself for the first time—and I felt exactly like that!" Several other children nodded in agreement as Joe spoke.

Although I knew my students would identify with this poem, I didn't anticipate the volume in their voices as they read the poem aloud with me. But their loud voices didn't bother me at all. As a matter of fact, I relished every minute of this shared reading experience, because it was the first time everybody joined in with great enthusiasm and expression during the initial shared reading of a poem.

Taking the additional few minutes to read silently helped my students gain more fluency and confidence in their oral reading. I'll continue to implement this new procedure until most students don't need this scaffold to be successful.

LESSON FIVE

Introduction of a Color Word

> ### The Cardinal
>
> After the snow stopped
> the garden was white
> and sparkled like crystals of sugar.
> Whiteness was everywhere
> except for one bird,
> a cardinal,
> like a drop of blood
> in the snow.
>
> —*Charlotte Zolotow*

What I Was Thinking

Although wintertime in Maine is long and arduous, I can't deny the beauty of newly fallen snow. During the day, the world looks pristine. At night, the snow that blankets the ground and frosts the branches of trees glistens in the moonlight. In her poem "The Cardinal," Charlotte Zolotow captures these images through her use of effective similes. Through this poem, I believed my students would be able to see how vivid diction helps language come alive.

Materials

The poem "The Cardinal" by Charlotte Zolotow, handwritten on manila tag chart paper in large, neat print and attached by rings to a wooden chart stand

Collection of sight-word cards previously presented

One 3" x 5" card printed with the word *white* in large lowercase letters

A picture of a cardinal

What This Lesson Looks Like

✿ Review the collection of sight words. Explain to your students: "When I believe you're able to read a poem without my support, I'll invite you to try it. And this poem is one I believe you can read all by yourself. But before you read, let's review all the sight words you've learned, because you may encounter some of them in this poem. As I show you the word, please read each word aloud in one big voice." Hold up the set of cards for all to see. Proceed through the cards at a steady pace.

✿ Introduce the color word *white*. As you hold up the set of previously learned sight words, say, "I have a new word to add to this collection." Then hold up the card printed with the word *white*. Say, "Read it if you know it." After an accurate response is given, confirm those students' accuracy by saying, "This word *is* the color word *white*." Invite your students to look at the sound features in the word: "Look carefully at the letters in this word. Who can identify the spelling pattern of this word?" If no one is able to remember the initials, say, "It's a CVC*e* pattern. The *C* stands for the word *consonant*." Point to the consonant digraph as you say, "The *wh* is the consonant because it makes one sound. What's this digraph's sound?" Call on a capable student to answer. Then continue the explanation by pointing to the vowel *i*. Say, "*V* stands for *vowel*, and the letter *i* is the vowel in this word. Repeat the initials you have just discussed by pointing to the three successive letters [*w, h,* and *i*] as you say: "*C . . . V . . .*" Then, as you point to the consonant letter *t*, name the next initial in the spelling pattern by saying, "*C*." Ask your students, "What does this *C* stand for?" When someone says that this initial *C* also stands for the word *consonant*, explain: "The letter *t* is a consonant." Finally, ask, "And what's "at the end of this word?" When your students identify the letter *e*, add, ""A silent *e*." Remind your students: "The silent *e* gives all its power to the other vowel." Follow with: "What does that mean?" Hold up the card printed with the word *white*. Call on a student to demonstrate its meaning. Ask, "What does the vowel *i* say in this word? Why?" After the student correctly answers, ask, "What does the vowel *e* say?" Invite your class: "Let's slowly blend the sounds in the word *white*." Accompany your class by saying, "/wh/ /?/ /t/." Direct your students' attention to the poem: "The word *white* is located in two different lines. It's located at the end of one line. And in another line, it's inside a bigger word. It's the first part of the word. You'll be able to figure out the second part of the word by yourselves." Invite your students: "See if you can find this word in one line of the poem and tell me what it says." Call on a student to identify its location and read the word aloud.

☀ Introduce the poem. Point to the title as you say, "Today's poem is called 'The Cardinal.' " Point to the bottom of the chart paper as you say, "It's written by Charlotte Zolotow, who has written many poems for children. This poem focuses on a special sighting she observes in the world around her. She uses simple describing words to express what she sees, so that children, like you, will be able to understand and respond."

☀ Invite your students to share information about the cardinal: "What's a cardinal?" If someone identifies it as a bird, ask your students, "Who can give us some information about this bird?" After your students have shared what they know, provide relevant information that was not covered: "The cardinal is the only redbird present during the winter and sometimes is called the Winter Redbird. The cardinal is found year-round from Maine to Texas. They can be seen near the edges of woodlands, in gardens, and around bird feeders." Hold up a picture of the cardinal and say, "This is a photo of the male cardinal. The male is brilliant red in color and has a black-masked face, while the female is mostly brown with some red on her wings."

☀ Check your students' understanding of the information shared about the cardinal by asking: "Why is the cardinal sometimes called the Winter Redbird?" Follow with: "Name some places the cardinal visits."

☀ Explain to your students: "This information may help you figure out some words you don't know in the poem. I'd like you to read this poem to yourselves. If you don't know a word, try to make sense of it. Do the best you can. When you finish, please signal me by putting your hand on your head. Please begin reading."

✻ When several students have signaled you, say, "Thank you for letting me know you've finished. You may take your hands off your head now, and patiently wait for your other classmates to finish."

Note: It's best to stop the silent reading when you see the first sign of restlessness—even if there are some students who haven't finished reading the poem. Those students probably will be relieved to move on to the next activity.

✻ Invite your students to share new words with their classmates. Say, "I'd like you to identify a word you figured out all by yourself when you read this poem. And for those of you who could read all the words, I'd like you to point out a word you believe would be helpful for your classmates to know." Call on a student, and say: "Please read your word as you sweep the pointer across it." Allow time for all students who would like to share a new word.

✻ After the word-sharing is completed, say, "Now let's review all of these words together. When I point to a word, read it aloud in one big voice." Also point out any of the following words that weren't identified by your students: *garden, sparkled, crystals, sugar, everywhere, except,* and *blood.* Before you point out these words, say, "There are some words in this poem that aren't too easy. Let's see who knows these words. First, I'll point to the word. If nobody knows it, we'll read the line together to see if we can make sense of the word. Ready?" Then point to each word for your students to read aloud.

✻ Invite the class to read the poem chorally: "Now that you've read the poem silently, and you've reviewed some hard words, you should be able to read this poem more fluently. Read this poem aloud with me in one big voice." Point to the title with your pointer and begin.

✻ When the shared reading is completed, say, "Tell me about your mind-pictures. What did you picture in your mind as you read the poem? What words in the poem helped you visualize the scene more clearly?"

✻ Invite a girl and a boy who would like to read the poem independently to take turns reading.

❧ Reflection ❧

MacAllister, who is a natural little actress, raised her hand when I asked for a volunteer to read "The Cardinal" independently at the end of the lesson. I suspected she could read this particular poem aloud well, but I didn't realize the depth of her feeling until she began. When she read, she spoke as if it were a story she was telling. Then, when she paused and emphasized the words *a cardinal*, Kate, a capable reader, looked up at me and smiled, because she, too, recognized that MacAllister had been able to masterfully convey Zolotow's message and skillfully attend to the punctuation marks. MacAllister made the language come alive. It was a phenomenal performance by a student who had learned to appreciate and love poetry. And to think, this is only January!

LESSON SIX

Introduction of the r-Controlled Vowels ar, er, and ir

What I Was Thinking

Whenever my students encountered a word containing an irregular vowel, I would casually identify it as an *r*-controlled vowel and say its sound. Then we'd move on to the task at hand, and my students would dismiss it from their minds. Although I had mentioned the *r*-controlled vowel *er* and the /êr/ sound numerous times, my students never recognized it or remembered its special sound in unfamiliar words they attempted to decode. It was obvious that casually pointing out the *r*-controlled vowel wasn't helping my students to retain this information, but before I focused on any of the irregular vowels, I wanted to be certain my students had acquired a solid understanding of CVC and CVC*e* words.

Because the poem "The Cardinal" contained a number of *r*-controlled vowels, it would be an appropriate poem to use for an introductory lesson about these irregular vowels. But I didn't want to make a hasty decision and move too quickly to introduce a more complex skill if my students hadn't internalized the basic vowel sounds. After pondering the outcome of my previous word studies, I believed my students were ready to learn about irregular vowels, but I felt it was important to proceed slowly and cautiously. Since there are so many variations of these vowel sounds, I knew I'd have to implement future word studies. But first, my students needed to be able to recognize *r*-controlled vowels in words by themselves.

Materials

The poem "The Cardinal" by Charlotte Zolotow, handwritten on manila tag chart paper in large, neat print and attached by rings to a wooden chart stand

Red, blue, and green Vis-à-Vis pens

Set of students' names on craft sticks

Plastic sheeting to attach over the poem "The Cardinal"

One 3" x 5" card printed with the *r*-controlled vowel *ar* in large lowercase letters

One 3" x 5" card printed with the *r*-controlled vowel *er* in large lowercase letters

One 3" x 5" card printed with the *r*-controlled vowel *ir* in large lowercase letters

What This Lesson Looks Like

✸ Read the poem aloud with your class. Say, "When you read this poem aloud yesterday, you wowed me with your fluency. What made it even more special was your classmate's performance of this poem when he [or she] read independently. [Name of student] read with such feeling—as if he [or she] had witnessed the wonder of this sight, too. I especially liked how [name of student] varied the tone of his [or her] voice and paused before he [or she] identified the bird. [Name of student]'s reading brought the poem alive." Then invite your students: "I'd like you to use a conversational tone as we read the poem aloud together. Pretend you're describing this awesome sight to a friend." Sweep your pointer across the title as you say, "Now let's read 'The Cardinal.' "

✸ Reinforce the sight words in the poem: "I enjoyed listening to you read aloud so much, I'd like to hear it read again. Before you find out who will be chosen to read the poem aloud to the class, let's practice reading all the sight words in this poem and see how fast you can recognize them." Direct your students: "I'll name a sight word for you to find. Raise your hand as soon as you see it, but be certain you know exactly where the word is located, because if you don't point it out immediately, I'll choose someone else to show us. It's important to know how to read these words quickly and automatically." Then ask, "Who sees the word *the*?" Call on the first student who signals you. Follow the same procedure for the remaining sight words: *and, for, in, like, of, one,* and *was.*

✺ Invite a student to select a classmate to read the poem aloud independently: "Please choose a craft stick from the set I'm holding. You can't see the names because my hand's covering them. After you choose one, pull it out, and read the name aloud."

✺ When the student finishes reading aloud, give the child specific feedback about his or her performance. For example, if the student identified all sight words with automaticity, you could comment on the student's fluency by saying, "Since you know many sight words now, your reading's becoming fluent. You no longer read word by word." If you notice improvement in the student's expression, you could say, "You tried your best to use a conversational tone. With more practice, your voice will sound even more natural."

✺ Introduce *r*-controlled vowels through a story, "The letter *r* is sometimes called the bossy *r*. Sometimes the bossy *r* takes control of the vowel that stands next to it. It won't let the vowel say its regular sound, and it forces the vowel to change its sound. But it is nice to the vowel, because the bossy *r* always lets the vowel be first, and then it takes its place after the vowel. I'll show you what I mean." Explain through the *ar* combination.

✺ Then introduce the *r*-controlled vowel *ar.* Write the word *cat* on the board. Ask your students: "What's this word?" Follow with: "What does the vowel *a* say in the word *cat*?" When you hear your students make the /ʔ/ sound, say, "Yes, the vowel says its regular sound. Now watch what happens when the *r* follows the *a.*" Erase the *t* from the word *cat*, and replace it with an *r*. Direct your students: "Listen to how the vowel sound is changed now that the letter *r* follows the *a.*" Say the word *car.* Then ask, "What does the vowel say now?" Remark: "That letter *r* is bossy!"

✺ Continue the demonstration by writing the word *hen.* Ask your students, "What's this word?" Follow with: "What does the vowel *e* say in the word *hen*?" When you hear your students make the /ĕ/ sound, say, "Yes, the vowel says its regular sound. Now watch what happens when the *r* follows the *e*." Erase the *n* from the word *hen*, and replace it with an *r*. Direct your students: "Listen to how the vowel sound is changed now that the letter *r* follows the *e*." Say the word *her*. Ask, "What does the vowel say now? The letter *r* likes to take control, doesn't it?"

❅ Hold up the card printed with the *r*-controlled vowel *ar*. Direct your students: "Repeat after me: *a r* says /är/." Then hold up the card printed with the *r*-controlled vowel *er*. Continue the echo recitation by saying, "And *e r* says /ûr/."

❅ Explain to your students: "There's another *r*-controlled vowel that says /ûr/— just like *er* does. Watch!" Write the word *fin* on the board and ask, "What's this word? What does the vowel *i* say in *fin*?" After your students say /ĭ/, erase the letter *n* and replace it with an *r*. Inform your students: "This word says *fir*, as in a fir tree. How did the *r* change the vowel's sound?" When someone responds that the letter *r* directly follows the vowel *i*, ask, "Then what's the name of this *r*-controlled vowel?" As the answer is given, underline *ir* in the word *fir*. Then, confirm a correct response by saying, "Yes, the *r*-controlled vowel is *ir*."

❅ Explain the purpose of the word study. Attach the three cards printed with *ar*, *er*, and *ir* to the white board, and then explain: "There are several words in this poem with these particular *r*-controlled vowels. This lesson will help you become more aware of these vowels in words."

❅ Use *ar, er,* and *ir* vowel cards as a visual aid to clarify directions for the lesson. Point to the *ar* card and say, "If you find a word containing *ar*, please use a red felt-tip pen to circle this *r*-controlled vowel." As you speak, circle the *ar* on the card with a red Vis-à-Vis pen. Next, point to the *er* card, and say, "If you find a word containing *er*, please use a green felt-tip pen to circle this *r*-controlled vowel." Circle the *er* on the card with a green Vis-à-Vis pen. Finally, point to the *ir* card and say, "And if you find a word containing *ir*, please use a blue felt-tip pen to circle this *r*-controlled vowel." Then circle the *ir* on the card with a blue Vis-à-Vis pen.

❅ Remind your students: "Before you circle an *r*-controlled vowel in a word, check these cards for the correct pen color you should use."

❅ Invite your students to search for *r*-controlled vowels in the words in the poem.

Point to each card as you say, "Please raise your hand if you see a word with *ar, er,* or *ir.*" Call on a student who signals you and ask, "Where did you find an *r*-controlled vowel?" Follow with: "How do you know it's an *r*-controlled vowel?" When the student points to one, ask, "What's the sound of [name of *r*-controlled vowel]?" Support the student if necessary. Then say, "Now blend the sounds and tell me the word." After the student identifies the word, invite the student to look at the cards on the board, "Which colored pen do you need to use to circle [name of *r*-controlled vowel]?" Follow the same procedure for the remaining *r*-controlled vowels. If your students understand the procedure after they watch a few of their classmates circle different *r*-controlled vowels, allow them to proceed independently and give support only when it's needed. When the word *sugar* is identified, explain: "Sometimes the *ar* vowel sounds like *er* and *ir.* In upcoming word studies, we'll look at other words with the same variation."

❧ Reflection ❧

As soon as I pulled over the plastic sheeting to begin the lesson, I heard several of my students whisper to their classmates along the lines of, "Oh, good! I like when we use the plastic cover to circle things." Their positive reaction alleviated my concern that this lesson might lack the excitement of others. When I heard their comments, I knew my students would remain engaged throughout the lesson.

Not only were they engaged, but most were able to follow the multistep directions independently. When I designed the lesson, I did consider the pace, but I didn't expect it to flow so smoothly. Using the vowel cards as visual aids helped my students become independent, which in itself positively affected the flow of the lesson. The children knew what to do, and they successfully circled the *r*-controlled vowels with the appropriate pen color without any reminders from me.

Because I did have to provide some assistance with the *sounds* for these irregular vowels, I wondered if it might help my students to better understand the sounds if they learned a key word for each irregular vowel sound. I thought it might help them determine other words with the same pattern. It was definitely worth a try.

FEBRUARY

LESSON ONE

Action Words

Cold Fact

By the time he's suited
And scarved and booted
And mittened and capped,
And zipped and snapped
And tucked and belted,
The snow has melted.

—*Dick Emmons*

What I Was Thinking

If *I* was tiring of observation poems about winter, I knew my students must be weary, too. But I didn't want their enthusiasm to wane. I knew I had to find a poem that would rekindle their delight in poetry about the world around them.

In order for my students to develop a love for all kinds of poetry, it was important to explore different kinds: poems with strong rhythms and rhymes, free-verse poems, and poems with figurative language.

When I read this poem for the first time, I knew my students would be able to appreciate its tone—especially the last line! Emmons's poem even made me laugh, because it brought to mind the daily scene I witness each day after lunch during the biting, blustery days of winter: kindergartners sprawled out in the coat area, surrounded by their numerous pieces of outerwear, and at times overwhelmed by the enormity of the task of dressing for outdoor recess. Although they begin to dress five minutes *before* any other class, the kindergartners are always the last children to get outside. Not only does the snow melt by the time they're suited up, my lunch gets stale, too!

I thought my students would enjoy this poem as much as I did, and I couldn't wait to see and hear their reactions.

Note: If these winter poems don't reflect your region's climate, they still may be used to discuss regional climate differences (e.g., weather, temperature, and clothing) or the seasons of the year. You might consider finding rhyming and free-verse poems that reflect your particular region's climate.

Materials

The poem "Cold Fact" by Dick Emmons, handwritten on manila tag chart paper in large, neat print and attached by rings to a wooden chart stand

What This Lesson Looks Like

❋ Begin with: "After watching you get ready for outside recess, I know you'll get a kick out of this poem. Sometimes poets like to surprise us at the end of the poem. Just wait until you hear the surprise ending of this poem by Dick Emmons."

❋ Read the poem aloud to the class. Then ask, "Did the last line take you by surprise? Do you think the snow has really melted?" Explain: "This big exaggeration is called a *hyperbole*." Then ask: "What was Emmons suggesting?"

❋ Ask your students, "Do you share the same feelings as this poet? Why or why not?" Then ask, "What do you put on to get ready to go outside?" Prompt them to elaborate by asking, "What piece of clothing do you put on first? Then what?" And so on.

❋ Explain to your students, "Poets sometimes use words we normally wouldn't use when we speak. For instance, Dick Emmons doesn't say, 'By the time he's put on his mittens.' Instead, he makes up his own action word: *mittened*."

❋ State the purpose for rereading the poem: "Listen as I reread the poem, and be ready to tell me the different action words he uses to demonstrate what clothing he puts on."

❊ Call on different students to name different action words. Point to each word on the chart paper when a student identifies it.

❊ Review the action words: "When I point to an action word, I'd like you to read it aloud." Point to each action word in order.

❊ Explain: "Watch carefully as I act out one of the action words you read aloud. If you know what I'm doing, raise your hand. I'll ask you to identify my action, and if you're correct, I'll ask you to point to the word in the poem." Imitate different action words in the poem.

❊ At the end of the lesson, invite your students to read the poem aloud with you: "You've done such a great job reading the different action words mentioned in this poem. I know you're ready to read it in its entirety with me. Please join me in reading 'Cold Fact' by Dick Emmons."

❧ Reflection ❧

My students surprised me at the end of my miming activity. Believing I had completed all the action words, I stopped and started to address my students. One of my students yelled out, "Wait a minute! You forgot one." Puzzled by his comment, I began to review each article of clothing. When Isaac perceived my confusion, he clarified his thinking: "It's not an action word about putting anything on. You forgot to act out the word *melted*. *Melted* is an action word. See, watch this!" He proceeded to fall to the ground and lay flat on his tummy. When the class and I saw him on the floor, we burst out laughing, because he had definitely made his point. By overlooking an action word, I discovered that at least one student understood the meaning of action words.

I'm glad I took the time to thoroughly review the action words in this poem. It enhanced the probability for a successful lesson tomorrow.

LESSON TWO
-ed Ending

What I Was Thinking

Since every verb in this poem has the same ending, it seemed to me to be the obvious choice for our word study. Although my students automatically pronounced the correct –ed ending whenever they made sense of these verbs in their reading, they hadn't made the connection when they wrote verbs that ended with –ed during their daily writing workshop. Instead, my students wrote the sounds they heard, e.g., /t/ or /d/. So I thought a lesson focused on this specific ending would not only help them as readers, but also as writers.

Materials

The poem "Cold Fact" by Dick Emmons, handwritten on manila tag chart paper in large, neat print and attached by rings to a wooden chart stand

A red marker

A black marker

A white board

Magnetic tape or masking tape

Ten 4" x 1.5" strips of card stock with a different action word from the poem printed on each card: *suited, scarved, booted, mittened, capped, zipped, snapped, tucked, belted, melted*

- ✿ Use a black marker to print most of each word; use a red marker to print the *-ed* ending.

- ✿ Attach a magnetic strip on the back of each piece of card stock if your white board is magnetic; otherwise use masking tape.

What This Lesson Looks Like

- ✿ Review the set of sight words by reading them aloud together.

- ✿ Call on students: "Please come up to the chart stand and point to a sight word you can see and read 'just like that' [snap your fingers]. As you read it aloud, sweep across the word with the pointer."

✿ Invite students to read the poem "Cold Fact" aloud with you.

✿ Review the action words in the poem. Ask your students, "Who remembers an action word the poet, Dick Emmons, uses in this poem?" Each time a student responds, point to the identified verb and say, "Read it with me." Then read the word as you sweep across the word with the pointer.

✿ Then explain to your students: "Now *I'll* point randomly to the action words. When I point to one, I'd like *you* to read it aloud."

✿ Point out the *–ed* ending in the different action words on the chart. Explain: "This ending is used when an action is completed. This ending can be confusing because it has three sounds: /t/, /d/, and /ed/." Write these sounds on the white board, leaving a big space between each sound heading.

✿ Pass out word cards printed with action words from the poem to different students. Direct your students: "If you were given a word card, please take a moment to whisper your word aloud." Then ask, "What sound do you hear at the end? Does it say /t/, /d/, or /ed/?" Continue with these directions: "When you're ready, please raise your hand to read the word aloud and then place the word card under the correct heading."

✿ When all words have been read and sorted, invite the class to reread each list of action words. Instruct your students: "Let's read the action words that end with /ed/." Follow this procedure for the remaining columns.

✿ Explain to students how the cards will be removed from the board: "Now we'll remove the cards one by one. To remove a card, I'll name an action word for you to remove. When you've located the word, keep your eyes focused on it while you raise your hand, and I'll choose the first student I see who seems to know its location." Call on a student who hasn't yet had a turn to remove a card from a column you specify.

✿ After the action words have been collected, invite students to read the poem in one big voice.

✿ Ask your students, "Who would like to read this poem to the class?" Remind your students to stress the word *and* each time it's read. To avoid gender bias, call on a boy *and* a girl to each read the poem independently.

LESSON THREE

Vocabulary Review and Color Words

The Wind Woman

The Wind's white fingers
Are thin and sharp.
And she plays all night
On an icy harp.

On her icy harp
Of stiff, black trees,
She plays her songs,
And the rivers freeze.

—*Barbara Juster Esbensen*

What I Was Thinking

In the poem "The Wind Woman," the poet, Barbara Juster Esbensen, uses powerful poetic diction. As literal thinkers, my students would have difficulty understanding Esbensen's use of figurative language. To help them better understand this poem, I wanted to wait for a bone-chilling winter day to read it. And in Maine, frigid air usually arrives during the month of February, freezing rivers and lakes.

I knew I'd need to carefully prepare my lesson in order to address potential trouble spots. By asking my students to describe their mind-pictures, I'd get a sense of their understanding, and then I'd know how I should proceed. I'd discuss only the lines that caused confusion, but just in case their interpretation was completely inaccurate, I wanted to be prepared for the worst-case scenario.

Materials

The poem "The Wind Woman" by Barbara Juster Esbensen, handwritten on manila tag chart paper in large, neat print and attached by rings to a wooden chart stand

One 3" x 5" card printed with the word *black*

A picture of a harp

What This Lesson Looks Like

☼ Invite your students to share words or lines they immediately recognize: "What words do you see in this poem that you can read just like that [snap your fingers]? Remember, you must be able to read the word immediately. You must say it as soon as you touch it with the pointer." Pass the pointer to a volunteer and say, "Read each word you know as you touch it with the pointer." When the reader has finished, ask the class, "Do you see any other words you can read?" Continue this procedure until no more words can be read.

☼ Review all the words that were identified by the students. Invite your students: "Read these words aloud with me as I point to them."

☼ Introduce the color word *black*. Hold up the word card printed with *black* and say, "This is a color word. Look at all the letters in this word carefully before answering." Then ask, "Who knows its name?" Call on a student to answer. When you hear a correct response, explain: "The color words *black* and *blue* both begin with the *bl* blend." Then ask, "What helped you distinguish this word from the color word *blue*?" Accept all reasonable responses.

✻ Explain to your students: "This poem is about something ordinary Barbara Juster Esbensen observes in her everyday life, and she takes time to think about it in a thoughtful and different way. As I read the poem aloud, try to visualize what Esbensen sees."

✻ Ask your students to describe their mind-pictures.

✻ Then give them additional information that will help them better understand the poem's meaning. Explain to your students: "Whenever a cold front passes through, the temperature drops, and the wind shifts to the northwest, giving a blast of very cold Arctic air. Barbara Juster Esbensen uses personification to describe this winter wind event. Who remembers what *personification* means?" When someone correctly responds, or if no one can define the word, say, "*Personification* is giving human qualities to something that isn't human." Then explain: "She uses personification in both stanzas of her poem." Prompt by giving clues: "Both the beginning and the ending of this poem contain personification." When a student explains that the wind doesn't have white fingers that are sharp and thin, say, "You're right. But a cold wind can feel sharp—just like sharp fingernails." If no one is able to identify the other example, read the line "She plays her song" and say, "This is another example of personification. We know the wind doesn't really play songs. What's the wind really doing?"

✻ Read the last line of the first stanza, then say, "We know the wind doesn't really play a song on an icy harp. Listen carefully as I reread the poem, because she compares an icy harp to something in nature. Be ready to tell me what she is comparing to an icy harp."

✻ After the reading, ask, "What's a harp?" Show the class a picture of the musical instrument. Ask, "How is the harp played?" Follow with: "In the poem, the harp is being compared to what?" If no one answers, point to the second line of the second stanza and read "*stiff, black trees.*" Ask, "How are a harp and a tree alike?" Elaborate on a student's answer by saying, "Esbensen imagines the wind moving the branches of a tree just as a person would stroke or move the strings of a harp to make its distinctive sound."

 Read the poem for a final time. Invite your students: "Chime in whenever you can, and read with me."

❧ Reflection ❧

Whoa! As soon as my students began describing their mind-pictures, it was evident they had no idea what this poem was about. Most students saw a woman dressed in a flowing white gown, standing by a frozen river. One student mentioned she had a harp. When I asked if anyone knew what a harp was, I was shocked to discover that not one student knew it was a musical instrument. Needless to say, I was relieved I had anticipated the potential trouble spots because I was thoroughly prepared to help my students grasp the meaning of this poem. Although I spent more time discussing the poem than I had planned, by the end of our discussion, more students seemed to have a better understanding. It's time well spent if, when I read this poem again tomorrow, my students can picture the bitter cold wind whistling through the rigid tree limbs at night.

LESSON FOUR
Introduction of New Sight Words

> ### Valentines
>
> I gave a hundred Valentines
> A hundred, did I say?
> I gave a *thousand* Valentines
> one cold and wintry day.
>
> I didn't put my name on them
> or any other words,
> because my Valentines were seeds
> for February birds.
>
> —*Aileen Fisher*

What I Was Thinking

I thought it would be easy to find a Valentine's Day poem to use, but how wrong I was! Most of the ones I found wouldn't interest my boys, because the message was either too sentimental or too romantic. In my mind I could hear them groan and see them roll their eyes when I read the line *I love you*. Other poems were humorous, but they didn't contain a suitable message to my liking. For example, one humorous poem contained the word *hate*, which is a word my students aren't allowed to use in my class. I work so hard to develop a positive tone in my classroom; that word (*hate*) makes my hair stand on end whenever I hear it. After browsing through several poetry anthologies, I finally discovered the poem "Valentines" by Aileen Fisher. Since we had recently hung special treats on an evergreen tree on the school property for the birds to eat, I thought it would appeal to every child in my classroom.

To ensure their engagement and motivation to read, I thought I'd implement an activity I knew my kindergartners loved. When we read big books during reading workshop, I often have the children use their small notepads to make predictions of various words I cover in the poem. I thought, "Why not use them to predict words in poems?" I was ready for a change, and I was betting my students were more than ready!

Materials

The poem "Valentines" by Aileen Fisher, handwritten on manila tag chart paper in large, neat print and attached by rings to a wooden chart stand

A small notepad for each student

A pencil for each student

Three 3" x 5" cards printed with the words *because, one,* and *put* in large lowercase letters

Construction paper strips to cover parts of words:

- ✻ *ousand* in *thousand*
- ✻ *ay* in *day*
- ✻ *ame* in *name*
- ✻ *irds* in *birds*

What This Lesson Looks Like

- ✻ Pass out a small notepad and a pencil to each student.

- ✻ Direct your students to look at the poem on the chart stand. Ask, "What do you notice about this poem?" When someone says that parts of some words have been covered with paper, confirm the observation. Then explain: "You should carefully listen as I read this poem aloud. When I come to a covered word, you'll write your prediction of the covered word on a blank page in your notepad."

- ✻ Explain the expectations for this activity. To emphasize each point, illustrate as you speak: "To be successful, you need to be good listeners [draw a head with big ears], focus on your own work [draw big eyes near the top of the head], and keep your lips zipped [draw a simple mouth with diagonal lines through it]." Also emphasize: "When you've written your prediction, you should hold up your notepad for me to see. If your prediction is correct, I'll give you a thumbs-up, and if it isn't I'll give you a thumbs-down. Please remember, I don't expect correct spelling, but you must supply enough letter sounds to make your word readable. When I say, 'All pencils down,' you *must* stop writing. I'll take your pencil if you don't follow my direction. But I *will* give the pencil back to you after your classmates have completed one more entry, because I always give my students a second chance." If a consequence has to be given for not following your directions, before you give the pencil back to the student, ask, "What will you do next time you hear me say 'pencils down'?"

✲ Read the poem aloud, pausing at each word to be predicted. Reread a line so students can make sense of the covered word. If all students have predicted correctly, ask, "What's the word?" When there are wrong answers, choose a student who has made an accurate prediction to respond. Remove the paper strip to reveal the correct word.

✲ After the two words in the first stanza have been identified, direct the class: "Let's read the first stanza together." When the last two words have been identified, read the second stanza chorally.

✲ For the final reading, say: "I'd like the girls to read the first stanza, and I'd like the boys to read the second stanza."

❧ Reflection ☙

As soon as Joseph saw me begin to hand out notepads to the class, he exclaimed, "Oh, boy! I love this activity!" Like Joe, I was pleased with my decision to deviate from my standard practice when introducing a new poem. This activity allowed me to quickly assess my students' phonological awareness. Although they had recorded every sound they heard in each word, only Kate had applied the rules she had learned about *r*-controlled vowels and silent *e*. This observation made me keenly aware that I need to be on the lookout for poems that contain a sufficient number of silent *e* or *r*-controlled words to reinforce these skills. The sooner, the better!

Every Child a Reader

LESSON FIVE

Making Predictions to Identify Words and Confirming Meaning

> **But Then**
>
> A tooth fell out
> and left a space
> so big my tongue
> can touch my FACE.
>
> And every time
> I smile, I show
> a space where some-
> thing used to grow.
>
> I miss my tooth,
> as you may guess,
> but then—I have to
> brush one less.
>
> —*Aileen Fisher*

What I Was Thinking

Since February is Dental Health Month, I wanted to find a tooth poem, but I didn't expect to find one that would allow me to integrate health science and literacy. Once again, my favorite poet, Aileen Fisher, came through for me with her poem "But Then." I knew my students would be able to identify with it. For young children, losing a tooth is a magical moment—especially their *first* tooth. To them, it's a rite of passage from being little to becoming a big kid!

Whenever someone loses a tooth, classmates will rush to admire the child's new look as he or she smiles broadly to reveal the big space where the tooth once lived. Kindergartners never seem to tire of inspecting a gaping space and wishing they, too, would lose a tooth. This poem captures this universal experience to a tee.

Although I found many tooth poems, my decision to read this one was easy because it had it all: humor, a health connection, and a personal connection. I couldn't wait to share it with my class!

Materials

The poem "But Then" by Aileen Fisher, handwritten on manila tag chart paper in large, neat print and attached by rings to a wooden chart stand

Two strips of construction paper to cover the word *tooth* in the first and last stanzas of the poem

What This Lesson Looks Like

* Invite the class to read the title of the poem. Touch each word with the pointer as they read the title aloud. Remind the students: "We know most titles are short, and they usually give the reader an idea what the story or poem is about." Look mystified as you ask, "Does this title help us know what the poem is about?" When students emphatically respond "No!" explain: "Sometimes poets draw readers in by using important words from their stories or poems. Do you see these two words somewhere else in the poem?" Invite a student to point out the phrase *but then* found in the eleventh line of the poem.

* As you point to the covered words, explain to your students: "The words I've covered are identical." Then ask, "Why do you think I've covered these words?" After a student correctly explains the class has to guess the word, confirm the student's thinking, and then instruct the class: "You're right! The word identifies what this poem is about. I bet you'll know the word by the time I get to the last line."

* Invite your students to listen to the poem "But Then" as you read it aloud.

* Pause for a moment after reading the last line, and then ask, "What's the missing word?" When a student makes a prediction, explain: "I'll read the sentence with the word you think it is, to make sure your guess makes sense." Then ask the class, "Does anyone have a different prediction?"

Every Child a Reader

Read the sentence again with the second prediction. Ask the student who suggested the word, "Does your word make sense?" If it does, say, "Let's check the first letter to give us a clue about the real word." Then reveal the first letter. Say, "Now what do you think the word is? Why do you think so?"

* Invite a capable student to spell the predicted word: "Before I reveal the correct word, who would like to spell the word the class has predicted?" To ensure a standard spelling, offer support if needed: "Because we'll check the accuracy of your prediction, the spelling needs to be correct so we can see if both words are the same or different. I'll help you with the spelling if you don't know all the letters." As the student spells, write the letters on the paper strip.

* After the student finishes spelling, invite her or him to remove the paper strip and place it above the printed word in the poem. Ask, "Is it the same word?" If the word is the same, say, "Read the word." If the prediction isn't correct, point to the revealed word and ask, "Who knows this word?" Call on a capable reader to identify the right word. Then say, "This poem is about a missing *tooth*!" Emphasize the word as you point to it.

* Before discussing the poem, explain the purpose of rereading it: "I'm going to read the poem again. Listen to the poet's thoughts about losing a tooth and be ready to compare your own experience with the poet's."

* Read the poem aloud again.

* Invite your students to share their tooth stories. Initiate the discussion by asking, "How many of you have lost a tooth?" Encourage those students to participate by saying, "Tell us what it's like to have a missing tooth." After each student shares a tooth story, ask, "Were you able to identify with the speaker?" Probe a student's thoughts by asking why or why not.

* Prompt students by asking, "Do you have a big space left by losing a tooth? Can you push your tongue through the space to touch *your* face?" Challenge students who have a missing tooth to see if they can push their tongue through the space.

* For the final reading, invite students who were successful at completing the challenge to act out each stanza of the poem as you read it. Explain to the

remaining members of the audience: "I'm going to read aloud most of the poem by myself. When I pause at the last word in each stanza, I want you to supply the rhyming word."

☀ Read the poem aloud, using appropriate tone and pacing.

◦ Reflection ◦

Just as soon as I finished reading the first stanza aloud, one of my kindergartners, Isaac, turned to his classmate Maddy and exclaimed, "That's you!" And like Isaac, I, too, immediately thought of Maddy when I first read this poem. Since Maddy's front tooth left a cavernous space when it fell out, I knew she'd be a perfect model for this poem. Her classmates closely watched her as she acted out each stanza—especially during the second stanza, when she pushed her tongue through the gaping hole in her mouth.

I didn't expect the children to be ready to read this poem aloud independently, but this time they surprised me. After they completed supplying the rhyming words, some pleaded with me to let them read it aloud by themselves. How could I say no? Having kindergartners excited to read, I couldn't allow this golden opportunity to slip away. When they read, I didn't have to help them apply different strategies to figure out unknown words. Although they hesitated when they came to the word *space* in the first stanza, they eventually made sense of the word. They continued on and fluently read the remainder of the poem.

When they finished, they looked at me, waiting for my feedback. But I was speechless. They didn't need verbal praise from me, because they knew they had read the poem masterfully. For a few minutes we kept smiling at one another. I can't say who was prouder, I or they! Perhaps using Maddy as a visual aid helped my students remember the words more easily. No matter what, I do know this: *They've come a long way, baby!*

Every Child a Reader

MARCH

LESSON ONE
Word Identification

> ### It's Time for Spring
>
> My sweater's tight and itchy.
> My snow pants are too small.
> Last week I lost a mitten.
> I can't find my scarf at all.
>
> My woolen socks have lost their toes.
> My boots have lost their tread.
> And I have lost the love I had
> for words like "skis" and "sled"!
>
> But . . . my fishing rod still fits.
> And . . . my baseball bat still hits.
> I have a kite that wants to fly.
> So . . . Winter, call it quits!
>
> —*Bobbi Katz*

What I Was Thinking

In Maine, the winter season is fickle at best. Some winters are mild with little snow or ice, while others are brutally cold with record snowfalls and icy roads. The latter aptly describes this past season. With one major snowstorm after another pounding the coast of Maine, even kindergartners grew weary of winter. No longer did a snowstorm excite them; at the first sight of a snowflake, they would often groan and become sullen. No longer did they enjoy sledding at recess, because it meant they had to wear their snow pants. They grew tired of layers of clothing and often complained about having to dress for the weather.

Because their disenchantment grew stronger with each passing day, I thought my students would be able to relate to this poem and read it aloud with genuine feeling. Finding the ideal poem to read makes it even more enjoyable to present.

Materials

The poem "It's Time for Spring" by Bobbi Katz, handwritten on manila tag chart paper in large, neat print and attached by rings to a wooden chart stand

* ✿ Fold up the bottom edge of the chart paper to cover the body of the poem; hold it in place with paper clips.

A strip of construction paper to cover the word *Spring* in the title of the poem

Highlighting tape

What This Lesson Looks Like

* ✿ Call attention to the title with your pointer. As you sweep the pointer across the line, ask, "What's this heading called?" When your students answer, repeat their answer with emphasis: "That's right. It's the *title*. How does a title help the reader?" Paraphrase a student's response by saying, "A title either gives us an idea about the content of the poem or it draws us in by making us wonder what the poem is about."

* ✿ Focus your students' attention on the covered word in the title. Invite your class to read the words in the title: "Let's read the words in the title to see if we can predict the last word."

* ✿ Invite your students to predict the covered word: "What do you think it's time for?" Accept all responses. Explain, "Without knowing the content of the poem, sometimes it's difficult to make a prediction. We need clues from the text to be able to make a good prediction. Once you hear the poem read aloud, it'll be easier to guess the covered word because you'll know what the poem is about."

* ✿ Remove the paper clips to reveal the body of the poem. Read the poem aloud to the class.

* ✿ Then point to the covered word in the title and ask, "What's it time for?" When your students have exhausted all reasonable predictions, reread the

title with the first prediction that was suggested. Continue to reread the title until every prediction has been used.

 Explain to your students: "Every prediction makes sense. Let's listen to each prediction again. Tell me the letter you hear at the beginning of each word I say." After you say each prediction, pause to allow them time to respond with the beginning letter. Then say another predicted word. Continue this procedure until all predictions have been analyzed.

 After your students have stated each beginning letter, reveal the first letter in *spring*. "The first letter of the word and the context help us make a correct prediction. What's the word?"

 Invite a student to spell the word *spring*. Support the student by saying, "Listen to the sounds in the blend as I slowly say it aloud: /s-p-r/." Then ask, "What three letters make up this blend?" Write the blend on the paper strip as the student names each letter. Complete the sounding-out of this word by saying the phonogram *-ing*. Ask, "What three letters spell *ing*?" Write the chunk on the paper strip as the student spells it to complete the word *spring*.

 Invite the student who spelled the word to remove the paper strip to reveal the correct word: "Would you like to remove the paper strip for us?" Instruct the student to check the accuracy of the prediction. "Are both words the same?" Tell the student to read the whole title aloud.

 Discuss the content of the poem. Explain: "Sometimes winter seems long. How does the poet suggest this feeling?" If needed, prompt their recall by asking, "What's happened to the poet's *snow pants*?" When someone correctly responds, tell the student to point out the second line and read it aloud. Then reread the same line to validate the student's response. Highlight *snow pants* with highlight tape. Invite the class to identify some other winter clothes: "What are some other clothes mentioned by the poet?" Each time an item is recalled, ask, "What's his complaint about the item you mentioned?" Follow with: "Please point to the specific line in which this piece of clothing can be found, and read it aloud." Reread the appropriate line to verify the student's answer. Continue to follow this procedure for the remaining pieces of clothing. Highlight the name of each piece of winter clothing as it's identified.

- When the word *boots* is recalled, ask, "What happened to the speaker's boots?" When someone mentions the word *tread*, ask, "Who knows what this word means?" If no one volunteers to define the word, prompt your students by saying, "The treads on a tire are the unique ridges that give the tire traction on different surfaces." Then ask, "Where can you find the treads on a boot?"

- Explain to your students: "The first two stanzas describe the speaker's complaints about winter clothing. The last stanza's tone is more hopeful as the speaker describes spring activities. What's the speaker anxious to do?" When a student mentions fishing or baseball, ask, "What do you use when you fish?" Highlight the words *fishing rod* in the poem. Tell your students, "Read this line with me." Follow the same procedure for *baseball bat*.

- Invite your students to share their own feelings about winter: "How do you feel about winter ending soon?"

- Then direct your students' attention back to the poem: "Look at the words I highlighted in the poem. I'm going to act out one of these highlighted words. Guess what it is." Then act it out. Ask your students, "What's this?" When a student correctly guesses, invite him or her to point to the appropriate highlighted word and read it aloud. Then announce to the class: "Now let's read the whole line together." Continue to follow this procedure until all items have been identified.

- Invite the class to read the poem aloud with you: "Since you read each line with such ease, I'd like you to read 'It's Time for Spring' in its entirety. Let's read it aloud together with feeling."

❧ Reflection ❧

I didn't think anyone would be able to predict the word *spring* in the title of the poem before it was read, but I was wrong. With a twinkle in his eye, Nolan announced that it had to be the word *spring*. Since I didn't want to ruin the rest of the lesson, I waited until we read the poem aloud before I confirmed the accuracy of his prediction. Believe me, it was extremely difficult to maintain a neutral demeanor and continue the lesson when, in reality, I wanted to stop immediately and ask, "How did you know?" But I knew the point of the lesson (i.e., context clues) would be lost if I gave in to my curiosity.

When we uncovered the first letter in the word and discovered it was an *s*, I looked at Nolan and smiled. When I asked him how he knew it was the word *spring* even before we read the poem, he said, "For a lot of reasons." When I asked him to elaborate, he said, "Everybody's tired of winter, and I know spring's almost here. Since it's March now, I figured you'd do a spring poem instead of another one about winter." And he was right.

LESSON TWO

Seeing Small Words Inside of Bigger Words to Identify Unknown Words

What I Was Thinking

Since my students could now recognize most one-syllable words with automaticity, I thought they were ready to learn another strategy—looking at the structure of the word—to help them determine unknown words. By focusing on all the letters, they might discover little words they already knew to facilitate the decoding of the unknown word.

Although this strategy can't be applied to all words, I could use several words in this poem to show when it does work. I planned to highlight them in the poem before the lesson began, to draw my students' attention to just these words. After the children had applied this new strategy a few times, I'd take time to point out a word in the poem that would be mispronounced if this strategy were used. And because of the importance of reading for meaning, I planned to model how to cross-check meaning with pronunciation.

Materials

The poem "It's Time for Spring" by Bobbi Katz, handwritten on manila tag chart paper in large, neat print and attached by rings to a wooden chart stand

Highlighting tape to highlight the words *itchy, mitten, scarf, baseball,* and *winter* before the lesson

What This Lesson Looks Like

- Explain your rationale for the necessary change in the lesson's procedure: "Today I'm going to show you another strategy you can use to figure out words you don't know. Because I don't want you to become *too* familiar with the words in this poem, I'm going to begin with our word study. Then, we'll practice reading the poem."

- Inform your students: "I'm going to show you a new strategy you can use to decode unfamiliar words. Now that you know many little words, you're ready to learn how to put this knowledge to use. This strategy involves looking closely at all the letters in the word to find little words that may help to decode the unknown word."

- Direct your students' attention to the poem and ask, "What do you notice?" Call on a student to answer. When the student mentions the highlighted words, say, "Yes, I did highlight some words I want to discuss with you. These words have something in common. What do you think it is?" Someone may recall your explanation of the new strategy and guess that they contain little words. Respond to the student's conjecture by saying, "Yes, each word I highlighted contains a little word you already know. You're going to use that word to help you figure out the bigger word."

- Point to the highlighted word *itchy*. Ask, "Look closely at all the letters in this word. Who sees a little word they know?" Call on a student to answer. Then point to the word *it* and say, "Yes, the word *it* is at the beginning of this word. Now all you have to do is blend the other two sounds to identify this word. Let's do it together." Slowly sweep your finger across the word *it* as you and your class say the word aloud. Then, as you move your finger under the letters *ch*, say, "It /ch/." Then ask, "What's the word?" When someone says the word *itch*, say, "But we need to add one more sound before we know what this word is." Then ask: "What's the sound of *y* at the end of a word?" When someone says it could be the /?/ sound or the /?/ sound, verify the answer by saying: "Yes, you're right. When the letter *y* is at the end of a word, it represents a vowel sound." Follow with: "Does it say /?/ or /?/ in this word?" Instruct your students: "Listen as I add the last sound to *itch*. I'll first use the /?/ sound at the end and then I'll use /?/. Is it *itch* /?/ or *itch* /?/?"

Every Child a Reader

❁ Point to the highlighted word *mitten* as you say, "I see two little words inside this word. What are they?" Call on a student to identify the words. If the student sees only one of the words, accept the student's response, and then sweep your finger under the letters that make up that word. Then ask, "Who knows the other word?" When someone correctly responds, say, "Now let's put both words together." Sweep your finger across the word *it* and say, "It." Then sweep your finger across the word *ten* and say, "Ten." Invite your students: "Let's put these two word parts together by saying them quickly." Say, "-*itten*." Ask, "What still needs to be added?" When someone correctly responds, say, "That's right. All you need to do now is add the beginning sound, and you'll be able to say the word." Then ask, "Who knows the word?" Call on a student to identify the word.

❁ Point to the word *scarf* and ask, "Who would like to point out a little word they see inside this bigger word?" Call on a student and say, "Please sweep your finger across the word as you say it." Then invite the student: "Knowing the word *car* will help you figure out this unfamiliar word easily. What other letter sounds do you need to add to the word *car*?" When the student states that the beginning letter sound and the final sound still need to be added, direct the student: "Show us how to blend these sounds with the word *car*." Follow with: "What does this word [point to the word *scarf*] say?"

❁ Point to the word *baseball*. Introduce the term *compound word*: "This word is called a *compound word* because it's made up of two smaller words. What two words make up this word?" Call on a capable student to identify the words. As the student says the first word, cover the other smaller word so the class can see the first word. Then cover the first word and ask the student, "What does this say?" Direct your students: "Now let's read this word together." Cover the word *ball* and say, "Base." Then cover the word *base* and say, "Ball." Invite your students: "Let's put these two word parts together by saying them quickly: *baseball*."

❁ Invite a student to demonstrate how to implement this strategy. Point to the word *winter* and ask, "Who would like to show us—step-by-step—how to figure out this word using this new strategy?" Call on an articulate student to explain the process.

✿ Explain to your students, "Now that you understand how to use this strategy, you should also understand that this strategy won't work with all words." Point to the word *sweater* and say, "For example, let's take a look at this word. Inside this word, I see the word *eat* [sweep your finger across the word]. I also see the *sw* blend [point to the blend] at the beginning of the word, and the *r*-controlled vowel *er* [point to the two letters] at the end of this word." Demonstrate how to blend the word *eat* with the other two sounds: "Listen as I blend the beginning sound and the final sound with the word *eat*: /swē/ /t/ /ûr/." Announce the mispronunciation of the word: "Sweeter." Then explain: "Now I'll read the first line to see if it makes sense." Replace the word *sweater* with *sweeter* when you read the first line aloud: "My sweeter's tight and itchy." Exclaim, "That doesn't make sense! But my mispronunciation still helps me figure out what the word has to be." Ask your students: "What word do you think would make sense?" When someone says *sweater*, explain: "The word *sweater* does make sense. Listen as I read the line again." Read the line correctly by saying, "My sweater's tight and itchy." Say, "Sometimes a mispronounced word will help you figure out what would make sense, so always cross-check the meaning with your pronunciation."

✿ Invite your students to read the poem aloud with feeling: "To end our lesson, I'd like *you* to read this poem aloud in one big voice. I'll just do the pointing. I want to hear you make this poem come alive by using great expression. Give it all you have. First, read through the poem silently to yourself, and then show me you're ready by focusing your eyes on the title. When I see everybody's eyes on the title of this poem, I'll begin sweeping my pointer." Wait until *all* students demonstrate they're ready to begin before you sweep the pointer across the title.

❧ Reflection ❧

The pace of this lesson sped up after I modeled the strategy using the word *sweater*. My students had such fun hearing the mispronunciation and supplying the mispronounced word as they reread the line. They discovered that even mispronunciations could sometimes help a reader determine the unknown word through the meaning.

I wanted to end the lesson at that point, but Nicco interrupted me to declare he had found another word that contained a little word that didn't help with the pronunciation. Curious to see what word he had discovered, I asked him to come up to the poem and point it out to the class. When he pointed to the sight word *their*, I knew Nicco already knew this word. However, because I also knew many of his classmates didn't know it, I wanted him to continue with his demonstration. Pointing to the word *their*, he proceeded to cover the last two letters to reveal the little word *the*, and then he pointed to the letters *ir* and said their sound. When he read the line again using his mispronunciation, I heard some of his classmates immediately call out the word *their*.

Nicco's discovery had a domino effect on the class; other students started sharing their insights. For example, Joe pointed out the little word *is* in the word *skis*, and Isaac pointed out the word *ant* in the word *wants,* both of which resulted in mispronunciations. Because each student enthusiastically modeled the strategy, I extended the length of the lesson. Why not continue? They were practicing a necessary skill and having a great time doing it.

LESSON THREE
New Sight Words, End Punctuation

March Alarm Clock

Huh?
What time is it, anyway?
Hey, you big-mouth birds—
I'm trying to sleep here.
Get lost!
Go away!
Come back some other day!

Wait a minute.
Hold on.
Could it be?
Holy crow!

Birds.
Birds in the morning.
Birds in the morning in March.
Spring is around the corner.

—*Brad, Asa, Dylan, Michael,*
Jonathan, Sheldon, & Nancie
CTL 1992 Fifth-Grade Class
Collaboration

What I Was Thinking

At the Center for Teaching and Learning, we begin each day with a schoolwide assembly called morning meeting. Each teacher takes a turn leading morning meeting for a week. During this time, he or she is responsible for finding poems to read aloud and songs to sing for our daily community gathering. Since it would soon be my turn to be in the chair (as we affectionately term this duty), I decided to browse through CTL's assortment of poems printed on chart paper to find the

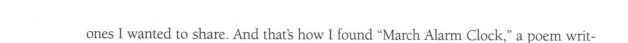

ones I wanted to share. And that's how I found "March Alarm Clock," a poem written by Nancie Atwell and several CTL fifth graders.

As soon as I read the stanzas, I knew I had found a golden nugget. This poem had it all: voice, simple vocabulary, and humor. And since many of my students enjoyed reading expressively, I knew they'd love "March Alarm Clock." Not only would this poem enhance my students' oral reading skills, it would also reinforce their understanding of end punctuation marks. In addition, the simple vocabulary and cumulative lines in the last stanza would enable my students to read this poem without any support from me. What a lucky find for my class *and* for me!

Materials

The poem "March Alarm Clock" by CTL fifth graders and Nancie Atwell, handwritten on manila tag chart paper in large, neat print and attached by rings to a wooden chart stand

Purple, red, and yellow Vis-à-Vis pens

Plastic sheeting to attach over the poem

Four 3" x 5" cards printed with the words *around, could, hey,* and *minute* in large lowercase letters—one word per card

What This Lesson Looks Like

✾ Introduce this poem by explaining its origin and your rationale for selecting it. "One day in March, Nancie met with some fifth-grade students at lunch recess to write this poem [point to the title with the pointer as you read], 'March Alarm Clock.' As soon as I saw the title they chose for their poem, I couldn't wait to find out what this poem was about. And when I read it, I also loved the words the fifth graders used. This poem has such voice that in my mind I could hear them say the words. Notice that this poem contains the three types of end punctuation you've learned about: periods, question marks, and exclamation points. Since you're beginning to use a lot of expression when you read, you'll be able to practice modulating your voice, depending on the sentence you read aloud in this poem. Most of the words are easy, so I think you'll be able to read this poem without any problem. But before I ask you to read, I want to focus on a few words you might not know."

☼ Introduce the sight words *around, could, hey,* and *minute.*

- Remind your students: "If you know the word I hold up, I'd like you to read it aloud in a strong voice. If you don't know this word, just listen."

- Hold up the word card *around* and say, "If you know this word, please read it."

- After it's read aloud either by a student or by you if no one identifies it, discuss the sound features in the word. Direct your students: "Let's clap out the parts of this word. Ready?" Clap out each syllable as you say it: "A-round." Ask, "What sound did you make at the beginning of the word *around*?" When your students respond, "/ŭ/," invite them to supply the missing letter as you talk. Say, "The *a* sounds like the letter *u*." Explain: "Sometimes words that consist of more than one syllable and start with the letter *a* say /ŭ/ at the beginning. Listen as I say some *a* words." Clap as you slowly say each syllable. Stress the /ŭ/ sound as you say the first syllable in the following words: America, Amanda, away, awake, and appear. Then point to the letters *ou* in the second syllable. Ask, What's the sound of *ou* in the word *around*?" When you hear a correct response, say, "Yes, the vowel combination *ou* has the same sound as *ow*. They both say /ow/. Now that we've discussed these specific sounds, you'll be able to sound out this word. Let's say the sounds together as I point to the letters." As you point to the letters, say the sounds aloud with your class. Ask, "What's the word?" Invite your students to spell and cheer the word. Point to each letter as they spell, and then cheer the word by raising your arm as you say the word aloud (Cunningham, 1995).

- Hold up the word card *could.* Tell your students, "This word can't be sounded out. You have to take a picture of it in your mind." Invite students who know this word to read it aloud. Ask, "Which three letters in this word don't make the sound you'd think they'd make?" When someone suggests *o, u,* and *l,* ask, "What vowel sound did you

Every Child a Reader

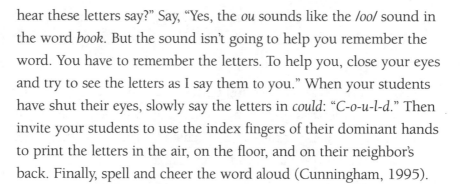

hear these letters say?" Say, "Yes, the *ou* sounds like the /oo/ sound in the word *book*. But the sound isn't going to help you remember the word. You have to remember the letters. To help you, close your eyes and try to see the letters as I say them to you." When your students have shut their eyes, slowly say the letters in *could*: "C-o-u-l-d." Then invite your students to use the index fingers of their dominant hands to print the letters in the air, on the floor, and on their neighbor's back. Finally, spell and cheer the word aloud (Cunningham, 1995).

- Hold up the word card *hey*. Ask, "Does anyone know this word?" If no one does, explain: "You've learned a sight word that rhymes with this word: *they*." Call on a capable student to spell the word *they*. As the student names each letter, record the letters on the white board or chart paper for the class to see. Then write the word *hey* below it. Invite your students to check the letters in both words. Ask, "What do you notice? Which letters are the same?" Explain to your students: "If you know that the word *they* is spelled *t-h-e-y*, then drop the *t* so that the beginning letter is an *h*, and you have *hey*." Invite your students to spell and cheer the word *hey* (Cunningham, 1995).

- Hold up the word card *minute*. Ask, "Does anyone know this word?" If no one answers, ask your students: "Do you see a little word you know inside this word?" When they indicate they see the word *in*, point to the letter *m* and say, "Make the beginning sound." When you hear your students correctly respond, tell them, "Now blend the beginning sound you just made with *in* and what do you have?" Then say, "That's right: *min*." Ask them, "What do you think the word could be if you know the first part says *min*?" Sweep your finger slowly under the word as you say the first part, and then point out the second syllable by sweeping across the remaining letters with your finger. Tell your students the word if no one is able to figure it out. Invite them to read it aloud with you: "Read this word with me."

✦ Invite your students to locate these four new words in the poem. Shuffle the word cards a few times. Then say, "Read this word." After the word has been identified, tell your students to look at the words in the poem,

"Where do you see [name the word]? Call on a student to identify it using the pointer and read it aloud. Follow this procedure for the remaining words.

✽ Focus your students' attention on the end punctuation. "Who sees an end mark they can identify by name?" Then ask, "Who sees a different punctuation mark at the end of a sentence? There's one more mark that's different from the ones already mentioned. What's its name?"

✽ Review the function of the period, question mark, and exclamation point. Call on different students to complete the sentences you start. Say, "A period comes at the end of a _____ sentence [telling]. A question mark comes at the end of an _____ sentence [asking]. An exclamation point comes at the end of an _____ [exclamation]."

✽ Invite your students to locate the different punctuation marks. Instruct your students: "Raise your hand if you see a period." Then call on a student and direct him or her: "Please circle each period with the red Vis-à-Vis pen. A period is a full stop." After the student has finished circling the last period, ask, "Do our voices go up or down when we read a telling sentence?" Reiterate what has been correctly answered: "Yes, our voices go down at the end of the telling sentence." Continue this procedure by circling all the question marks with a yellow Vis-à-Vis pen and then the exclamation points with a purple Vis-à-Vis pen. Upon completing the task of circling the question mark, ask, "What happens to our voices when we read an asking sentence?" After you hear a correct response, say, "Yes, our voices go up." When the third student completes circling every exclamation point, ask, "What should our voices sound like when we read an exclamation?" End with: "That's right: LOUD!"

✽ Draw their attention to the words in the poem: "I'm going to give you a few minutes to read this poem to yourselves. When you've finished, please put your hands on your head. When most of you have signaled me you've finished, we'll whip around the class to point out a word that you can read which you think will help your classmates when we read this poem together."

Every Child a Reader

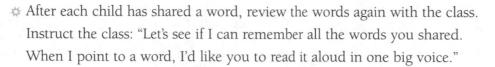

✿ After each child has shared a word, review the words again with the class. Instruct the class: "Let's see if I can remember all the words you shared. When I point to a word, I'd like you to read it aloud in one big voice."

✿ For the first reading, tell your class, "I'd like to invite you to take turns reading one line each until the poem is completed." Remind each volunteer: "Remember to look ahead to the punctuation mark so you'll change your voice appropriately. Who would like to begin by reading the title?" Call on a student who is willing to read. Then continue calling on volunteers to read the next consecutive lines in the poem until they reach the end. Some students may have more than one turn if no one else is interested in reading a particular line.

✿ Compliment each reader by giving specific positive comments (e.g., "I like the way you remembered to raise the volume of your voice in order to sound angry.").

✿ Read the poem again to the class, so students are able to hear it read without interruptions: "Listen as I read 'March Alarm Clock.' I'll try to use as much expression as I can as I read it aloud. In order for me to successful, I've got to pay attention to the punctuation mark I see at the end of each sentence. Be ready to tell me why the title is so perfect for this particular poem."

✿ After reading the poem, ask your students, "What's an alarm clock? Why did the students decide to title this poem 'March Alarm Clock'?"

✿ Ask your students, "What kind of bird was making all the noise?" Follow with: "How do you know it was a crow?"

✿ Initiate a discussion by asking, "Have you been awakened by the morning songs of birds?" Allow your students time to describe their own personal experiences with hearing the sounds of birds early in the morning.

✿ Invite your class to read the poem aloud with you. Remind them to use appropriate inflection and tone.

❧ Reflection ❧

Sometimes I feel my kindergartners teach me as much as I teach them. And this lesson proved to be such a time. Everything was going as planned until my students started to read the poem aloud. When we read the line *Holy crow*, several students began to giggle. Since I just thought they were amused by their animated interpretation of this line, I didn't stop to question their reaction until we had finished reading the poem aloud. That's when I discovered my students had comprehended the poem better than I had.

Because Lucas was the first student to giggle, I decided to call on him to provide his reason for all the joviality. He continued to giggle as he explained that Nancie had replaced the obvious phrase, *holy cow*, with *holy crow*, because the crows were some of the birds making the noise. I must admit that when I read the poem, I never once thought about Nancie's choice of words.

Although I was embarrassed to have missed this word-surprise, I was pleased my students immediately recognized the word substitution and understood the poet's purpose for making the change.

Note: I revised my original lesson so that it now includes a question about the word *surprise*.

LESSON FOUR

Review of <u>r</u>-Controlled Vowels <u>ar</u>, <u>er</u>, and <u>ir</u> and Introduction of the <u>r</u>-Controlled Vowel <u>or</u>

What I Was Thinking

When I was trying to decide what type of word study to use, I noticed that several words in the poem "March Alarm Clock" contained the same *r*-controlled vowels I had previously introduced. Because these irregular vowels trip up many of my students, I knew I needed to provide more opportunities to study words containing *r*-controlled vowels in order for my students to be more comfortable with them.

Since my students had already participated in a partner activity as well as a whole-group activity focused on these vowels, I thought they were ready to work on an independent task. I planned to use this time to observe my students as they worked, with the hope of detecting problem areas that could be addressed in future word studies.

Materials

The poem "March Alarm Clock" by CTL fifth graders and Nancie Atwell

Six 3" x 5" cards handwritten with the words *alarm, birds, corner, March, morning,* and *other* in large, neat print—one word per card

A photocopy of the poem for each student

A yellow highlighter for each student

The four new sight-word cards: *around, could, hey,* and *minute*

A pocket holder

What This Lesson Looks Like

❋ Review the four new sight words in the poem: "Before we read the poem aloud, I'd like to review the sight words I pulled from this poem. First, we'll read the word cards together. Next, I'll ask you to locate the words in the poem. After you point out each word, I'd like you to read the line in which you found the word." Shuffle the word cards, and then hold them up one at a time at a steady pace for your students to read aloud. Then, after shuffling the word cards again, begin the exercise.

❋ After reviewing the new sight words, invite your class: "Let's read this poem aloud with feeling."

❋ After the shared reading of the poem, ask, "Who would like to read the poem aloud to us?" Choose a more skilled student to read first to allow a less skilled student more opportunity to become familiar with the words in the poem. After he or she finishes reading, invite someone else to read the poem aloud.

❋ Explain to your students: "Today I'm going to give each of you a copy of the poem and a yellow highlighter. Six words in this poem contain some type of *r*-controlled vowel. I'd like you to highlight each word you find. Before you come back to the meeting area with your completed work, I'd like you to practice reading each highlighted word."

☀ Discuss different strategies to determine unknown words: "If you don't know a word, what can you do?" If someone mentions sounding out the word, say, "Yes, you can sound it out as long as you know all the sounds in the word." Follow with: "What could you do if you don't remember the sound of the *r*-controlled vowel in the word?" If someone says to ask the teacher, clarify the response by saying, "Yes, you can ask me to identify the word, but first you need to try every strategy you know to figure it out by yourself. Who knows a different strategy to try besides sounding out the word and asking me to identify the word?" When someone suggests to read for meaning, elaborate on the student's statement by saying, "Yes, you could read the line, and skip the unfamiliar word. Then you would read the line again, and supply the word that makes the most sense based on the meaning and the letters in the word." As you hand a copy of the poem and a highlighter to each student, say, "No more than four children should sit together at a table. Make sure you sit at a table with good working partners, because to do your best work, you need to be able to concentrate and focus."

☀ Walk around and observe individual students as they work, and ask yourself the following questions:

- Can they quickly locate words with *r*-controlled vowels?

- Who can read the highlighted words with automaticity?

- What strategies do most students use to determine unknown words?

- Which *r*-controlled vowels continue to be problematic?

☀ As soon as you observe several students returning to the meeting area with their completed work, inform the others: "I'd like all of us in the meeting area when the big hand of the clock is on the [name a number], whether you're finished or not."

☀ When the time has expired, invite those students who are still working to join you and their classmates in the meeting area: "The hand is now on the [name the number], so you must stop working now; there's no more time left to work. Please join us now—even if you haven't finished."

✸ When all of your students have returned to the meeting area, direct them: "Please put your paper on the floor in front of you so you'll be able to identify a word you highlighted if I call on you."

✸ Introduce the /ôr/ sound. Hold up the card printed with *morning*. Ask your students, "What's this word?" When someone identifies the word, say, "Yes, it *is* the word *morning*. This word contains an *r*-controlled vowel we haven't discussed yet. Who sees it?" Call on a student who signals. When the letters *o* and *r* are named, say, "Yes, the word *morning* contains the *r*-controlled vowel *o-r*. It looks and sounds just like a word made up of these two letters. Does anyone know what word *o-r* spells?"

✸ Hold the cards printed with *alarm, birds, corner, March,* and *other* in your hand. Then, call on a student to identify one of the words he or she has highlighted. When the student identifies a word, ask, "Will you please spell that word for me? To spell it, just look at the letters in the word and name them from the beginning of the word to the end." As the student spells, look for the word in your set. When the student finishes spelling, hold up the card printed with that word and ask, "What's the *r*-controlled vowel in this word?" Follow with: "What's the sound of [name of *r*-controlled vowel]?" Then invite the class: "Let's read this word aloud together." Call on a different student to identify a second highlighted word. Follow the same steps with this student as you did with the first student. Continue the same procedure with different students for the remaining three *r*-controlled vowels.

✸ Invite your students to read the different *r*-controlled vowel words aloud, chorally. Before you begin reading, address those students who didn't finish highlighting all six words by saying, "Raise your hand if you didn't finish highlighting all six words." Then direct each of these students to pair up with a classmate who completed the task. Ask a student who has all six words highlighted, "Would you please share your paper with [name of student]?" Continue this process until those students have been paired up. Then say, "Let's practice reading all six words aloud together. Please pick up your paper from the floor now. We'll start from the beginning of the poem and read just the highlighted words aloud in the order they appear." Then read all six words chorally.

✸ Close the lesson by playing a visualization game. Invite your class: "Let's play a game called Read My Mind." Place the six word cards printed with *alarm, birds,* corner, March, morning, and other into the pocket holder. Say, "I'll give you clues about one of these word cards. If you think you know my word, please raise your hand. I'll continue to call on students until someone correctly identifies the word I described. Then I'll invite that student to point to the correct word in the pocket holder, so you can see what I was describing." Follow this procedure for all six words. Provide the following clues:

1. "This word contains two *r*-controlled vowels: *or* and *er*. /Ôr/ is inside the word and /ûr/ is at the end of the word. Read my mind." (*corner*)

2. "This word contains the *r*-controlled vowel *ar*. It begins with the uppercase letter *M*. Read my mind." (*March*)

3. "This word contains the *r*-controlled vowel *ir*. It begins with the letter *b*. Read my mind." (*birds*)

4. "This word contains the *r*-controlled vowel *er*. It's at the end of the word. This word begins with the vowel *o*. Read my mind." (*other*)

5. "This word contains the *r*-controlled vowel *or*. It ends with *i-n-g*. Read my mind." (*morning*)

6. "This word contains the *r*-controlled vowel *ar*. It begins with the vowel letter *a*. Read my mind." (*alarm*)

❧ Reflection ☙

When I observed my students working independently, they appeared to understand how to recognize words with *r*-controlled vowels, because it didn't take long for most students to locate them in the poem. However, I noticed many children were rereading lines in the poem to help them figure out some of the highlighted words, which indicated to me that they were having difficulty reading the words in isolation.

Based on this observation, I decided to revise my original plan. In lieu of a sorting activity, I decided to play a visualization game. I thought this particular activity would benefit my students more, because it required more complex thinking than merely categorizing sounds.

Every Child a Reader

LESSON FIVE

Playing With Tricky Words

Invitation to the Wind

Dance
with me
now
in the Springlight
dance
with me under the sky.
Dance
on
your
tiptoes and turn me and
whirl me and lift me
and teach me to fly!
Carry me
on your wild shoulders
I'll
catch all the petals
that spill!
Dance with me,
Wind,
like
you
dance
with the kites
Like you dance with those kites
on the hill!

—*Barbara Juster Esbensen*

What I Was Thinking

Since March is notorious for its windy weather, I wanted us to read a poem that addressed this topic. When I discovered "Invitation to the Wind by Barbara Juster Esbensen," I knew I couldn't bypass this wonderful poem. Its short lines and repetitive words would facilitate my students' success in reading the poem independently. In addition, because the line breaks (i.e., white space) in "Invitation to the Wind" create such a strong rhythm that rises and falls like a gust of wind, my students would realize how line breaks create the specific cadence the poet intended and help a reader know how a poem should be read aloud.

For a shared reading experience, I thought I'd invite the boys and the girls to take turns reading lines of the poem aloud, so that the rise and fall of the rhythm would be more pronounced.

Materials

The poem "Invitation to the Wind" by Barbara Juster Esbensen, handwritten on manila tag chart paper in large, neat print and attached by rings to a wooden chart stand

Three 3" x 5" cards printed with the words *dance, shoulders,* and *wild*

What This Lesson Looks Like

☼ Introduce three tricky words: *dance, shoulders,* and *wild*. Sweep your pointer across the title as you say, "Today you're going to read a poem called 'Invitation to the Wind' by Barbara Juster Esbensen. This poem contains a few tricky words I'd like to review with you before you read it silently."

  • Hold up the word card printed with *dance*. Direct the class: "Read this word aloud if you know it." When you hear a correct response, sweep across the word as you repeat the response. Say, "Dance." Then ask, "Why would *dance* be considered a sight word?" Reiterate the correct answer given by a student: "Yes, you would expect the silent *e* to make the letter *a* sound like its name—/?/, but instead it says /?/." Then inquire: "Who can explain why the letter *c* says /s/?" Call on a capable student to explain the phonics rule. Then say, "That's right! Whenever the letter *e* or *i* follows the letter *c*, the *c* will say /s/."

- Before you hold up the word card printed with *shoulders*, say, "This word can't be sounded out." As you hold up the word card, cover the last three letters to reveal only the word *should*. Say, "And even though the word *should* is located inside this unknown word, it won't help you determine the word." Remove your fingers from the last three letters of the word *shoulders* and ask, "Does anyone know this word?" If no one responds, say, "Since you probably haven't seen this word in your reading, I'll give you a clue to help you. This word is the name of a body part." Then hold up the word card. If no one correctly identifies the word, point to the thirteenth and fourteenth lines of the poem and say, "Let's see if you can make sense of this word by reading these two lines aloud with me." After reading the two lines aloud, say, "I mentioned to you that it's a part of your body. On which part of the body could you be carried?" When someone identifies the word correctly, invite your students: "Let's all say this word." Then direct your students: "Listen to the sounds in this word as I slowly say the word: /sh/ /?/ /l/ /d/ /ûr/ /s/. There's one letter that makes no sound. Which letter is silent?" After someone accurately responds that the letter *u* is silent, print the word *shoulders* on the white board. Invite your students: "Let's say this word slowly." As they say the word, draw a line under the letters that correspond to the sounds they utter: *sh, o, l, d, er,* and *s.* Then, as you circle the letter *u*, say: "The word *shoulders* is tricky because the letter *u* makes no sound." Direct your students: "Focus your eyes on the letters in this word, and read it aloud again."

- Hold up the card printed with the word *wild.* Direct your students: "If you know this word, say it." After the word is correctly identified, invite your students: "Look closely at the letters in this word. Why do I call it a *tricky* word?" Call on a capable student to explain his or her reasoning. Elaborate if necessary by saying, "When there's only one vowel in a word, the vowel's usually short. If this word followed the rule, the vowel would say /ĭ/, but the vowel says /?/ in this word."

✹ Fan out the word cards with the printed side facing you. Call on a student to select one. After he or she has selected one, ask, "Which word did you select?" Follow with: "Would you please find [name of word] in the poem for us? Point to the word each time you see it." Follow the same procedure for the remaining cards.

✿ Invite your students: "I'd like you to take a few minutes to read 'Invitation to the Wind' to yourselves. Since this poem is long, I had to use two charts to copy it. As soon as you've finished the first page, please signal me by putting your hands on your heads. When most of you are ready for page 2, I'll turn the chart over so you're able to read the rest of the poem."

✿ After your students have silently read the poem, explain the procedure for the second reading. Say, "Now that you've had an opportunity to practice reading the words to yourself, I'd like you to read the poem aloud." As you speak, sweep across the corresponding line with the pointer. "To feel its strong rhythm, we'll alternate between the girls and the boys. The girls will read the first line; then the boys will read the second line. Who's going to read the third line?" Confirm the answer by repeating what was said: "That's right! The third line will be read by the girls." Sweep across this line. Then, as you sweep across the fourth line, ask, "Who will read this line?" Follow with: "What kind of reading pattern will we be creating?" If someone identifies it as a girl-boy pattern, justify his or her answer by saying: "It *is* a girl-boy pattern, or it can be described as an *AB* pattern." Before beginning to read, ask, "Any questions?"

✿ Invite your students to take turns reading the lines in the poem: "Girls, you're going to begin the reading. Please start by reading the title aloud, as well as the first line. Boys, follow along with your eyes, so you'll know when to take your turn." Point to the title with your pointer as you request: "Girls, will you please start reading?"

✿ After the shared reading, discuss the poem's meaning. Invite your students: "Picture in your mind a kite flying high in the sky on a windy day. All of a sudden a gust of wind comes up. What's happening to the kite?" After your students share their mind-pictures, ask, "What does the speaker of this poem want the wind to do to him or her?" Invite the class: "Let's recall the action words in this poem." List the verbs on the board as students offer them.

☼ Discuss the purpose of white space in poems: "The white space signals the reader to pause before reading the next line. In this poem, the line breaks produce a rhythm simulating a gust of wind." Then ask, "Have you ever felt a gust of wind? What happens when a gust of wind comes up?" Call on different students to recall a windy day and invite them to share their stories. End with: "As you can see from your own experiences, a gust of wind can suddenly pick up and be powerful. And just as quickly, it can die down."

☼ For the final reading, invite your students: "Let's take turns once more reading the poem aloud, but this time, I'd like the boys to read first and the girls to read second. Remember, since you take turns reading *lines*, it's important to stay focused to know when to begin reading." Point to the title, and say, "Boys, please begin by reading the title."

◈ Reflection ◈

When reading the lines, alternating between girls and boys worked beautifully. More importantly, this pattern allowed my students to hear the rise and fall of the rhythm more easily because of the natural delay between each group's readings. Not only did they understand the importance of attending to line breaks, but they also recognized the music of poetry. They read confidently, expressively, and joyfully. What more could I ask for?

LESSON SIX
Sound Sort for the Letter i

What I Was Thinking

As I scanned the words in "Invitation to the Wind," I was astonished to find a multitude containing the *i* vowel. It was obvious what our word study should focus on, but once again I faced the dilemma of designing a meaningful word study—one that would target my students' present stage of reading development.

Although a word sort would definitely utilize all the words I selected, I wanted to be certain it was the best choice of activity for a word study. After thinking about it, I realized that implementing a *closed* word sort would help my students gain a deeper understanding of graphemes, improve their word knowledge, and help them discover recurring patterns among the words. These potential benefits proved to me that I wouldn't be able to find a more worthwhile activity.

I decided to implement a whole-class word sort to determine how skilled my students were with the different /i/ sounds and with various words from the poem before I assigned an independent sorting task.

Materials

The poem "Invitation to the Wind" by Barbara Juster Esbensen, handwritten on manila tag chart paper in large, neat print and attached by rings to a wooden chart stand

Fourteen 3" x 5" cards written with the words *fly, hill, in, I'll, kites, lift, light, spill, spring, tip, whirl, wild, wind,* and *with*—one word per card (Duplicate words if necessary, so there is one card for each student.)

Three 3" x 5" cards written with the symbols *?, ĭ,* and *ir*

What This Lesson Looks Like

✲ Read the poem together. Remind your students: "Remember to pause whenever you see white space. These line breaks enhance the sound of the poem."

✲ Hold up the stack of word cards for the class to see. Then explain: "I chose several one-syllable words from the poem because they have a vowel in

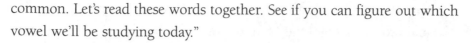

common. Let's read these words together. See if you can figure out which vowel we'll be studying today."

- Hold up one card at a time and have your students read the word aloud together.
- After your students have read the last word aloud, ask them, "Which vowel did you see in each word you just read?" If no one responds, hold up the words, one at a time, and ask your students, "What vowel letter do you see in each of these words?" Continue showing different cards until someone answers correctly.
- Remind your students that this vowel makes different sounds. Ask your students, "What sounds can the letter *i* say?" As a specific sound is given, hold up a card with the corresponding sound symbol (i.e., */?/, /ĭ/, /ir/*).
- Identify any sound(s) your students are unable to recall. As you say the sound, hold up the corresponding symbol card. Then place the symbol cards in a line on the floor, leaving a good space between each card.
- Direct your students: "Please make a semi-circle, so that everyone is able to see the word cards."
- Explain the directions of the activity, "Today you'll sort these words by the vowel sound you hear. I'll give each of you a word card. When you get your word, whisper it to yourself, so you can hear the vowel sound. When it's your turn, place your word under the appropriate symbol heading. For example, if you have the word *wild,* place it in this column [point to the */?/* heading] because you hear the vowel say */?/*."
- Give each student a word card. Allow a few moments for them to figure out which *i* sound they hear in their word.
- Explain the procedure for the word-sorting activity: "We'll whip around the class, beginning with [name of student] and ending with [name of student]. When it's your turn, you should read your word aloud before placing it in the appropriate column. I'll call on some of you to explain your reasoning for placing. Any questions?" When your students' questions have been answered, begin the sorting activity.

✿ After the word sort has been completed, discuss the results. Ask, "How many words contain the /ʔ/ sound?" Instruct your class: "Let's read the words in this category." Beginning at the top of the column, point to each word as it's read aloud. Follow this process for the remaining *i* sounds. Then ask, "Which sound occurs most often? Which sound occurs the least?"

✿ Call on a student to pick up the /ʔ/ word cards. Tell him or her, "Before you can pick up a card, you must read it aloud." Then choose a different student to follow this procedure for the /ĭ/ column. Complete the activity by inviting a third student to read aloud and pick up the remaining word cards from the floor.

✿ Invite a student to read the poem "Invitation to the Wind" aloud independently. Remind the student: "Each time you come to the action word *dance*, emphasize it by reading it aloud with a big voice to give the feeling of a gusty wind."

❧ Reflection ❧

Because my students had made progress in their phonological awareness, I knew most would be comfortable participating in this type of activity. My only reservation was that reading these words in isolation might pose a challenge for some. However, my concern wasn't warranted. When we began reading the word cards prior to the sorting activity, I noticed *all* my students participating in the vocabulary review, which doesn't often happen. Usually one or two students remain passive during our vocabulary practice and allow their classmates to do the work for them. The total-group participation helped the sorting activity flow smoothly from the beginning to the end of the lesson.

What was even more impressive was listening to various students explain their decisions for categorizing their words. Through this lesson, they discovered for themselves that they clearly understood how words work. And I had the pleasure of witnessing my students' facility with words. It doesn't get much better than that.

Every Child a Reader

LESSON SEVEN

New Sight Words

To a Red Kite

Fling
yourself
upon the sky.

Take the string
you need.
Ride high.

high
above the park.
Tug and buck
and lark
with the wind.

Touch a cloud,
red kite.
Follow the wild geese
in their flight.

—Lilian Moore

What I Was Thinking

I chose this poem because it seemed to nicely complement "Invitation to the Wind." And I was looking forward to our discussion regarding the similarities and differences between the two poems.

Once again, I felt my students would be able to read the poem easily. They had learned the necessary concepts and skills from prior word studies to know how to decode unfamiliar words contained in "To a Red Kite." As I was studying the words, I realized that soon my students would no longer need word studies to facilitate their reading success; they were blossoming into fluent readers. I knew they'd be able to read the words, but I wondered if they'd comprehend the meaning of the poem. To check their understanding, I planned to cover the word *kite* and invite my students to predict the obscured word. Their predictions would be the starting point of our discussion.

Materials

The poem "To a Red Kite" by Lilian Moore, handwritten on manila tag chart paper in large, neat print and attached by rings to a wooden chart stand

Four 3" x 5" cards printed with the words *above, high, lark,* and *touch*

A strip of construction paper covering the word *kite* in the title

A strip of construction paper covering the word *kite* in the second line of the last stanza

What This Lesson Looks Like

❋ Introduce the poem "To a Red Kite": "For this particular poem, the poet, Lilian Moore, uses a form called a *poem of instruction.* She speaks directly to the subject of the poem as if the subject were right there listening to her instructions. As you can see, I've covered one word in the poem—the subject of the poem—for you to guess. Lilian Moore's choice of words allows the reader to feel what it would be like to be this particular object. She must have closely watched this subject, or personally experienced using it, before she wrote her poem, because she was able to capture its actions so beautifully."

❋ Review the meaning of the word *lark* before reading the poem. Hold up the card written with the word *lark.* Ask your students, "Who knows this word?" Children will use their phonological knowledge to determine the word. When someone correctly responds, sweep across the last two lines in the third stanza. As you read, emphasize the word *lark*: "And *lark* with the wind." Then ask, "What does the word *lark* mean?" Explain its meaning in this context if your students don't know it: "Here, *lark* means 'to play pranks.' In other words, the subject of the poem is being mischievous in a fun-loving way with the wind."

Every Child a Reader

Introduce the new sight words *above, high,* and *touch.* Explain to your class: "Before you read this poem, I'd like to discuss a few words you can't sound out. And you may not even be able to make sense of these words through the context."

- Remind them: "When I show you the word, please say it aloud if and only if you know it. If you don't know the word yet, please don't guess, because it will be confusing to hear different words." Then hold up the word card *above.* When someone correctly reads the word, repeat the word: "This word is *above.*" Invite your students to examine the word's two syllables. Ask them, "From previous word studies, we know the vowel *a* can sound like which vowel at the beginning of a word with more than one syllable?" When someone correctly responds, confirm the student's response by saying, "Yes, the letter *a* does sound like the short vowel *u.*" Invite your students to think of other multisyllabic words that begin with the letter *a.* As students share a word, write each word on the white board or on chart paper for all to see. To reinforce the special sound of *a,* read the list aloud, emphasizing the first sound. Then refocus your students' attention to the word *above.* As you sweep across the second syllable, say, "Now let's look at the second syllable, *bove.* I see the letter *e* at the end of this syllable. Listen as I slowly say both syllables in this word." As you say the word, stress the second syllable: "A-*bove.*" Then ask your students, "Does the second syllable, *bove,* follow the silent *e* rule?" As soon as you hear students say no, follow with: "But you *can* remember this word by thinking of a word you do know that rhymes with *bove* and has the same spelling pattern." Prompt them by saying, "*Bove* rhymes with l____?" Write the word *love* on chart paper or the white board. Below it, write the syllable *bove.* As you underline the letters *o-v-e* in *love* and *bove,* repeat the sound /ŭv/.

- Hold up the word card *high.* Listen to your students' responses. Point to the *-igh* chunk and ask a student who correctly responded: "What does the chunk *i-g-h* say?" When the student answers, point to each letter as you reiterate to the class: "Whenever you see the chunk *i-g-h,* say /ī/." Continue the discussion by writing *-igh* words on the white

board for your students to read aloud. After you write *high, sigh,* and *thigh,* invite your students to read each word aloud as you point to it. After the students read the list, underline the *-igh* chunk in each word, and repeat the sound it makes. Then say, "Let's try some words that contain *-igh*." Write *fight, light, might, night, right,* and *sight.* Finally, write some words containing blends such as *flight, bright, slight,* and *fright* on the board or chart paper for your students to read aloud.

- Hold up the last card printed with the sight word *touch* for your students to read aloud. Ask, "Why is this a sight word?" If someone states it can't be sounded out, probe for more information. Invite the student to be more specific: "What do you mean it can't be sounded out? What letter combination does not make its usual sound?" Follow with: "What vowel sound do you hear in the word *touch*?" Then pronounce it slowly again to help the class distinguish the sounds in the word. Ask, "Which vowel says /ŭ/?" When you hear someone answer correctly, confirm the response by saying, "That's correct." Point to the letter *u* in the word *touch.* "The vowel letter *u* says /ŭ/. And the vowel *o* in this word doesn't make a sound; it's silent." Then spell and cheer the word *touch* (Cunningham, 1995).

✿ Review the sight words by inviting your students to locate each one in the poem. Instruct your students: "When I show you a word, I'd like you to read it aloud, and then find its location in the poem. I'll call on you if your eyes are focused in the appropriate location." Shuffle the word cards. Hold up one card for the class to read aloud. Ask, "Who sees where [name of sight word] is located in the poem?" Choose a student whose hand is raised and whose eyes are focused on the appropriate location on the chart paper. Say, "Please come up to the chart and show your classmates where the word [name of sight word] is located." Follow this procedure for the remaining sight words. When a student points to the word *high,* invite him or her to find its location elsewhere on the chart.

✿ Invite your students to silently read the poem. Explain: "As you can see, the words in this poem are easy to read. We've already discussed the troublesome words, so you should be able to read this poem—just like that

Every Child a Reader

[snap your fingers]! I'd like you to take a few minutes to read this poem to yourself. Let's see if you can figure out the subject of this poem by using clues from it. Be ready to share lines that helped you determine the unknown word. When you've finished reading, please put your hands on your head to signal me that you're ready to share your findings."

* When most students have finished reading, call on a student to make a prediction for the covered word. Then ask, "Why do you think it's [name of predicted word]? What are some words or lines from the poem that helped you make your prediction?" As the student reads a word, phrase, or line aloud, point it out on the chart paper. If the student's prediction is accurate but his or her reasoning doesn't makes sense, call on a different student who concurs with the first student's prediction to discuss his or her reasoning. However, if the student hasn't made an accurate prediction, continue calling on students until someone correctly identifies the covered word. Invite that student to share the word clues he or she found in the poem that helped him or her determine the unknown word. Direct the student to spell the word *kite*. Support the student as needed to correctly spell *kite*. As the student names each letter, write it on the paper strip. When the word *kite* has been printed on the strip, invite the student to remove the paper strip to reveal the identity of the covered word. Ask, "Was your prediction correct?" When the student gives an affirmative response, ask, "How can you tell?"

* Discuss the poem's meaning by asking, "What's the poet telling the kite to do?" As a student identifies an action from the poem, locate the line and read it aloud. Continue until all actions have been named and the corresponding lines have been read aloud.

* Invite the class to share their own kite stories. Initiate the discussion by asking, "Who has ever tried to fly a kite? What was it like?" If no one has flown a kite, ask, "Have you ever watched someone fly a kite? Have you or someone you watched ever had trouble getting the kite to fly?"

* Tell the class: "Let's create an *AB* pattern to read this poem aloud. The girls will read the first stanza, the boys will read the second stanza. Who will read the third stanza?" When you hear the word *girls* uttered, ask, "Who

will read the last stanza?" Remind them: "When the girls are reading, the boys should be listening and following the pointer with their eyes, so they'll know when it's their turn to read aloud. Then the girls should listen to the boys read the second stanza aloud and keep their eyes focused on the words the boys read aloud." Ask, "Are there any questions before we begin reading?"

❧ Reflection ❧

Everything about this poem was easy for my students: the vocabulary, the prediction, and the meaning. Because the lesson flowed seamlessly, we had extra time to read several old favorites. However, if I hadn't taken the time to discuss the troublesome words and the meaning of the word *lark* in this poem, my students wouldn't have had as much success as they did. Again, this lesson validates how important it is to be prepared for any potential trouble spot.

APRIL

LESSON ONE

Suffixes -ble, -dle, and -tle

The Muddy Puddle

I am sitting
In the middle
Of a rather Muddy
Puddle,
With my bottom
Full of bubbles
And my rubbers
Full of Mud,

While my jacket
And my sweater
Go on slowly
Getting wetter
As I very
Slowly settle
To the Bottom
Of the Mud.

And I find that
What a person
With a puddle
Round his middle
Thinks of mostly
In the muddle
Is the Muddi-
Ness of Mud.

—*Dennis Lee*

What I Was Thinking

Mud season arrives during the early weeks of April in Maine. No matter how hard children try to stay out of the mud, their pants, as well as their boots and shoes, are often coated when they come in from recess. Although they don't necessarily sit in mud puddles, there are times when they do slip and fall into puddles and muddy patches of grass. So they know just what it feels like to have soggy pants, as well as mucky shoes and socks. I knew my students would relate to this hilarious poem by Dennis Lee and enjoy reading it.

The many words in this poem ending in *-le* enhanced my motivation to use it. Since my students could proficiently decode one-syllable words, I knew they were ready to begin to learn how to decode multisyllabic words. I now needed to show them how a word can be broken into recognizable chunks. I thought beginning with the spelling pattern consonant *-le* would be an appropriate starting point.

Materials

The poem "The Muddy Puddle" by Dennis Lee, handwritten on manila tag chart paper in large, neat print and attached by rings to a wooden chart stand

> ✿ Fold up the bottom edge of the chart paper to reveal only the title of the poem; use paper clips to keep the paper in place.

Three 3" x 5" cards printed with *-ble, -dle,* and *-tle*

Five 3" x 5" cards printed with the words *bubble, puddle, middle, muddle,* and *settle*

> ✿ Use a black marker to print the first syllable of each word.

> ✿ Use a red marker to print *-ble, -dle,* or *-tle* in each word.

What This Lesson Looks Like

> ✿ Point to the title as you say, "Today's poem is called 'The Muddy Puddle.' I've covered the words to the poem, because I'd like to get your ideas about muddy puddles first. Then you'll see what Dennis Lee has to say when you read the poem. Perhaps you'll find his experience with mud puddles is similar to yours." Initiate a discussion by saying, "Young children love mud puddles. Let's think of different things children do when there's a

puddle nearby." When ideas begin to wane, tell your students, "This poem describes what *sitting* in a mud puddle is like. Maybe you haven't intentionally sat in a mud puddle, but you may have accidentally slipped in the mud and fallen down. Who has ever slipped in mud? What happened when you fell?"

☀ Following the discussion, say, "Before we read the poem to find out how the speaker describes his or her experience sitting in the mud puddle, I want to show you some words from the poem that end with a similar spelling pattern."

☀ Hold up the word card printed with *-ble*. Explain to your students: "Some longer words end with this chunk. If you recognize it right away, you'll be able to figure out the word easily." Say, "The letter combination *b-l-e* says /bl/." Invite your class to repeat what you just said. Then hold up the word card printed with *bubble*. Cover the first syllable (i.e., *bub*) with your hand and ask, "What does this say?" When the class says /bl/, remove your fingers from the first syllable and cover the final syllable (*-ble*). Direct your class: "Look at the letters that make up the first part of this word." Point to each letter as you name it: "*b-u-b*." Ask, "What does this part say?" Call on a student to identify it. Then invite your students to say it aloud. As soon as they say *bub*, reveal the final syllable. As you sweep your fingers across *-ble*, ask, "What does this say?" Follow with: "Let's put these two parts together: *bub-ble*. What's the word?" Follow the same procedure for *-dle* and *-tle*.

☀ Review the sounds of *-ble, -dle,* and *-tle*. Hold up the card printed with *-ble* and ask your students, "What does *b-l-e* say?" Follow the same procedure for *-dle* and *-tle*. After your students have practiced saying all three chunks, ask, "Which letter is silent?"

☀ Remind your students: "Usually when *le* is at the end of the word and another consonant letter comes before the *le*, the consonant plus *le* make up the last part of the word."

☀ Then shuffle the word cards printed with *bubble, puddle, middle, muddle,* and *settle* and invite your students: "Let's read these words again."

❄ Invite the class to read the poem silently: "I'd like you to take a few minutes to read 'The Muddy Puddle' to yourself. Since this poem is long, I had to use two charts to copy it. As soon as you've finished the first page, please signal me by putting your hands on your head. When most of you are ready for page 2, I'll turn the chart over so you're able to read the rest of the poem." Remove the paper clips to reveal the body of the poem.

❄ Use the whip-around procedure to read the poem aloud for the first time. Invite your students: "Let's take turns reading the lines of this poem. You'll read a line in the poem, and then your neighbor will read the next line until the poem is completed. Since there are 24 lines including the title, everyone will get at least one turn to read." Sweep your pointer in a zigzag motion across the rows of students as you say, "[Name of student] will begin by reading the title and [Name of student] will be the last to read one line."

❄ After reading the lines of the poem aloud, say, "Although this humorous poem uses simple language, Dennis Lee's choice of words helps to create vivid images in your mind. What did you picture in your mind as we read this poem aloud?"

❄ Inform your students, "Dennis Lee is known as the Wizard of Words because he uses words in ways that are memorable and clever. Which word surprised you?" If your students can't recall the word *muddle*, prompt them by saying, "The word is in the last stanza. Who sees it?" Call on a student who signals you to point to the word in the poem. Ask, "What do you think the word *muddle* means? Why do you think he uses the word?"

❄ Invite your class to read the poem aloud with you: "Let's read this poem together to end Poetry Time on a high note. Although this poem has few rhyming words, its rhythm brings it to life. Try to read at a steady pace to keep the rhythm throughout the poem."

❧ Reflection ❧

What transpired during this lesson took me by surprise. I had planned to do a step-by-step demonstration to show my students how to divide a word into recognizable chunks. When I began the demonstration, I could sense a bit of restlessness. At that point, because I wondered if they thought this demonstration was unnecessary, I decided to bypass this step to see if my instinct was correct. As soon as I held up the word *bubble*, I knew I had made the right decision. My students spontaneously read that word and every other word I held up.

Could the highlighting of the second syllable have facilitated the reading? I wanted to be certain my students could recognize these particular consonant *-le* chunks before I moved on to a different word study. Since my curiosity was raised, I had to find out the answer as soon as possible. Although I had planned to just practice reading the poem in Lesson Two, I wanted to supplement the lesson by reviewing the consonant *-le* chunks to verify my students' competency.

LESSON TWO

Introduction of New Sight Words and Review of the Suffixes -<u>ble</u>, -<u>dle</u>, and -<u>tle</u>

What I Was Thinking

Although I hadn't originally intended to do a follow-up lesson to the word study I introduced in Lesson One, I changed my mind when I thought about what had transpired the day before. I wanted to be certain that my students understood how to divide a word into recognizable chunks. To verify their understanding, I decided to have them play a dice game using *different* words ending with *-ble, -dle,* or *-tle.* But before they performed this independent activity, I planned to reinforce this skill with a quick review of the words in "The Muddy Puddle" that ended with *-ble, -dle,* and *-tle.*

Materials

The poem "The Muddy Puddle" by Dennis Lee, handwritten on manila tag chart paper in large, neat print and attached by rings to a wooden chart stand

A black fine-point pen

Previously learned sight word card: *pull*

Class set of Popsicle sticks, one for each child printed with the student's name

Three 3" x 5" cards printed with *-ble, -dle,* and *-tle*

One pencil for each pair of students

Four 3" x 5" cards printed with the words *full, most, very,* and *what*

A 1-inch cube printed with *-ble, -dle,* and *-tle* for each pair of students

   ❀ Use a black fine-point pen to print each consonant *-le* chunk.

   ❀ Print each chunk twice on the sides of the cube.

A 1-inch cube printed with *mar, peb, rid, bun, lit,* and *bot* for each pair of students

   ❀ Use a black fine-point pen to print each beginning syllable.

   ❀ Print each beginning syllable once on the sides of the cube.

One 8?" x 11" sheet of white paper for each student, numbered from 1 to 6

Chart paper or white board

What This Lesson Looks Like

   ❀ Introduce four new sight words: *full, most, very,* and *what.* Say, "This poem contains four sight words that are important for you to know, because you'll undoubtedly encounter them in your learning as well as in your reading. For example, two of these words are math terms."

   • Hold up the card printed with the previously learned word *pull* and direct your students: "Tell me the word." When your students say the word, inform them, "If you know this word says *pull,* then this word must say [hold up the card printed with *full*]." When a correct response is heard, say, "The word *full* is a math word." Call on a student and ask, "[Name of student], how do you know this word says *full*?" After the student finishes his or her explanation, write the word *pull* on the board, and below it, write the word *full.* Underline the chunk *-ull* in both words as you say, "Because both words contain -*ull* at the end of the word, they sound the same. Words that sound the same at the end of the words are called *rhyming* words. What would **b**-u-l-l say?" Follow with: "Let's spell and cheer the word *full* before I show you another word." Accompany your class in naming each letter you touch with your finger. Then announce, "Cheer it!" At this moment, your students should extend one of their arms toward the ceiling with a fist and cheer, "*Full!*" (Cunningham, 1995).

- Hold up the card printed with *most*: "This is another math word. What is it?" When someone identifies it correctly, confirm the student's answer by saying, "Yes, it does say *most*. This word is tricky, because it looks like the vowel should say /ŏ/ since the word contains just one vowel." Invite your students: "Let's spell and cheer this word." Accompany your class in naming each letter you touch with your finger. Then announce, "Cheer it!" At this moment, your students should extend one of their arms toward the ceiling with a fist and cheer, "*Most!*" (Cunningham, 1995). Explain: "Actually, the word *most* isn't in this poem." Point to the word *mostly* as you say, "An ending called a suffix has been added to the word *most*. What letters make up this suffix or ending?" Call on a student to answer. Confirm the student's correct response by covering the *l*-*y* suffix. Say, "Here's the word *most*." Follow with: "Who knows what *ly* says?" Call on a capable student to answer. Confirm the student's accurate response by saying, "Yes, it does say /lē/." As you sweep your finger under the word *mostly*, ask your students, "What does this word say?"

- Say, "I selected this word for two reasons. You probably see this word often in your reading, *and* it's a word you often use when you write." Then hold up the card printed with the word *very* and ask, "What's the word?" After a student identifies it, say, "The word *very* isn't really a sight word, because it can be sounded out. But the *e*-*r* [sweep your finger under the letters] may trick some readers because they might try the /ûr/ sound: /v/ /ûr/ /ē/. However, it's close enough to the correct pronunciation that a reader most likely will self-correct the error when he or she uses the word in context." Direct your students' attention to the word *very* in the poem: "Listen as I begin reading the second stanza containing the word *very*. I'll mispronounce the word *very*, because I want you to see how reading for meaning will help you correct a miscue you might make." After reading the stanza and mispronouncing the word *very*, reread the lines correctly.

- Hold up the card printed with *what*. Say, "I bet you see a little word inside of this word. What do you see?" When someone mentions the word *at*, explain, "The word *at* won't help you figure it out, because this word can't be sounded out; it's a sight word." Then ask, "Who knows this word?" Call on someone who signals you. If the student is correct, say, "You're right. It's the word *what*—not /wh/ /?/ /t/. The vowel in the word *what* sounds like a . . ." Pause to allow your students to complete the sentence. Then say, "That's why you need to take a picture of it in your mind. The word *what* is a question word. Most question words begin with *wh*. Watch as I write them on the board." Write the words *what, who, when, where,* and *why* on the white board or chart paper. As you write each of them, underline the letters *wh*, and then use the question word in a sentence. After your demonstration, direct your students: "I'd like you to close your eyes and try to picture the word *what* in your mind. First, picture the letters *wh*, and then picture the little word *at* after the letter *h*. Keep your eyes closed as we say the letters. Ready?" After spelling the word *what* with their eyes closed, invite your students: "Let's open our eyes and use our pointy fingers to write the word *what* on the floor within our own personal space. Say the letters as you write them." After the class has completed the writing exercise, ask, "How do you spell *what*?"

✿ Fan out the word cards with the printed side facing you. Call on a student to select one. After he or she has selected one, ask, "Which word did you select?" Follow with: "Would you please find [name of word] in the poem for us?" Use the same procedure with the remaining three word cards.

✿ Read the poem chorally with your students. Invite your students: "Now that we've spent some time focusing on the new sight words in this poem, let's turn our attention to all the words and read this delightful poem aloud."

✿ After the shared reading of the poem has ended, ask your students, "Who would like to read this poem aloud by himself or herself?" When some students begin to raise their hands, say, "Please keep your hand raised until I find your name on one of these Popsicle sticks." Observe which students raised their hands, and as you say someone's name aloud, remove the Popsicle stick printed with the name of that student from the class set. Follow this procedure for every student who would like a turn to read.

Every Child a Reader

☼ After you've gathered the appropriate sticks, be certain your hand covers the names printed on them. Then call on a student who didn't want to read independently to select one of the Popsicle sticks. Say, "Please pull out one stick and read the name aloud." As the student begins to pull one out, ask, "Who's going to be the lucky one to read the entire poem aloud?" The student should then read aloud the name of his or her classmate. Hand the pointer to the student who is selected and say, "Please sweep across each line as you read it aloud."

☼ After the student finishes reading the poem, provide appropriate positive feedback to him or her: "[Name of student] fluently read the words we discussed when I introduced the poem—words that ended with *le*."

☼ Review the words in the poem that contain the consonant -*le*. Hold up the cards labeled with -*ble*, -*dle*, and -*tle* one at a time and invite your students: "Say these sounds with me." Point to the word *bubble* in the poem and say, "The chunk -*ble* is at the end of . . ." Pause to allow your students to read it aloud. Follow the same procedure for *puddle, middle, muddle,* and *settle.*

☼ Select a student to model the partner activity with you: "Today you and a partner are going to play a fun word game using dice. I'd like [name of student] to be my partner as I demonstrate how to play this game." Invite the student to sit on the floor beside you, so that all your students will be able to see the demonstration.

☼ Hold up the die printed with the three different consonant -*le* endings as you explain: "One die has three different endings of words: -*ble,* -*dle,* and -*tle.* Each is printed twice on the die." Turn the die to demonstrate this feature. Then hold up the second die and say: "A different beginning syllable or part is printed on each side of this die. In all, there are six different beginning syllables."

☼ Hold up the sheet of paper numbered from 1 to 6. Say, "There are six different words that can be rolled with a pair of dice. You'll record each different word you make on your sheet of paper. The game ends when you roll all six different words. Before you can record the word, you and your partner must agree that it's a real word."

☼ Describe the materials required to play the game: "To play this word game, you and your partner will need your own paper to record the real words you roll on your turn." Hand a recording sheet to your partner and place one in front of you. Then say, "You and your partner will share a pencil and the dice. Place the pencil and the pair of dice between you and your partner."

✻ Model the game with your partner. Pick up the dice and say, "I'll roll first." Roll the dice and then read the side that turns up on each die. Say, "On this die I rolled *–ble*, and I rolled *mar* on this one. I know *-ble* is found at the end of a word, so I'll place it after *mar*. The dice need to touch in order to form a word." Read the word that results from putting the two parts together: "I made the word *marble*." Ask your partner, "Do you agree that *marble* is a real word?" When the partner responds affirmatively, say, "Since I rolled a real word, I have to record it on my paper next to number one. However, if I didn't make a real word, I couldn't record it on my paper. My turn would be over." After you've printed the word neatly next to number one, hold up the paper for everybody to see. Emphasize: "If your partner has made a real word, you must wait until your partner has finished recording the word before you can roll the dice. If you roll the dice before your partner is done, it won't count. You'll have to roll again." Look at your partner and say, "Now it's your turn."

✻ Explain to your students: "You'll play this game for 10 minutes. Some of you might be able to roll all six words, while others won't be so lucky. But it doesn't really matter. When we come back to our meeting area to discuss the different words you rolled, I'm sure all six words will be identified."

✻ Using your prepared list of partners' names, say, "When I read your name aloud, please stand up." Read the names of the first pair of students. When the two students stand up, explain to them, "Since you'll be working together as partners, I'd like you to find a personal space on the floor to play this game together." Then hand each of them a recording sheet and say, "[Name of student], please take a pair of dice for both of you to share. And [Name of student], please take a pencil to share." Follow the same procedure for each pair of students.

✻ Circulate around the classroom to observe students as they work. Take note of your students' automaticity in reading the words they roll.

✻ At the end of 10 minutes, explain, "It's time to stop playing. After you've returned your pencils to their home, please join me in the meeting area with your recording sheets."

✻ When your students have gathered in the meeting area, ask, "Did anyone roll all six words?" Then call on a student and ask, "What word did you roll?" If it's authentic, neatly print the word on the white board. Then ask, "Did anyone roll a

Every Child a Reader

different word?" Call on someone else who signals you and ask, "What word did you roll?" If the student also identifies a different authentic word, print it below the first word. Continue to make a list until all six words have been identified. If they're not all identified, say, "Since no one rolled all six words, We'll complete the list by matching up the first part with the correct consonant -le ending." Print a list of the first syllables in one column and a list of the endings in the second column. Point to *mar* and ask: "Which ending would make a real word if it came at the end of *mar*?" Then draw a line from *mar* to -*ble* in the second column, Then ask:"Who can make another real word?" Continue until all six words are identified.

☀ Invite your students to read the completed list of words with you.

❧ Reflection ☙

Because my students were so engaged in playing this game, they were disappointed when it was time to stop. Rather than extend the activity time, I believed it was more important to come together as a group to allow closure to the lesson by discussing the words.

Needless to say, no student rolled all six words in the allotted time. That fact alone motivated my students to name each word they did roll. However, when no one could identify the fifth and sixth words, I knew I needed to intervene, but I didn't want to steal their thunder by just telling them the words. That's when a lightbulb went off in my head. I made a list of the six beginning syllables in one column and the six consonant –*le* endings in a second column and hoped that they'd be able to figure out the remaining words by matching up a beginning syllable with a consonant –*le* ending.

As I watched my students use this strategy with ease and read the list of words with confidence and automaticity, I realized I could move on to another word study. More importantly, I recognized that word studies may not be needed for much longer if my students continued to demonstrate the same fluency and proficiency with words that I observed today.

Note: I revised my original plan to reflect the changes I made during the lesson.

LESSON THREE

Introduction of Tricky Words

Keep a Poem in Your Pocket

Keep a poem in your pocket
and a picture in your head
and you'll never feel lonely
at night when you're in bed.

The little poem will sing to you
the little picture bring to you
a dozen dreams to dance to you
at night when you're in bed.

So—
Keep a picture in your pocket
and a poem in your head
and you'll never feel lonely
at night when you're in bed.

—*Beatrice Schenk de Regniers*

What I Was Thinking

Although we celebrate poetry every day at CTL, I wanted my students to gain a broader perspective and realize that people throughout the United States value poetry as much as we do. I noticed that another teacher had displayed a poster announcing that April is National Poetry Month. This poster was the impetus I needed. I decided to use Beatrice Schenk de Regnier's famous poem "Keep a Poem in Your Pocket" as a tribute to this genre. I hoped my beliefs about the power of poetry would be confirmed when we discussed de Regnier's message. Would my students have special poems in their heads? I was counting on it.

A P R I L

Materials

The poem "Keep a Poem in Your Pocket" by Beatrice Schenk de Regniers, handwritten on manila tag chart paper in large, neat print and attached by rings to a wooden chart stand

Three 3" x 5" cards printed with *dozen, head,* and *picture*

What This Lesson Looks Like

✿ Introduce three tricky words: *dozen, head,* and *picture.* Remind students: "When I hold up a word that you don't know, just listen as it is read aloud. Hearing different words being called out may cause confusion."

• Say, "The words I chose might be troublesome when you encounter them in this poem. They contain some sounds you wouldn't expect if you tried to sound them out. I want to review them now so you'll be able to read the poem easily." Hold up the word card printed with *dozen.* "If you know this word, say it." If no one responds or if the response is incorrect, identify the word for the class. Then ask, "Which letter doesn't make its usual sound?" When someone identifies the letter *o,* follow with, "What letter does the *o* sound like?" Then discuss the meaning of the word *dozen:* "How many items make up a dozen?" Prompt your students by saying, "Think of a dozen eggs or a dozen donuts." Confirm a student's answer by reiterating, "A dozen is a collection of twelve objects: a dozen eggs means twelve eggs, a dozen donuts means twelve donuts."

• Hold up the word card printed with *head.* Say, "If you know the word, read it aloud." After someone identifies it, invite the class to analyze the sounds in the word *head.* Ask, "Why would I consider this word to be troublesome?" When someone points out the letters *ea,* say, "You're right! We learned this particular vowel digraph says /?/, but in some words it says /ĕ/. And *head* is one of these words. Tomorrow we'll focus our attention on this particular vowel digraph." Then say, "Watch me as I chant and cheer the word *head.*" To chant the word *head,* pat your head with one hand each time you say each letter in the word. Then pat your head with both hands as you say the word *head.*

- Hold up the word card printed with *picture*. Ask, "Who knows this word?" Call on a student who raises his or her hand. When the word is correctly identified, instruct them: "Look at the printed word as I slowly pronounce it. Listen carefully to the sounds I say. Be ready to explain why this word can't be sounded out." Then slowly emphasize the sounds in the word *picture*. Follow with: "There are two reasons why this word can't be sounded out." (The silent *e* does not follow the rule. The letter *t* does not make the /t/ sound; instead, the *ch* digraph is heard.) Ask, "Who can explain one reason why this word can't be decoded?" When someone correctly states one reason, validate the student's response by demonstrating what the word would sound like if the standard phonics rule applied. Then ask, "Who heard another sound in the word *picture* that doesn't make sense—knowing what you know about letters and sounds?" End the discussion by imitating the action of taking a picture with a camera as you explain, "You have to picture this word in your *h-e-a-d—head*." Then instruct your students: "To do this, close your eyes and try to see each letter I say: *p-i-c-t-u-r-e*."

- Shuffle the word cards a few times. Then instruct your students: "Please read the word I hold up. Then look for it in the poem. Raise your hand once you've located it. I will call on you if your eyes are focused in the correct location." Hand the pointer to a student and say, "Sweep across the word with the pointer as you read the word." Allow the student to locate the word elsewhere in the poem if it's applicable. Continue this procedure until all four words have been located and read aloud.

✿ Direct your students to read the poem silently: "Please take a few moments to read the poem silently. When you finish, signal me by putting your hands on your head. As soon as most of you have finished reading the poem, we'll share words you think will help our reading flow better."

✿ When most of your students have finished reading, invite each student to identify a word from the poem. Say, "There are words in this poem you may not have encountered before in your daily reading. Who would like to share a word you believe would help our reading of this poem?" Remind them, "The word needs to be one we haven't seen in other poems." Call on a student to come up to the chart and point to a word: then have him or her read it aloud. Continue calling on students until everyone who would like to share has had a turn. Accept all words, even if the word has been shared already.

✻ Review the words shared by the class members. Inform the class, "Let's see how well I remember the words you shared. When I point to a word somebody shared, I want all of you to read it aloud together. If I forget any words, you can tell me when I've finished."

✻ Invite the class to read the poem aloud with you: "Now that we've identified the words that might cause difficulty, I think we're ready to read the poem together. Please read along with me in one big voice." Read each word aloud as you point to it with the pointer.

✻ When you've finished reading the poem aloud with the class, tell them, "Now I'd like you to listen carefully to the poem, because when I finish reading, I want you to explain in your own words the meaning of this poem."

✻ Read the poem aloud with feeling. Use the pointer to sweep across each line as you read it aloud.

✻ Direct your students' attention to the poem by pointing to the first and last stanzas. Ask your students, "How are these two stanzas the same?" When someone says that the lines repeat in the last stanza, stress, "Not every line repeats." Ask, "Who can identify the words the poet switches?"

✻ Ask your students, "What do the lines 'keep a poem in your pocket and a picture in your head' mean?" Paraphrase a student's thinking by saying, "Poems often create pictures in our minds."

✻ Read the first three lines of the last stanza aloud: "So—'keep a picture in your pocket and a poem in your head.' " Discuss the meaning of these lines by asking, "What do you think this means?" Elaborate upon a reasonable response by saying, "A picture will bring to mind a poem. For example, what poem comes to mind if you see children climbing up a steep hill with their sleds?"

- Invite your students to share poems they've memorized: "Do you have any poems in your heads?" If students respond positively, ask, "Which poem do you know?" Follow with: "I'd love to listen to you recite it if you're willing."

- At the end of the poetry recitations, announce to your students, "It's obvious that poetry is in your hearts as well as in your minds. I hope you'll always have deep pockets filled with favorite poems for sharing, soothing, and remembering."

- For the final reading, call on a capable student to read the poem "Keep a Poem in Your Pocket" to the class.

❧ Reflection ❧

Typically, when I design a lesson, I'm confident it will be successful. But this time I had a few doubts. To add to the challenge, a prospective kindergarten student and her parents were visiting with us that morning. I feared they'd witness a total disaster.

Before the lesson started, I had difficulty deciding which approach would be best to introduce the poem. Each time I read it, my interpretation of the poem's meaning changed. Because of this, I decided to ask open-ended questions so there would be no right or wrong answer. I also wondered whether it was the right time to ask if they had favorite poems in their heads. Last year several children recited their favorite poems during the final days of kindergarten. I knew it was risky to ask so soon, but it would make this poetry experience especially meaningful even if just *one* student had memorized a favorite poem and was willing to recite it.

What transpired during this lesson was beyond my wildest dreams! My students articulated their thoughts about the poem's meaning with great skill and insight. Just listening to their discussion made me realize how much they had learned about poetry this year. And the visiting parents were impressed with my students' knowledge.

More importantly, when I inquired if they had poems in their heads, a flood of different titles poured out of my students. Although most children volunteered to share rhyming poems, what astonished me was that *every* child recited a favorite poem. This memory will be forever ingrained in my heart. Until now, I didn't realize how much they enjoyed the poems I chose for Poetry Time. I still get teary

Every Child a Reader

when I think about their recitations—especially the meaty free-verse poems. For example, MacAllister's superb performance of the poem "My Book" by David Harrison amazed everyone. Likewise, Lucas, who volunteered to recite "January" by Bobbi Katz, performed it with such feeling.

Although Lucas entered kindergarten with a limited knowledge of letters, he loved bringing home his poetry notebook every weekend to read the poems aloud to anyone who would listen. And now he has become a fluent reader as well as a lover of poetry. It's amazing to witness his tremendous growth in literacy, which I believe is a direct result of our word work with poetry.

This lesson validated for me the importance of choosing poems to which young children can make a connection. Their poetry notebooks allow my students to reread poems many times. I believe this continual reading markedly enhances their recall of poems as well as outstanding gains in their reading development.

To think that I had doubts about this lesson . . .

LESSON FOUR

-ead and -ed Phonograms

What I Was Thinking

At the end of each school week, I spend time gathering ideas for potential lessons I can do next. There I sat at a table in the Primary Reading Room deep in thought, studying the words in the poem "Keep a Poem in Your Pocket." No matter how hard I tried, I couldn't think of an appropriate word study.

Ted, my colleague who teaches a combined first- and second-grade class, heard my sighs and came in to see if he could help. I am one teacher who doesn't have trouble accepting help when I'm perplexed. As soon as he saw the words *head* and *bed* in the poem, he suggested I design a word study focused on the two phonograms *-ed* and *-ead*. He thought these particular phonograms were important ones to introduce. Since most of my students no longer decoded words letter by letter, I agreed with him.

However, my next problem involved how to present a word study that would provide adequate practice, when there were only two words in the entire poem with these phonograms. I decided that since my students had total command of rhyming words, I could design a lesson using all the rhyming words I could think of with these two spelling patterns. I knew a game would engage my students, but I needed to design a fast-moving activity to maintain their engagement. When I could come up with only nine -ead words, I thought that by choosing only nine -ed words, the game would not drag on for too long. And if the player had to place the word he or she pulled out of the feely box on the appropriate cut-out pocket, it would increase the level of excitement and cut down the number of turns it would take to complete the game. I just hoped it would work the way I imagined.

Materials

24 3" x 5" cards printed with *bed, fed, led, red, wed, fled, bled, sled, bred, shed, shred, sped, Ted, Ed, Fred, dead, lead, read, spread, dread, tread, head, bread, thread*—one word per card

Nine strips of paper printed with *bed, red, fed, led, fled, sled, shed, shred,* and *sped*

Nine strips of paper printed with *head, lead, read, dead, dread, tread, bread,* and *spread*

A feely box (a plastic peanut butter jar placed inside a tube sock)

One sheet of 12" x 18" red construction paper cut into a large pocket shape

  ✼ At the top of the pocket, print in uppercase letters: *-ED*.

  ✼ Print the numbers one through five along the left edge of the pocket, beginning near the top of the paper pocket. ✼ Print the numbers six through nine approximately seven inches from the left edge. Try to line up the numbers to make them symmetrical.

One sheet of 12" x 18" blue construction paper cut into a large pocket shape

  ✼ At the top of the blue pocket, print in uppercase letters: *-EAD*.

  ✼ Print the numbers one through five along the left edge of the pocket, beginning near the top of the paper pocket.

Every Child a Reader

✴ Print the numbers six through nine approximately seven inches from the left edge. Try to line up the numbers to make them symmetrical.

What This Lesson Looks Like

✴ Read the poem "Keep a Poem in Your Pocket" together.

✴ After the class has finished reading the poem aloud, point to the words *head* and *bed*. Inform your students: "I'd like you to listen carefully as I say these words." Sweep across the word *head* as you say it aloud. Follow the same procedure for the word *bed*. Then ask, "What did you hear?" When someone responds, "They rhyme," point to the words again and say, "Yes, both words do sound the same at the end, but what else do you notice?" If no one responds, explain to your students, "Sometimes rhyming words don't have the same spelling pattern, but they still sound the same. What spelling pattern does the word *head* contain? What about the word *bed*?"

✴ Invite children to think of other words that rhyme with *bed*. When a child names a rhyming word, scan the word cards for that particular word and hold it up for the class to see. Ask, "What's the spelling pattern in this word? Your rhyming word contains . . ." Pause to allow the student to supply the phonogram. After the student identifies the phonogram, remove the card from the set.

✴ If there are words left in the set that were not named, hold up one card at a time for your students to read chorally. After a word has been read aloud, call on a student to identify the phonogram.

✴ Review all words by inviting the class to read them aloud with you.

✴ Tell the class, "We're going to play a game with these particular phonograms. To play, we need to make two teams." Divide the class in half.

✴ Explain the directions for the sorting game. Point to one team as you place the oversized red pocket cutout labeled with *-ed* on the floor next to them. Point to each phonogram in the label as you say, "You're the *e-d* phonogram team." Glance over at the other team as you place the oversized blue pocket cutout labeled with *-ead* on the floor next to them. Then point to each letter in the phonogram as you say, "You're the *e-a-d* phonogram team."

Show the set of paper strips to the class and say, "I've chosen nine words with the *-ed* phonogram and nine words with the *-ead* phonogram for this game. Now, I'll place these strips into the feely box and thoroughly shuffle them. The goal of this game is to collect all nine words containing your team's phonogram before the other team collects their nine words." Continue by saying, "A member of the *-ed* team will choose a strip from the bag, read it aloud, and identify the word's phonogram. If it contains the *-ed* phonogram, he or she may place it next to number one on his or her team's pocket. If it's an *-ead* phonogram, he or she must place it on the *-ead* team's pocket. Then a member of the *-ead* team has a turn to choose a paper strip and follow the same procedure. The game will continue until one team collects all nine words containing their assigned phonogram."

☼ When a team has collected all nine words, invite the members of that team to read their collection of words aloud.

☼ Then pull out the remaining words one at a time to read aloud. Invite different students to place each word onto the appropriate pocket until there are no words left in the feely box.

☼ Invite the team whose pocket was just filled to read their words aloud in one big voice.

☼ Invite the *-ed* team to read the *-ead* words aloud.

☼ Invite the *-ead* team to read the *-ed* words aloud.

❧ Reflection ❧

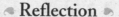

The game was the highlight of the lesson. The children enjoyed the suspense of pulling out a word from the feely box and discovering whether they had to give the word to the other team or keep the word for their own pocket. This rule also helped the children to focus on the spelling pattern of each word.

Although my students preferred playing the game to brainstorming rhyming words, the rhyming activity that preceded the game was worthwhile. They were able to see the different spelling patterns many times. In addition, reading the words aloud reinforced their fluency with this particular spelling pattern. My students persevered during this activity, because they enjoyed seeing the set of cards decrease in size whenever I removed cards printed with words they suggested. No matter how hard they tried to think of all the words, two cards still remained in my hand: *thread* and *shred*. But that didn't matter. I wanted to give my students exposure to these two spelling patterns. And I did just that.

LESSON FIVE

Introduction of New Sight Words

If You Find a Little Feather

If you find a feather,
a little white feather,
a soft and tickly feather,
    it's for you.

A feather is a letter
from a bird,
and it says,
"Think of me.
Do not forget me.
Remember me always.
Remember me forever.
Or remember me
at least
until
the little feather
is lost."

So . . .

. . . if you find a little feather,
a little white feather,
a soft and tickly feather,
    it's for you.
    Pick it up
        and . . .
            put it in your pocket
                —*Beatrice Schenk de Regniers*

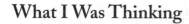

What I Was Thinking

The title "If You Find a Little Feather" immediately attracted my attention. What young child doesn't love finding bird feathers? When I read this poem, its stanzas pulled at my heartstrings. I could just imagine how my students would react when they discovered what a feather symbolizes. Perhaps it would become a class favorite—at least, I hoped it would. I knew I'd never tire of it. And I didn't think my students would either.

Materials

The poem "If You Find a Little Feather" by Beatrice Schenk de Regniers, handwritten on manila tag chart paper in large, neat print and attached by rings to a wooden chart stand

Three 3" x 5" cards printed with the words *always, feather,* and *remember*

What This Lesson Looks Like

✿ Introduce the poem: "Today's poem is called 'If You Find a Little Feather' by Beatrice Schenk de Regniers. How many of you have found a bird's feather lying on the ground?" When students raise their hands, invite them to share their stories. Begin the discussion by asking, "What did you do with the feather after you found it?" When the last student has shared a story, inform the class, "You'll look at a feather differently once you read this poem."

✿ Introduce three new vocabulary words: *always, feather,* and *remember.* Explain: "There are three words I'd like to review before you begin reading. Let's first look at the words that are often repeated in this poem."

• Hold up the card printed with the word *feather*. Provide the class with a clue: "This word is the subject of this poem." Instruct the class: "Tell me the word." Explain to your students: "The word *feather* is repeated nine times in this poem." Invite the class: "Let's be word detectives and find where the word *feather* is located in the poem." Call on a student and say, "Let's see how many times you can find the word *feather* in this poem. Your classmates and I will keep track of the counting. Your job is to locate the word." Then look at the class and say, "You should also look for the word *feather* and remember the word's location in case your classmate overlooks it somewhere in the poem." If this does happen, call on a student who appears to know the location and ask him or her to point it out. When the word *feather* has been identified throughout the poem, invite your class to practice reading it aloud. Instruct your class: "Each time I point to the word *feather*, I'd like you to say it."

- As you hold up the card printed with the word *remember*, cover the first syllable *re-* with your fingers. Explain: "This is a word I noticed inside of this word. It may help you to figure out the word more easily." Ask your class, "Who knows what this says?" If there's no response, tell the class, "It says *member*." Then reveal the first syllable, and ask: "What do the letters *r-e* say?" Remind the class: "The first syllable has the same spelling pattern as the sight words *he, me, she,* and *we*. Spelling patterns help you figure out unknown words." Instruct your class, "Listen as I say these two parts: *re-member*." Then ask, "What's the word?" After your students identify *remember*, direct their attention to the second stanza of the poem: "The poet repeats this word in consecutive lines to elevate the sentimental tone of the poem. Do you see three lines in a row that contain the word *remember*?" Call on a volunteer to identify it in the consecutive lines. Then instruct the student: "Take a look at the word that follows *remember* in each of those lines. What do you notice?" When she or he points out the word *me*, invite the student to read the repetitive phrase in the consecutive lines.

- Say, "Now let's look at the last word." Hold up the card printed with the word *always*. Ask, "What little word do you see inside this word?" If someone mentions the word *a*, explain: "Yes, that *is* a word, but the word *a* doesn't help us to figure out this word. The word that will help us is a three-letter word." When someone identifies the word *way*, say, "Spell *way*." As soon as the student says the letter *w*, cover the first two letters, *a* and *l*. When the spelling of *way* is completed, cover the final letter *s* to reveal just the word *way*. Then show the final letter and ask, "Now what's the word?" As soon as your students call out the word *ways*, cover it up with your fingers. Then reveal the letters *a* and *l*. Say, "You might think this says /ăl/, but it doesn't make sense when you say

Every Child a Reader

the two parts together. Listen: /ăl/ /w?z/. Let's see what word *would* make sense. By reading the line in which it is used, we most likely could figure it out." As you show the word on the card, ask, "Who sees this word in the poem?" Invite a student to locate *always* in the poem. When the student points to it, explain: "Read the line aloud. When you come to this word, pronounce it as /ăl/ /w?z/. By doing this, you'll be able to hear what the word should be." After the student makes sense of the word, invite him or her to read the line again.

✿ Explain the procedure for reading the poem: "Today we'll read and discuss one stanza at a time. The first stanza will tell you the type of feather to find. I'd like you to take a few moments to read the first stanza. As soon as you finish reading it to yourself, please signal me by putting your hands on your head. When most of you finish, we'll talk about what you've read, and then we'll read it aloud together."

✿ As soon as most students have finished reading, check their understanding. Say, "The poet describes the feather in the first stanza." Invite your class to list its distinctive features by asking, "What does this feather look like?" Call on a student to answer. As the student describes the feather, point out words to corroborate the student's description. Prompt your students with different attribute clues if necessary.

✿ Invite the class to read the first stanza with you.

✿ When you finish reading the first stanza aloud with your class, point to the second stanza and say: "This stanza explains why a bird leaves a little white feather behind. It moves me every time I read it. Please take a few minutes to read it silently, and then we'll discuss what the feather represents."

✿ When your students have finished reading, ask them, "Finding a little white feather is like receiving what? What's the bird trying to tell us?"

✿ After your students contribute relevant information, invite a capable student to read: "I'd like you to read this touching passage aloud. Try to evoke as much feeling as you can." Immediately following the student's reading, invite the class to read the second stanza aloud: "Your classmate read with wonderful expression. Now, let's read this stanza aloud with the same kind of feeling."

❈ Point to the last stanza and sweep your pointer down the margin of the first four lines. Then ask, "What do you notice about the words in these lines?" When someone says, "They're the same words as the words in the first stanza," invite them to read the last stanza with you. Say, "Since you know these words, I'd like you to read the last stanza aloud with me."

❈ Invite the class to read the poem chorally: "Please join me in reading this beautiful poem from beginning to end."

❧ Reflection ❧

Certain poems allow us to see ordinary things differently and find significance in them. When children are able to make personal connections with a particular poem, the writing becomes even more memorable, which became readily apparent after my students read "If You Find a Little Feather" by Beatrice Schenk de Regniers.

When we discussed the poem's meaning, all of my students adamantly declared they had never seen a *white* feather. The only ones they had ever collected were gray-and-white seagull feathers found at the beach. Because I loved the sentiment of this poem and wanted my students to love it as much as I did, I knew they had to be able to relate to the poem.

To help them connect with this poem, I dramatically announced how special it was to find a *white* feather, because it brings with it a tender message from the bird. Even though it might be hard to find a white feather, I told them it would be worth their effort. A few days later, Katie ran up to me holding a little white feather in her hand. She exclaimed, "Look, Helene, what I found on my bed this morning: a little white feather from a bird. I don't know how it got there, but I don't really care. All I know is I'm going to keep this special feather forever, because that bird wants me to remember him always. And I will." I chuckled to myself, because I knew exactly where the feather had come from—her down feather pillow. But I wasn't going to spoil the moment. The poem is now instilled in Katie's heart forevermore.

LESSON SIX
Compound Words

What I Was Thinking

Since my students now could recognize small words automatically, compound words would be my next focus. My students had already heard me mention the term *compound words* in previous lessons, but it was time for them to work with this type of word. With compound words, they could practice using the strategy for attacking unknown words by attending to the little words within a bigger word.

I planned to have my students create compound words by giving each of them one word. They'd be responsible for locating a classmate who held a card that would create a compound word if they put the two cards together. Because this interactive lesson had the potential of causing havoc, I recognized that some precautionary steps would be needed to maintain a sense of order (and to preserve my sanity!). Therefore, I planned to implement a highly structured procedure.

Materials

The poem "If You Find a Little Feather" by Beatrice Schenk de Regniers, handwritten on manila tag chart paper in large, neat print and attached by rings to a wooden chart stand

Three 3" x 5" cards printed with the words *for, get,* and *ever*

For a class of 16 students:

16 3" x 5" green cards printed with the words *any, base, book, butter, cow, ear, every, finger, for, in, lip, lunch, snow, star, sun,* and *your* in large, neat print

15 3" x 5" red cards printed with the words *way, ball, mark, fly, boy, ring, where, nail, get, to, stick, box, fish, flower,* and *self* in large, neat print

- ☀ To make the first set of compound words, gather the green cards printed with the words *any, base, book, butter, cow, ear, every,* and *finger,* and the red cards printed with the words *way, ball, mark, fly, boy, ring, where,* and *nail.*

- ☀ To make a second set, gather the remaining green and red cards.

- ☀ Wrap a rubber band around each set of cards.

Note: Depending on the size of your class, you may need a different number of cards. And if you have an odd number of students, it's necessary for you to be an active participant in the activity; you should take a red card to complete a compound word.

What This Lesson Looks Like

☀ Divide the class into three sections: "Today I'm going to divide you into three groups to read the poem 'If You Find a Little Feather.' The first group, or line, will read the first stanza; the middle group, or line, will read the second stanza; and the third group, or line, will read the last stanza." Then invite your students to read their assigned stanzas.

Note: If you have enough space in your teaching area, it works best to have your students sit in three rows across, because the groupings are more distinctive.

☀ Call on a boy and a girl to each take a turn reading this poem aloud.

☀ Introduce the word study by saying, "Today we're going to study compound words." Explain the meaning of the term *compound word*. Ask, "Does anyone remember what a compound word is?" Call on a student who signals you to answer. If nobody knows, say, "A compound word is made up of two words joined together to form a new word."

☀ Demonstrate the process of forming a compound word. Hold up the card printed with *for*. Ask your students, "What's this word?" Then hold up the card printed with *get* and ask, "What does this word say?" Holding the card printed with *for* in your right hand and the card printed with *get* in your left hand, move the two word cards toward each other until they touch. Say, "These two words are now joined together to make a new word. What does this compound word say?" After the word *forget* is named, put down the card printed with *get* and pick up the card printed with *ever*. As you hold up this word card, ask, "What's this word?" Then slide it next to the word *for* and ask, "If this is the word *for* and this is the word *ever*, what new word has been made?" Repeat the word as soon as you hear it identified by saying, "Forever."

☀ Direct your students' attention to the poem, "Who can locate these compound words, *forget* and *forever*, in the second stanza of the poem?"

Look for those students who signal you with their eyes as well as their hands; their eyes are focused on the words, and their hands are raised. Call on one of these students to point out both words. When you hand the pointer to him or her, direct the student, "As you read the first word, please use the pointer to show us where the first word ends and the second word begins. Then read the second word aloud."

✻ Explain the purpose of the interactive activity: "Today you're going to create different compound words by joining two words." Hold up the first set of cards, flip through them, and say, "As you can see, half these cards are green, and the other half are red. It's a special code to help me as well as you. Who thinks they know why I made some red and some green?" If no one remembers what the color code symbolizes, prompt them by saying, "At the beginning of the year, I used the colors of the traffic light to help you understand the beginning, middle, and end of a word. Just as the color green on a traffic light signals you to go, I used the color green to signal the start of the word. What does a *red* light signal you to do?" Then respond, "That's right. A red light does tell you to stop. Just as a red light signals you to stop, I used the color red to signal the end of a word." Then ask, "How would the colors green and red represent a compound word?" Confirm a student's correct response by saying, "You're right. The green cards have words that start specific compound words and the red cards have words that make up the second part of specific compound words." Explain: "Your job will be to create a compound word by joining a green card and a red card to form a real word."

✻ Invite your students to stand up and make a circle. Then say, "Let's hold our neighbors' hands and move back as far as we can until our arms are outstretched as much as they can be without losing hold." As soon as your students' arms are adequately outstretched to provide a sufficient personal space between each student, say, "Please stop moving back." As soon as all students have followed this direction, say, "Please put your hands down to your sides." As you glance around the circle, say, "The circle is now the right size to play our activity."

✻ Explain the procedure for this activity. First, shuffle the first set of cards. Then walk around the circle, handing one card to each student. After you have distributed the cards to your students, direct them: "If you have a *green* card, take a big step back." Then say, "Children who have green cards will move around the circle looking for a red card that would form a compound word. And children who have red cards will remain still in their own personal space holding their cards so that their classmates can see them." Then ask, "How should the children with green cards move around the circle: run or walk?" Follow with: "Why should they walk?" Call on a student who would most likely move too quickly around the circle to explain why. Then ask, "What should you do if you see someone checking a card that you know would form *your* compound word?" Prompt students by asking, "Should you grab it out of your classmate's hands, or should you quietly wait until he or she has finished checking it?" Direct those students with red cards: "Show me how you should hold your cards so that your classmates can see your word." Reposition any card that's difficult to see. Explain: "As soon as a green card and a red card form a compound word, those two children should calmly sit down together, and watch until the activity is finished. Then invite each pair of students to share the compound word they formed." Inform your students: "We'll play the game again with a different set of cards to allow those students who held red cards during the first game to have green cards for the second game, so they'll have a chance to move around the circle, too." Write the names of students who are currently holding red cards on the board. Say, "This list will help me remember who should receive a green card when we play again."

❉ Begin the activity by saying, "Children with green cards may begin moving around the circle." Direct those students: "As you move, look at each red card. Say the word printed on the red card after you say the word printed on your card. When you've created a real compound word, please sit down with your partner."

❉ After every compound word has been identified, invite each pair of students to share the compound word they formed. Call on a pair of students to demonstrate the procedure. Say, "I'd like you to show the class what each pair of students will do when they share their compound word. First, stand before your class. If you have a green card, please stand here [make an X with masking tape]. And if you have a red card, please stand here [make a short horizontal line with masking tape]." When they're correctly placed, explain, "Now, [Name of student], since you're holding the *green* card, say your word first." As soon as the person with the green card says his or her word, say, "[Name of student], since you're holding the *red* card, you'll say your word immediately after your partner finishes speaking." After the student with the red card reads his or her word aloud, say, "Please move your cards together until they touch." Instruct both students: "In one big voice, announce the compound word you've formed." Following the step-by-step procedure, invite the next pair of students: "Now I'd like you to begin the sharing." When they've completed the procedure successfully, call on another pair of students to share their compound word. Continue to call on other pairs until everyone has had a turn to share.

✿ After everyone has taken a turn sharing their compound words, use the second set of cards to play again. Refer to the list to ensure that each of those students receives a green card.

✿ When every compound word has been formed, invite your students to read aloud the new compound words they formed. Follow the same procedure as described above.

❧ Reflection ❧

If someone asked me to rate my first experience with this lesson from zero to ten, I'd give it a nine. Even with the modifications I made to the game, one of my students still became a bit rowdy as he moved around the circle. As soon as he noticed the word he needed in order to form a compound word, he became overly excited. Instead of patiently waiting while another classmate was checking the word, he grabbed the card right out of the classmate's hand. After I spoke to him about his rudeness, I imagined how chaotic it would have been if I had allowed everyone to circulate around the classroom to find the word they needed to form a compound word. I thanked my lucky stars I decided to modify the lesson by having only students with the green cards move around the circle, because it would have driven me crazy to witness such confusion if everyone was searching for a word at the same time. And my students wouldn't have been able to concentrate on the task at hand.

With the exception of that one student, the activity produced the results I desired. However, the next time I use it, I'll demonstrate what students should look like and sound like as they search for the words they need. With this additional management technique, I could then rate the lesson a perfect ten.

Note: The lesson has been revised based on this experience

LESSON SEVEN
Exploring Literary Elements and Sight Words

> **Things to Do If You Are the Rain**
>
> Be gentle.
> Hide the edges of buildings.
> Plip, plop in puddles.
> Tap, tap, tap, against the rooftops.
> Sing your very own song!
> Make the grass green.
> Make the world smell special.
> Race away on a gray cloud.
> Sign your name with a rainbow.
>
> —*Bobbi Katz*

What I Was Thinking

How could I allow the month of April to pass without a poem about rain? Although I wanted to include one, I couldn't find one that would be suitable for a word study until my colleague Ted shared a poem he had read with his first and second graders called "Things to Do If You Are the Rain" by Bobbi Katz. Not only did this poem contain an imaginative message that would provide an opportunity to discuss how poets allow us to look at things in new ways, but it also contained interesting words that we could use to focus our attention on soft *c* and soft *g* words. More importantly, I noticed a few compound words, which would provide an opportunity to reinforce a concept recently introduced. Thanks to a colleague's willingness to share, my search for a purposeful poem was over.

Materials

The poem "Things to Do If You Are the Rain" by Bobbi Katz, handwritten on manila tag chart paper in large, neat print and attached by rings to a wooden chart stand

* Fold up the bottom edge of the chart paper to reveal only the title of the poem; use large paper clips to keep the paper in place.

Four 3" x 5" cards printed with the words *edges, gentle, race,* and *sign*

A double-thick sticky note to cover the word *rain* in the title of the poem.

What This Lesson Looks Like

* Begin the word study by saying, "Before you read this great poem by Bobbi Katz to yourselves, I'd like to discuss some tricky words you'll encounter when you read."

* Explain, "You know that the letters *c* and *g* stand for more than one sound. What two sounds can the letter *c* say?" Call on a student to pronounce the two sounds. Elaborate upon the student's answer by saying, "That's right. In some words, the letter *c* stands for the *soft* sound of *c,* or /s/, while in other words, the letter *c* stands for the *hard* sound of *c,* or /k/." Then ask, "What two sounds can the letter *g* say?" Call on a different student to pronounce the two sounds. Elaborate upon the students' answers by saying, "That's right. The letter *g* in some words can stand for the *hard* sound of *g,* or /g/, and in other words, it stands for the *soft* sound of *g,* or /j/."

* To help your students organize their thinking, first explain, "When the letters *c* and *g* are followed by an *e* or an *i,* the *c* usually says /s/, and the *g* usually says /j/."

* Then discuss the words *race, edges,* and *gentle.*

- Hold up the card printed with the word *race*. Ask, "Who knows this word?" Call on someone who signals you to identify the word. If no one knows the word, say, "This word is *race*." Ask your students, "What letter follows the *c* in the word *race*?" Direct your students: "Listen as I say the sounds in the word *race*: /r/ /?/ /s/." Then ask them, "Does the letter *c* say /k/ or /s/?" When you hear the correct response, point to the letter *e* and say, "The letter *c* says /s/, because *e* follows the *c*."

- Hold up the card printed with the word *edges*. Ask, "Who knows this word?" Call on someone who signals you to identify the word. If no one knows the word, say, "This word is *edges*." Ask your students, "What letter follows the *g* in the word *edges*?" Direct your students: "Listen as I say the sounds in the word *edges*: /?/ /d/ /j/ /?/ /s/." Then ask them, "Does the letter g say /g/ or /j/?" When you hear the correct response, point to the letter *e* and say, "The letter g says /j/, because *e* follows the *g*." Follow the same procedure for the word *gentle* until a student pronounces the /j/ sound. Then ask, "Why does the letter g say /j/ in this word?" Call on a student to explain the rule.

✿ Introduce the sight word *sign*.

- Hold up the card printed with the word *sign*. Inform your students, "This word is a sight word. No matter how hard you try, you can't sound it out. Either you know it or you don't." Then ask, "Who knows this word?" If no one responds, tell your students the word: "This word is *sign*. I'd like you to listen carefully to the sounds you hear in this word. Say it with me: *sign*." Then ask your students, "How many sounds did you hear?" Call on a student to answer. If the student is incorrect, say, "Listen carefully as I say the word slowly. Count each sound you hear: /s/ /?/ /n/." Follow with: "You heard *three* sounds, but this word contains *four* letters. Which letter is silent?" Remind your students, "I see only one vowel in this word. We learned that usually the vowel letter stands for the short sound, but in this word what does the vowel say?" Call on a student to pronounce the vowel sound. Confirm a student's accurate pronunciation by saying,

Every Child a Reader

"Yes, it says /?/." Invite your students: "Because the g is silent and the vowel doesn't say what you'd think it would, you need to take a picture of this word in your mind to help you remember this word." Direct your students: "I'd like you to close your eyes and try to picture the word *sign* in your mind. First, picture these letters: *s-i-g-n.*" Then say, "Keep your eyes closed as we say the letters. Ready?" After they spell the word *sign* with their eyes closed, invite your students: "Let's open our eyes and use our pointy fingers to write the word *sign* on the floor within our own personal space. Say the letters as you write them." After the class has completed the writing exercise, ask, "How do you spell *sign*?"

❀ Shuffle the word cards printed with *race, edges, gentle,* and *sign.* Say, "I'm going to whip around the class to review each of these words. When it's your turn to read, you'll read the word printed on the card I hold up. Each time three words are identified, I'll stop to shuffle the cards so that you won't be able to predict the word you'll get." After the cards have been shuffled a few times, use your pointer to zigzag to the last student in the last row. Say, "I'll start with [name of student] and end with [name of student]. Stay focused, so you'll be ready to read when it's your turn." Then begin the word practice.

❀ Introduce the poem "Things to Do If You Are the Rain": "Today we're going to read a great poem for the month of April. Hmm . . . Are you wondering what I'm talking about? As you can see, I covered an important word in the title. There are several specific clues in this poem to help you figure out the covered word. According to Nancie, 'Poets help us discover and uncover the world.' This poem will help you understand what Nancie means" (Atwell, 2007). Follow with: "Please take a few minutes to read this poem silently. Put your hands on your head to signal me when you've finished reading." Then remove the paper clips to reveal the body of the poem and say, "Please start reading now."

❀ When most of your students have finished reading, point to the covered word and ask, "Based on the clues you got from the poem, what's the subject?" Call on a student to make a prediction. Then ask him or her,

"Which line or lines helped you predict that the poem was about [predicted word]?" After the student points out the line(s), ask the class, "How many agree with [name of student]?" Call on a student who didn't agree and ask, "What do you think this poem is about?" Follow with: "Which line or lines helped you decide it had to be [predicted word]?" After he or she points out the line(s) that provided the best clues, invite the class: "Let's find out the topic of this poem." Remove the sticky note to reveal the word *rain*. Say, "This poem is about the rain."

☀ Read the poem chorally. Say, "Read softly to express a soothing tone. Let's pause at the end of each line to allow time to create a picture in our minds."

☀ After reading the poem aloud, discuss it by referring to Nancie's quote. Ask, "What do you think Nancie means when she says that 'poets help us to discover and uncover our world'?" If necessary, prompt them by saying, "Sometimes we don't really look closely at nature. We take things for granted and don't appreciate the marvels of nature." Then ask, "Which line in this poem gave you an 'aha' moment—the line that made you become more aware of what rain can do?"

☀ Review the term *personification*. Ask, "Who remembers what *personification* means?" If no one responds, write the term on the board and underline the word *person*. Say, "Sometimes poets make nonliving things seem human by having them do things only people can do. It allows us a chance to see the subject in a new way. How does Bobbi Katz make the rain seem like a real person?" Follow with: "Bobbi Katz uses personification in two lines of this poem. Which lines sound like things a person would do?" Call on a student who raises his or her hand and who appears to have his or her eyes focused in the correct location. Say, "[Name of student], please point out one of the lines and read it aloud." Then call on a different student to identify the second line in which personification is used.

☀ End the discussion by asking, "Which line do you like the most? I'd like each of you to take a turn to read your favorite line aloud, and then explain what makes that particular line special. Please use this sentence starter: 'I like'—then read your line—'because _____.' " Remind them: "There's no right or wrong answer. All of us are unique. None of us is the same. It would be a boring world if we all looked the same, sounded the same, and liked the same things. Please don't say what your best friend said if you liked a different line better. I want you to think for yourselves." Then say, "I'll give you a few moments to find your favorite line, so you'll be prepared to read when it's your turn." When your class appears ready, say, "We'll use the same whip-around procedure we used at the beginning of Poetry Time. We'll begin with [name of student] and end with [name of student]." Then say to the student who will begin the exercise: "Please use the sentence starter: 'I like'—then read your line—'because.' And then tell us why that line is your favorite." Initiate the whip-around procedure. When everyone has finished, discuss the results of the exercise. For example, you could identify the one line selected by the majority of your class or discuss an interesting comment made by a student.

✻ Invite a student to close the poetry session by reading the poem aloud: "When we read 'Things to Do If You Are the Rain' together, I enjoyed how [name of student] used a quiet, soothing voice as he or she read. Would you please read it again so that your classmates can hear how you use your voice to get across the peaceful tone of this poem?"

❧ Reflection ❧

Although some children already knew the tricky words in this poem, my students still benefited from the discussion about the rule for the consonant sounds of *c* and *g*. They'll now be able to use this information to decode other words that contain *c* or *g*. I realize my students will need more opportunities to apply the rule before they'll be able to internalize it.

For me, the best part of the lesson was hearing kindergartners share their thoughts about their favorite lines. Ella shocked me by her impressive memory of a term I had briefly introduced at the beginning of the year: *alliteration*. I remember how much she liked saying this word, but I didn't realize Ella understood the term until she shared the line "plip, plop in puddles." The majority of my students chose the last line of the poem as their favorite: "Sign your name with a rainbow." I'll always remember Josie's interpretation of this line. Josie, a deep thinker, thought it meant to always end each day with happiness. When I asked her to explain how she arrived at this conclusion, she said, "When I've finished a paper, the last thing I do is put my name on my paper. And seeing a rainbow in the sky makes me feel happy." Well, her interpretation made perfect sense to me. After all, this activity certainly put a smile on my face.

Every Child a Reader

MAY

LESSON ONE
Highlighting Tricky Words

May

Now children may
   Go out of doors,
Without their coats,
   To candy stores.

The apple branches
   And the pear
May float their blossoms
   Through the air,

And Daddy may
   Get out his hoe
To plant tomatoes
   In a row,

And afterwards,
   May lazily
Look at some baseball
   On TV.
      —John Updike

What I Was Thinking

Because of my students' growing independence as readers, they were ready to brave a new challenge. No more word studies and laborious discussions of sight words were necessary. Because I wanted to nurture their love of poetry, it was time to invite them to simply read poems so that they could discover for themselves how satisfying this experience could be. Through the vivid diction of good poems, language comes alive for my young students. The strong rhythms, the rhyming patterns, the repetition of words and phrases, the enticing sounds of language, and the small, fresh, meaningful stories all engage my students. And they can make connections between poetry and the world around them. I planned to start this new adventure with John Updike's poem "May" because the vocabulary is relatively easy, my students would be able to relate to the events in this poem, and I thought they'd enjoy the wordplay.

Materials

The poem "May" by John Updike, handwritten on manila tag chart paper in large, neat print and attached by rings to a wooden chart stand

What This Lesson Looks Like

* Introduce the poem "May" by inviting your students to read the title. Then ask your students to make predictions: "What do you think this poem is about?"

* Instruct your students: "Take a few minutes to read this poem silently. When you read this poem, you'll notice that the author, John Updike, repeats a certain word in each stanza. Be ready to tell me what it is. I'd like you to think about why he uses this particular word. Please put your hands on top of your heads to signal me when you've finished reading."

* Observe your students as they read silently. Take note of their reading behaviors (e.g., subvocalizes, sustains reading, gives up easily, distracts easily, demonstrates automatic word recognition, uses letter-sound cues and patterns, or self-corrects for meaning).

* When your students have finished reading the poem silently, invite them: "I'd like you to point out a tricky word you encountered in this poem and explain how you figured it out. It'll help everyone's reading become smoother, and you'll be helping a classmate who couldn't figure out the word that you solved." Follow with: "Who would like to share a tricky word?"

* Review the words identified by your students: "Let's read all the words that

were shared. If I miss any, please raise your hand at the end of the exercise to help me." Then point to each of the words with your pointer.

☀ Invite your students to read the poem aloud: "Now that you've had an opportunity to read the poem silently, I'd like you to read it aloud. Poetry is meant to be read aloud so that you can hear the appealing sounds of language. Because I'd like you to listen for connections between sound and meaning, we'll alternate turns between the girls and the boys." Use your pointer to draw an imaginary vertical line from the beginning of the first line to the beginning of the last line of the first stanza, and then repeat the action for the second stanza as you say, "The girls will read the first stanza; then the boys will read the second stanza. Who's going to read the third stanza?" Confirm the answer by repeating what was said: "That's right! The third stanza will be read by the girls." Use your pointer to indicate the lines of the last stanza as you ask, "Who will read this stanza?" Follow with: "What kind of reading pattern will we be creating?" If someone identifies it as a girl-boy pattern, justify his or her answer by saying, "It *is* a girl-boy pattern, but it also can be described as an *AB* pattern." Before beginning to read, ask, "Any questions?"

☀ Invite your students to read the poem aloud, "Girls, you're going to begin the reading. Please start by reading the title aloud, as well as the first stanza. Boys, follow along with your eyes so you'll know when to take your turn." Point to the title with your pointer as you request: "Girls, will you please start reading?"

☀ After your students have finished reading, ask them, "What word is repeated in each stanza?" Call on a student who signals that he or she can identify it. If the student is correct, invite him or her: "Please show us the word *may* in each of the stanzas."

☀ Discuss the meaning of the word *may*: "What does the word *may* mean in the title?" Direct your students: "Listen as I read aloud the lines that contain the word *may*. Let's see how the poet, John Updike, uses the word *may* in the body of the poem." After reading each line, ask, "What does the word *may* mean in each of the stanzas?"

✸ Explain, "As you can see, the word *may* has more than one meaning. The word *may* means *might*, and it's also the fifth month of the year." Then ask: "Why do you think John Updike chose to use the word *may* instead of the word *might*?"

✸ Discuss the events that were mentioned in the poem. Repeat each event as it's mentioned, and add: ". . . *may* happen, but it's not a certainty it would happen." After identifying the examples from the poem, ask your students, "What are some other things that *might* happen in May?"

✸ End the session with a shared reading of the poem.

◂ Reflection ▸

When I announced that word studies were no longer necessary because each one of my students now possessed the skills needed to read independently, my students' reactions were priceless. Several students high-fived each other, others clapped loudly, and everyone grinned broadly. They were not only relieved to be finished with word studies, but they were also proud of their achievement—especially Nolan.

Let me tell you a bit about Nolan. Ever since his parents told me during our first conference how uncomfortable Nolan felt during the poetry block, my mission had become to help him feel more at ease by building his self-confidence whenever I could. My plan was to wait until he signaled me that he wanted to participate in an independent reading. At first, he never volunteered, but gradually, over time, he raised his hand more frequently to read aloud on his own. When he offered to read aloud, he'd always be my first choice because I wanted him to realize his capabilities as a reader. Now he's a confident and skilled reader who eagerly volunteers to read every new poem aloud. I'm proud of all my students, but especially Nolan, because he never gave up.

Today's poetry session was extraordinary. Although I try to help my students feel at ease in our learning environment, in the past I've sensed a bit of tension because of students like Nolan who felt overwhelmed by their classmates' progress. I always felt their anxiety. But today, the atmosphere in the classroom was tranquil. I watched relaxed students savor the pleasure of reading a poem independently; they read it aloud with fluency. Then they enthusiastically participated in a great discussion about it. The deep satisfaction I felt made me recognize again the value of teaching.

Every Child a Reader

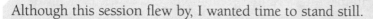

Although this session flew by, I wanted time to stand still.

Note: If your students require additional practice to increase their reading skills, an introduction of the two sounds of *ow* would be an appropriate word study to use with this poem.

LESSON TWO

Highlighting Tricky Words and Using Context Clues

To My Mother on Her Day

Preheat oven to a 78° May day.
Start with one beach of sparkling white sand.
Add a dash of salty air,
one bay of calm saltwater,
a half cup of brown seaweed,
one bucket overflowing with seashells and love,
one mother,
and one child.
Mix together gently
with a sprinkle of laughter
and a dash of ever-loving tenderness.
Serve in a bowl of happiness.

—*James Morrill*

What I Was Thinking

When I mentioned to Nancie that I hadn't been able to find a suitable Mother's Day poem, she suggested I look through her folder of poems written by former students as gifts for their moms. After spending some time browsing through the collection, I didn't think I'd find one my students would be able to identify with, because the topics were too mature. I was ready to give up when I spotted "To My Mother on Her Day" by James Morrill. Everything about this poem appealed to me: the length, the vocabulary, and the theme. But what caught my eye was the format Jimmy chose for his poem to his mother: a recipe. Because my kindergartners participate in weekly cooking activities, they'd easily understand and appreciate the setup for this loving poem.

Materials

The poem "To My Mother on Her Day" by James Morrill, handwritten on manila tag chart paper in large, neat print and attached by rings to a wooden chart stand

What This Lesson Looks Like

* Introduce the poem "To My Mother on Her Day": "This poem was written by James Morrill when he was a seventh grader at CTL. He wrote this poem as a present for his mom to honor her on Mother's Day. Because I'm a mom, I instantly connected with this poem. Its message allowed me to relive a special time I shared with my own children. As a child, I bet many of you also will be able to relate to the special place Jimmy and his mom both loved."

* Briefly review the tricky words: *calm, child, serve,* and *laughter.* Say, "Before you read on your own, I'd like to review some tricky words I discovered in this poem. When I point to a word with my pointer, I'd like you to read it aloud in one big voice. Let's see how many words you know by sight." If no one can identify a particular word, invite your class to read the word in context to provide a clue, "Let's read the line aloud that contains this word. When we come to the word, we'll say the beginning sound of the unknown word. That may help you think of what word makes sense."

✤ After the short review, invite your students to read the poem silently.

✤ When your students have finished reading the poem, ask them, "How is this poem different from all the other poems we've read?" If necessary, be more specific and ask, "What form did the poet use for his poem?" When someone mentions the words are arranged like a recipe, direct your students' attention back to the poem, and explain: "The first stanza contains the ingredients needed and the second stanza explains what to do." Follow with: "Why is a recipe format so fitting for this poem?"

✤ Then invite your students to read the poem aloud in one big voice. Say: "Let's read this recipe in two groups. The girls will read the list of ingredients and the boys will read the procedure." Then ask, "What do I really mean?" Call on a student to interpret your directions. After the student answers, confirm the student's explanation: "The girls will read the first stanza, and the boys will read the second stanza. Then we'll read the poem again. But this next time, the boys will read the first stanza, and the girls will read the last stanza."

✤ To check their understanding of the poem, ask your students the following questions:

- What place is the poet describing?

- What is the obvious feeling in the poem?

- What words does he use to convey this feeling? (As a student suggests a word, point it out in the poem.)

- What words did you especially like? (As a student suggests a word, point it out in the poem.)

✤ Invite your students to describe a special personal time they've shared with their own mothers. Ask, "How many of you love spending time at the beach with Mom? What makes this experience special?" To invite other children to participate in the discussion, ask, "Can you think of something else you do with your mom that's special to you?

✤ For the final reading, invite your students to read the poem chorally.

❧ Reflection ❧

When I read this poem, I recalled days long passed when my children were young and how the beach became our second home. Since we live on the coast of Maine, I assumed my students also would have spent many leisurely summer days at the beach. But this lesson taught me never to assume anything. I discovered that very few children had spent much time at the beach. At first, this disclosure surprised me, but then I realized most of my students' moms work outside of the home. These children spent their summer days either at day care or at a summer camp.

Because I loved this poem and wanted my students to like it, too, it was necessary for them to understand the poet's feelings and not get distracted by the setting of the poem. To achieve this, I invited them to think of a special time they spent exclusively with Mom. As soon as I said that, hands flew in the air. Many students shared their personal stories with a lot of heart. It was easy to sense the strength of their love. This discussion allowed my students not only to identify with the poet's feelings more easily, but also to like the poem almost as much as I did.

Note: If your students require additional practice to strengthen their reading skills, a review of compound words would be an appropriate word study to use with this poem.

Every Child a Reader

LESSON THREE
Linking Reading to a Science Project

The Seed

How does it know,
this little seed,
if it is to grow
to a flower
or weed,
if it is to be
a vine or shoot,
or grow to a tree
with a long deep root?
A seed is so small,
where do you suppose
it stores up all
of the things it knows?

—*Aileen Fisher*

What I Was Thinking

Learning becomes more meaningful to my students when I can integrate different subjects into a lesson. Since I was beginning a study of plants in science, I wanted to find a suitable poem to introduce this new unit. During my search I discovered numerous poems about the subject, but none of them stood out until I came upon "The Seed" by Aileen Fisher. Although my students would find this poem an easy read, I hoped it would jump-start our new science unit with a bang. It definitely should arouse my students' curiosity about the marvels of nature.

Materials

The poem "The Seed" by Aileen Fisher, handwritten on manila tag chart paper in large, neat print and attached by rings to a wooden chart stand

✤ Fold up the bottom edge of the chart paper to reveal only the title of the poem; use large paper clips to hold the paper in place.

A plastic container with a variety of flower, vegetable, and fruit seeds: one or two packages of each type of seed

Chart paper and a marker

What This Lesson Looks Like

✤ Introduce the poem: "Because May begins the gardening season, I found another wonderful poem by Aileen Fisher for us to read aloud called [point to the title of the poem] 'The Seed.' It's a perfect poem to launch our study of plants." Then ask, "What kinds of plants do people grow from seeds?" List the different types of plants your students suggest on the chart paper.

✤ Explain the procedure for distributing the seeds to your students, "I have a collection of different kinds of seeds in this container. I'd like you to take one seed that interests you. Please be considerate of your classmates. Don't take too long to decide since other children are waiting for their turn."

✤ Following the distribution of the seeds, invite your students to study their seeds. Then ask, "If you planted the seed that you selected, what would you wonder about?" Prompt them by supplying the first question, "Do you wonder what kind of seed you've chosen? Is it a fruit or a vegetable or a flower?" Follow with, "What are some other questions that come to mind as you examine your seed?" List your students' questions on the chart paper.

✤ Invite your students to read the poem aloud by explaining, "In this poem, Aileen Fisher also wonders about a seed she holds in her hand. Let's read this poem together to find out about her wonderings." Then ask, "What happens to our voices when we read a question?" When your students mention that your voice sounds higher at the end of the sentence, follow with: "This poem contains two questions. Be sure to look ahead to the end of the sentence to identify the punctuation mark, so that you'll be able to express the sentence just right." Then remove the paper clips from the sides of the chart paper to reveal the body of the poem.

☀ Read the poem chorally using an inquisitive tone.

☀ After the shared reading of the poem, begin the discussion by asking, "What was the poet curious about?"

☀ Invite a student who read the poem expressively to read it aloud to the class.

☀ After the student finishes, say, "To see if some of our questions can be answered, let's plant our seeds to discover each seed's magic." (Planting and caring for the seeds may be an activity in the science unit.)

❧ Reflection ❧

When I introduced this poem last year, it flopped miserably. After reading the poem, I initiated a discussion about the magic of seeds, but my students couldn't understand Fisher's sense of wonder, primarily because they didn't know much about seeds except for apple, sunflower, and pumpkin seeds.

However, I still thought it was a great poem to use at the start of my science unit. I knew I needed to change the format of the lesson if I was going to use this poem again with another class. After much thought, I decided that a hands-on experience (i.e., examining and then planting their own seeds) might help my students start wondering about the mystery of nature.

Distributing seeds prior to the reading of the poem sparked the sense of wonder that was missing the year before. One child after another shared their personal wonderings with the class. I heard children say, "I wonder if my seed will grow into a beautiful flower," "I wonder how tall my plant will be," "I wonder if my plant will have a lot of leaves," "I wonder how long it'll be before it'll pop up," and, my favorite one of all, "I wonder if my seed will grow at all!" Discussing their wonderings prior to the reading of the poem helped my students to better understand the poet's sense of wonder. And now the poem had meaning for them.

Note: If your students require additional practice to increase their reading skills, a review of high-frequency words would be an appropriate word study to use with this poem.

LESSON FOUR

More Tricky Words

Springburst

Flower!
the
slowly   slowly
the petal curling
the bud,
awakening,
Oh, the
up!
straight
I know!
Now
hm.
see.   hm   see
me   Hm   me
Let   Let
higher.
must reach
for the sky—
Now, must reach
I be!
I live!
up
tip
warmth
coolness
water,
food and
life growing,
life, being,
in the dark—
(seed style)
Spark
A

—*John Travers Moore*

Every Child a Reader

What I Was Thinking

When I introduced "Springburst" at a CTL Morning Meeting, the students from all grade levels—kindergarten through eighth grade—enthusiastically participated in the shared reading of this poem. But because I noticed many of my kindergartners had a difficult time maintaining the same reading pace as their older CTL peers, I wanted to bring it back to my classroom for just my kindergartners to read, so that they could experience the same depth of feeling as the older kids. In addition, "Springburst" is a perfect poem to follow "The Seed." Since this poem speaks from the heart, my students could deeply experience the wonder of nature. And they'd also learn about a plant's stages of growth. Double the pleasure, double the fun!

Materials

The poem "Springburst" by John Travers Moore, handwritten on manila tag chart paper in large, neat print and attached by rings to a wooden chart stand

What This Lesson Looks Like

✿ Introduce "Springburst" by discussing the poetic form. Invite students to look at the way in which the poet arranged the words: "What shape do you see?" Follow with: "So what do you think is the subject of this poem?" When someone mentions a flower, elaborate on the student's response by saying, "When a poet arranges the words in a shape related to the subject of the poem, he has written a *concrete* poem."

✿ Point out some potentially troublesome words in the poem: *straight, warm, style, awakening*. Invite your students: "I'd like to review some tricky words before we read this poem aloud. If you know the word I point to, please say it clearly so that your classmates can make sense of it." After each word is identified, discuss the special sound feature(s) of each word (e.g., the silent *gh* sound in *straight*, the /or/ sound in *warm*, and the little word *wake* and the chunk *ing* in the word *awakening*).

✿ Introduce the poem by saying, "The poet speaks in the voice of the subject, a flower, and expresses a moving account of a flower's awakening."

✿ Invite your students to read the poem aloud with you. Say, "As you read this poem, imagine yourself as a seed that has just burst open and is beginning to grow. How would you react if this were happening to you?" Follow with: "Make the poem become alive by reading it from your heart."

☀ Following the reading, ask, "What's the poet's purpose for starting the poem at the bottom and ending at the top?" Direct the students: "Find a line that gives us some information about the growth of a plant and read it aloud."

☀ After the discussion, invite the class: "For fun, let's read it from the top to the bottom of the page to see how it sounds. Do you think it'll make sense?" Then read it aloud with your class. As your students read, take note of their word-recognition skills. Is their reading automatic or is it hesitant? Which words cause difficulty?

❧ Reflection ❧

When my students noticed the poem "Springburst" displayed on my chart stand awaiting us, I heard several quiet *oohs* and *yays*. If only every lesson could be greeted with such a positive reaction, how easy my job would be! Throughout the entire lesson, my students' enthusiasm never wavered. They read with such heart that I knew they had comprehended the depth of the flower's feelings with its magical development from a seed. And how they loved reading the poem from the top to the bottom. Not only did my kindergartners enjoy the opportunity to read lines that made no sense, they also delighted in the fact that I would invite such silliness.

When it was time for someone to read the poem independently, everyone wanted an opportunity to read it aloud the wrong way. Although I didn't have time to honor every student's request on this particular day, I did promise that all of them would eventually get a turn. Because of my students' exuberant participation, it was obvious that this poem would be requested often as an old favorite. I didn't care how many times we read it, because I enjoyed listening to my students reading so fluidly and seamlessly. Knowing that they appreciated poetry made the experience even more enjoyable.

Note: If your students require additional practice to increase their reading skills, a review of *ow* sounds would be an appropriate word study to use with this poem.

Every Child a Reader

JUNE

LESSON ONE

Highlighting <u>oo</u> and Tricky Words

Cow

I approve of June
Fresh food to chew
         and chew
         and chew
Lots of room to move around
         or lie down
Not too hot
Not too cold
Not too wet
Not too dry
A good roof of sky over me and my calf
Who's now halfway up
         on new legs
He'll want a meal real soon
Yes, I approve of June

                    —*Marilyn Singer*

What I Was Thinking

It's a fact: my students and I work hard each and every day of the school year because I try to make use of every moment to maximize their learning potential. As a result of this joyful intensity, my students and I are ready for a break from the rigors of learning by the beginning of June. And since they now possess the skills necessary to be productive and competent first-grade learners, I don't need to push so hard; it's time to be playful.

When I first noticed this poem, I didn't think it was suitable for my students because the words were too simple. However, the moment I read it aloud, I realized its value. It would be the perfect vehicle to explore the music of language by hearing the song in the words. I'd have my students identify the words Marilyn Singer deliberately chose for this poem to develop the subject. And since children love animals and enjoy imitating animal sounds, I knew they'd love exaggerating the *oo* sounds of the different words in the poem to sound like a cow. It was a toss-up who would enjoy this poem more—my students or I. One thing was certain: we'd have fun performing it.

Materials

The poem "Cow" by Marilyn Singer, handwritten on manila tag chart paper in large, neat print and attached by rings to a wooden chart stand

A strip of construction paper to cover the title

Highlighting tape

What This Lesson Looks Like

✴ Introduce the poem to your students: "The poem we're going to read today is a persona [write the word on the white board] poem. There's a word inside the word *persona* that helps you figure out the meaning of the word. Do you see a word inside the word *persona*?" Validate any other words (e.g., *a, on,* and *son*) your students notice. Say, "You're right. The word [name of identified word] is inside *persona*, but that doesn't help us understand the meaning of the word." Prompt them if no one notices the word *person*. Say, "This word starts with the letter *p* and ends with the letter *n*." When someone correctly responds, underline the word *person* as you explain, "In a persona poem, the poet speaks in the voice of the subject. I've covered the title, because it's the subject of this poem. And I want you to use clues from the poem to identify the persona."

✴ Point out the tricky words: *approve, move, calf,* and *half.* Invite your students: "I'd like to review some tricky words before we read this poem aloud. If you know the word I point to, please say it clearly so that your classmates can make sense of it." After each pair of rhyming words is identified, point out the spelling patterns of each word (e.g., the *-ove* spelling pattern in *approve* and *move,* and the *-alf* spelling pattern in *calf* and *half*).

☀ Read the poem chorally.

☀ After the shared reading of the poem, ask your students, "What's the subject of this poem?" Call on a student to make a prediction. If the student is correct, ask, "Which line helped you know it was a cow?" Then ask, "Does someone have a different prediction?" Invite that student to share his or her reasoning for making the prediction: "Why do you think it's a [predicted word]?" Follow the same procedure for any student who has a different prediction.

☀ Point to the title of the poem. When there are no more predictions, say, "Now I'll let you see the beginning letter of the title." Reveal the first letter. Then ask, "Could it be a cow?" Call on a student to explain why. Then ask the student, "Would you please sound out the word *cow,* and write the sounds you hear in the word *cow* on the strip of paper?" After he or she spells the word *cow,* invite him or her to remove the paper strip.

☀ When the subject of the poem is revealed, explain, "The poet's choice of words also provides a clue." Then ask, "What vowel sound did you hear frequently throughout this poem?" If no one is able to identify the sound, read the poem again, exaggerating the */oo/* sound. Following your exaggerated reading, ask, "What sound did you hear?" Call on a student to identify the sound. Confirm the student's accurate response and then elaborate on the answer by saying, "Yes, Marilyn Singer deliberately chose words containing the */oo/* sound. Why do you think she chose these words?" When someone says the */oo/* sound reminds the reader of the sound a cow makes—moo—then elaborate: "You're right. The poet wants the person to sound like a cow."

☀ Invite students to identify all the words that contain the */oo/* vowel sound; mark each one with highlighting tape. Ask, "Which words contain the */oo/* sound in this poem?" Direct your students: "If you can identify one of these words, please raise your hand." Call on a student and ask, "What word says */oo/* in this poem?" If the student identifies one, highlight it each time it appears. Continue calling on different students until all /oo/ words have been identified and highlighted: *approve, June, food, chew, room, move, too, roof, who's, new,* and *soon.*

☀ Invite your students: "Let's practice stretching out the /oo/ to sound like a cow speaking. When I point to one of the highlighted words, stretch out the vowel sound." Then point to each highlighted word.

☀ Read the poem again with your students, exaggerating the /oo/ sounds as you read. Say, "I highlighted the /oo/ words to help you to quickly identify the appropriate ones to exaggerate. I'll point to each word as we read to help keep a steady pace to our reading." Direct your students: "Let's practice reading the first two lines. When you see the pointer move to the next word, you should move on to the next word so that we can read in one big voice." When your students read the first two lines well, say, "That's music to my ears. I think we're ready to read this playful poem. Let's start from the beginning of the poem." Point to the title and start reading with your students.

❧ Reflection ❧

When we first read the poem aloud, my students didn't hear the playful language. When I read it again and exaggerated the *oo* sounds, they immediately understood the poet's intent, and couldn't wait to perform it so that they, too, could exaggerate the *oo* sounds. But this reading didn't go smoothly. Even with the aid of my pointer, I had difficulty getting my class to read in one big voice. Some students got caught up in exaggerating the *oo* sound and prolonged it while others tried to maintain a steady pace. At one point, I had to stop and remind those students who continued to overly exaggerate the sound to pay attention to the pointer. Because of this problem, the next time we read this poem I'll take time to practice a few lines with my students, until they are able to maintain a steady pace. Then the shared reading will be a pleasurable experience for all of us.

Note: This lesson has been revised based on this experience. If your students require additional practice to strengthen their reading skills, sorting words with /oo/ sounds would be an appropriate word study to use with this poem.

Every Child a Reader

LESSON TWO

Voice Emphasis and Highlighting Tricky Words

A Swing Song

Swing, swing
        Sing, sing,
Here! my throne and I am king!
        Swing, sing
        Swing, sing
Farewell, earth, for I'm on the wing!
        Low high,
        Here I fly,
Like a bird through sunny sky;
        Free, free,
        Over the lea,
Over the mountain, over the sea!
        Up, down,
        Up and down,
Which is the way to London Town?
        Where? Where?
        Up in the air,
Close your eyes and now you are there!
        Soon, soon,
        Afternoon,
Over the sunset, over the moon!
        Far, far,
        Over all bar,
Sweeping on from star to star!
        No, no
        Low, low
Sweeping daisies with my toe.
        Slow, slow,
        To and fro,
Slow—slow—slow—slow.

—William Allingham

What I Was Thinking

Since poetry can create an enthusiasm for reading, I continually search for poems that will produce a positive response from my students. When I found "A Swing Song," I knew my students would appreciate its rhythm and rhyme. Without a doubt, they would read this poem with tremendous spirit.

This poem brought back memories of my favorite outdoor pastime when I was a child: I spent many summer days swinging on the playground. Because the strong rhythm of this poem simulates the back-and-forth motion of a swing, I felt like I was once again swinging high into the sky. If I felt the motion of the lines, I knew my students would feel it even more, because they're out on the swingsets every day at recess. And because I knew in no time that this poem would become part of them, I also visualized some of my students singing its words as they swung high into the sky on warm summer days.

Materials

The poem "A Swing Song" by William Allingham, handwritten on manila tag chart paper in large, neat print and attached by rings to a wooden chart stand

What This Lesson Looks Like

☼ Invite your students to read the title aloud with you. Point to the title as you say, "Today we'll read . . ." Then read the title with your students. Explain: "Because I want you to experience this poem without my influences, we'll talk about this poem *after* you've had a chance to read it on your own."

☼ Instruct your students: "Please take a few minutes to read it. Because it's fairly long, I had to use two pieces of chart paper to copy all the lines of this poem. When you've finished the first page, signal me by putting your hands on top of your head. As soon as I notice that most of you are ready, I'll turn the page." Then say, "Please begin reading silently."

☼ When several students have placed their hands on their heads, say, "Thank you for signaling me that you've finished. You may now take your hands off your head, because I know who hasn't finished. Please wait calmly while your classmates finish reading." Say to those students who continue to

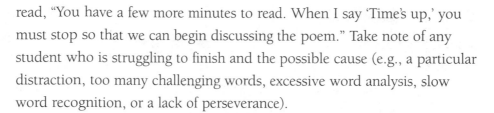

read, "You have a few more minutes to read. When I say 'Time's up,' you must stop so that we can begin discussing the poem." Take note of any student who is struggling to finish and the possible cause (e.g., a particular distraction, too many challenging words, excessive word analysis, slow word recognition, or a lack of perseverance).

✻ After your students have finished reading, invite them to share difficult words they encountered in the poem, "I'd like you to point out a tricky word you encountered in this poem and explain how you figured it out. It'll help everyone's reading become smoother, and you'll be helping a classmate who couldn't figure out the word that you solved." Follow with: "Who would like to share a tricky word?" Point out the words *earth, mountain, London,* and *eyes* if they weren't already shared. For each of these words, ask your students, "Who knows this word?" Call on a student who signals that he or she knows the word. After the word is correctly identified, ask that student, "What makes this word tricky?" Follow with: "If you didn't know this word, what strategy would you use to figure it out?"

✻ Discuss the meaning of the word *lea*. Point to *lea* as you ask, "What does this word say?" Say, "To help you understand the meaning of the word *lea*, I'll read two lines from the poem." Then read the lines "over the lea" and "over the mountain, over the sea." Ask, "Does anyone know what the word *lea* means?" Explain the meaning if no one is able to make an accurate guess from the context. Say, "A *lea* is a meadow or a pasture."

✻ Review the words identified by your students. Say, "Let's read all the words that were shared. If I miss any, please raise your hand at the end of the exercise to help me." Then point to each of the words with your pointer.

✻ Invite your students to read the poem aloud: "Now that you've had an opportunity to read the poem silently, I'd like you to read it aloud so that you can hear the strong rhythm. Because I want you to listen for connections between the rhythm and meaning, we'll alternate turns between the boys and the girls." Sweep across the first three lines of the poem as you say, "The boys will read the short lines and the girls will read the long lines." Sweep across any short line, and ask, "Who's going to read this line?" Confirm the answer by repeating what was said: "That's right!

The boys will read this line because it's a *short* line." Then sweep across any long line, and ask, "Who will read this line?" Again, confirm the answer by repeating what was said: "Yes, since this line is *long*, the girls will read it."

✹ Discuss the reading pattern. As you sweep across the first several lines of the poem in consecutive order, say, "Short, short, long. Short, short, long. This pattern for reading aloud is different from the one we used in previous lessons. What kind of reading pattern will we be creating?" If a student responds it's a *boy, boy, girl* pattern, say, "You're right! It is a *boy, boy, girl* pattern." Then ask, "How else could this pattern be described?" When someone says it's an *AAB* pattern, confirm the accuracy of the student's answer. Sweep across the first three lines as you explain the process, and say, "The boys will read *two* short lines and the girls will read *one* long line." Continue to sweep across the fourth and fifth lines as you say, "Then the boys will read *two* more lines." Sweep across the next line, and ask, "Who will read this short line?" Before beginning to read, ask, "Any questions?" Say, "Let's read the title together, and then the boys will begin the poem. Ready?" Point to the title to begin the reading.

✹ After the shared reading, ask, "How does this poem make you feel?" Follow with: "Where are you? What are you doing?" If no one responds, ask, "Didn't you feel like you were on a swing pumping hard in order to fly high into the air? The rhythm of this poem makes you feel like you're on a swing."

✹ Direct your students' attention to the length of the lines in the poem. Say, "The poet intentionally set up the lines of his poem to give you the sense of swinging on a swing." Ask, "What do you think the short lines are imitating?" If necessary, prompt them by asking, "What do you do to start your swing moving? When you start pumping, your swing moves a little." Then ask, "What do you think the long lines are like?" If necessary, prompt them by asking, "When you get your swing moving, how does this motion compare to the long lines?"

✹ Invite your students to share their stories about swinging: "Do you pump your legs to get your swing going or do you get pushed by a friend?"

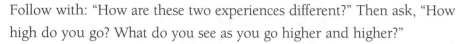
Follow with: "How are these two experiences different?" Then ask, "How high do you go? What do you see as you go higher and higher?"

☀ Read the poem chorally. Invite your students: "Let's pretend we're on a swing as we read this poem aloud." Direct your students: "Sway your body forward and back to the rhythm of the poem as you read it aloud. Watch me." Demonstrate the action as you read the first three lines of the poem. After your demonstration, ask, "Did I keep the beat with my body?" Then invite your students: "I'd like you to practice swaying your bodies as I read a few lines aloud." Emphasize to your students: "Just focus your effort on keeping a steady beat with your bodies. I'll do the reading." When your students demonstrate their ability to maintain a steady beat, say, "Now let's read *and* sway at the same time." Follow with: "Are you ready to sing your song as you swing? Let's try it."

❧ Reflection ❧

My kindergartners *loved* this poem. They belted out the words when they participated in the first group reading. And they interpreted the swinging and pushing motions beautifully by varying the speed of the words and phrases. Although they especially enjoyed their kinesthetic experience, for me it was frustrating to watch because some children had difficulty doing two things at the same time. When they focused on the rhythm, they didn't participate in the reading. And when I instructed them to read a bit louder, they were unable to synchronize their movements with their classmates. However, I knew I shouldn't be concerned with this, because they'd improve with practice. I reminded myself that my students did accomplish the goals of this lesson: to demonstrate proper rhythm and emphasis (e.g., varying the rate, pitch, and volume of their voices). And they performed these skills with expertise. Bravo!

Note: If your students require additional practice to strengthen their reading skills, a review of rhyming words (words that have the same spelling pattern vs. words that sound the same but have different spelling patterns) would be an appropriate word study to use with this poem.

LESSON THREE
Highlighting Tricky Words

> ### June
>
> June is
> > when your math book
>
> is completely lopsided:
> > > the pile of unfinished pages on the right
> > > is
> > > skinny
>
> but you need to use your left hand to hold down
> all the stuff you've already learned.
> > > And
> > > > June is
> > > > when the gentlest rustle
> > > > > of a leaf outside the window
>
> can drown out your teacher's voice
> > > and
>
> every word on the spelling test spells:
> S-U-M-M-E-R V-A-C-A-T-I-O-N!
>
> > > > > > —*Bobbi Katz*

What I Was Thinking

Believe it or not, I dread the arrival of June. Since my students know that the end of school is near, I no longer can relax and trust that our days will be smooth and productive, with every student enthusiastically immersed in schoolwork. My students are ready for school to end, ready to spend their days engaged in the joyful activity of play. Consequently, I can easily relate to Bobbi Katz's poem entitled "June."

Using this poem during the final days of school seemed fitting since it would not only celebrate summer vacation, but also all the learning my students had accomplished during the school year. However, I wondered how they would react

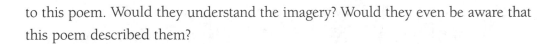

to this poem. Would they understand the imagery? Would they even be aware that this poem described them?

Materials

The poem "June" by Bobbi Katz, handwritten on manila tag chart paper in large, neat print and attached by rings to a wooden chart stand

☼ Fold up the bottom edge of the chart paper to reveal only the title of the poem; use large paper clips to keep the paper in place.

Class set of names on popsicle sticks

What This Lesson Looks Like

☼ Introduce the poem by saying, "The poet, Bobbi Katz, has written a list poem about a special occurrence that happens in this month." Point to the title and ask, "What's the name of the month?"

☼ Invite your students to make predictions: "What do you think the poem will be about?" Follow with: "What kinds of special things happen in the month of June?" After your students have shared their ideas, provide a clue by saying, "The speaker of this poem is a student like you. What do you think a student would be thinking about in the month of June?" Accept all responses, and then say, "Let's see if someone hit it on the nose." Invite your students to read the poem by instructing them: "Please read this poem silently to find out the answer. When you finish, keep your lips zipped. Allow your classmates time to find out the answer for themselves. Don't ruin the surprise!" Then remove the paper clips from the sides of the chart paper and say, "You may begin reading."

☼ When everyone's finished reading, ask, "What's the only thing on the speaker's mind?" Call on a capable student to respond. Direct your students' attention to the last line in the poem, and invite them: "Let's say the names of these letters together." Then ask, "What did you spell?"

☼ Invite your students to identify new words they encountered in the poem. Say: "I'd like you to point out a new word you figured out. First, identify it and then explain how you figured it out. It'll help everyone's reading become smoother, and you'll be helping a classmate who didn't know the word that you solved." Follow with: "Who would like to show the class a new word that he or she can identify?" Allow every child who would like to share a new word to take a turn. Explain to your students, "It's okay to point out the same word a classmate identified as long as you used a different strategy to figure it out. I want everyone to understand there's more than one way to attack a word."

✷ Review the words identified by your students, "Let's read all the words that were shared. If I miss any, please raise your hand at the end of the exercise to help me." Then point to each of the words with your pointer.

✷ Read the poem chorally with your students.

✷ After the shared reading, discuss the meaning of the poem.

- Ask, "What's this poem about?" If a student says that it's about the month of June, invite him or her to be more specific. Prompt the student if necessary: "The poet focuses on school life in June. What is she describing?"

- If no one understands the meaning of Katz's poem, explain: "The poet lists evidence that proves the end of school is near. One thing she describes is what a math book looks like in June." Instruct a student: "Imagine this is your math book. Open the book to show us what the poet means." When the student opens the book, ask, "How much work is left to do before school ends?" When the student points to a particular side, check the student's understanding by referring back to the poem and reading aloud the lines "the pile of unfinished pages on the right is skinny." Ask, "Which is the right side?" If the student confuses left and right, show him or her. Follow with: "How much work have we done this year?" When the student points to the left side, say, "Let's check to see if the poet's description matches what you're showing us." Then read aloud the lines: "But you need to use your left hand to hold down all the stuff you've learned." Then hold up the book and thumb through the pile of pages on the left side. Say, "Wow! We've learned a lot this year."

- Discuss the meaning of the word *drown* in the poem. Say, "The word *drown* has more than one meaning. What does the word *drown* mean in this line?" Sweep across the line with your pointer and read: "can *drown* out your teacher's voice." If no one can adequately explain the meaning, say, "It means to overpower the teacher's voice so you don't hear what she's saying." Say, "Can a leaf that gently moves make a sound loud enough to block out the sound of a teacher's voice?" When they respond, ask, "What is the poet suggesting?" If no one understands the vivid imagery of these lines, explain: "The poet is exaggerating to show how difficult it is for a student to listen when summer vacation is right around the corner. Is it getting harder for you to concentrate?"

- Survey your children by asking, "How many of you think that every word on the spelling test is summer vacation?" Count the number of students who raise their hands and record the total on the white board or chart paper. Follow with: "How many think the poet has something different in mind?" Count the number of students who raise their hands and record that total on the white board or chart paper. Compare the two totals. Ask, "What can you tell me about these numbers?" Say, "The children who thought the poet doesn't really mean that the spelling test repeated the words *summer vacation* are correct." Then ask, "What's the poet suggesting?" Confirm a student's correct response by saying, "Yes, the only thing the student can think about is summer vacation."

- Ask, "Do you agree with the poet? Does this poem describe you?" Follow with: "Why or why not?"

 After the discussion has ended, ask your students, "Who would like to read this poem aloud?" When some students begin to raise their hands, say, "Please keep your hand raised until I find your name on one of these Popsicle sticks." Observe who has his or her hand raised, and as you say someone's name aloud, remove the Popsicle stick printed with the name of that student from the class set. Follow this procedure for every student who would like a turn to read.

✸ After you've gathered the appropriate sticks, be certain your hand covers the names printed on them. Then call on a student who didn't want to read independently to select one of the Popsicle sticks. Say, "Please pull out one stick and read the name aloud." As the student begins to pull one out, ask, "Who's going to be the lucky one to read the entire poem aloud?" The student should then read aloud the name of his or her classmate. Hand the pointer to the student who is selected so that he or she can use it to sweep across each line as he or she reads it aloud.

❧ Reflection ❧

How my students loved reading this poem aloud—especially the last line! Although they read the words of this poem easily, they had difficulty understanding the meaning of some lines. The poet's use of imagery baffled them. Because my young students are literal thinkers, they couldn't comprehend what the poet suggests in the lines "when the gentlest rustling of a leaf can drown out a teacher's voice." The contrasting words *gentlest* and *drown* confused them. Using a book to demonstrate the poet's description of the math book was extremely helpful, because it allowed my students to envision the poet's intent.

When I first asked my students if they could relate to this poem, most of them emphatically said they couldn't relate to it because they didn't want school to end. Although I believe they did love school, I knew they were hiding their true feelings for fear of hurting me. However, one little boy wasn't afraid. Joe exclaimed, "I can't wait for summer vacation so I can play all day instead of working. My brain is tired." It was only then, after his open and honest sharing, that the rest of the class chimed in.

Note: If your students require additional practice to increase their reading skills, finding little words inside of bigger words would be an appropriate word study to use with this poem.

Every Child a Reader

LESSON FOUR

Discussion of Vocabulary Words: <u>Change</u>, <u>Autumn</u>, and <u>Crimson</u>

Change

The summer
still hangs
heavy and sweet
with sunlight
as it did last year.

The autumn
still comes
showering gold and crimson
as it did last year.

The winter
still stings
clean and white
as it did last year.

The spring
still comes
like a whisper in the dark night.
It is only I
who have changed.

—Charlotte Zolotow

What I Was Thinking

The poem "Change" by Charlotte Zolotow deeply affected me the first time I read it, because the meaning of the poem applied to me as well as to my students. And poetry was the change agent. Although I had found this poem months before,

I planned to wait until the last day of school to read it because it would provide a powerful ending to our year. I hoped this poem would be as meaningful to them as it was to me. But would my students realize how they had changed since the beginning of the year? I knew they'd be able to notice physical changes, but would they also notice the tremendous growth in their reading development?

Materials

The poem "Change" by Charlotte Zolotow, handwritten on manila tag chart paper in large, neat print and attached by rings to a wooden chart stand

> ✿ Fold up the bottom edge of the chart paper to reveal only the title of the poem; use large paper clips to keep the paper in place.

White board or chart paper

What This Lesson Looks Like

> ✿ Point to the title of the poem and ask, "What's the title of today's poem?" Then say, "Let's read it aloud together."

> ✿ Discuss the meaning of the word *change*: "What does the word *change* mean?" After someone mentions that something becomes different when it changes, invite your students: "Let's think of things in our natural world that change." Call on each student to share his or her idea. If no one mentions the seasons of the year, ask, "Do the seasons of the year change?" When your students respond affirmatively, follow with: "What are the names of the four seasons?" After the four seasons are identified, say, "Let's start with summer. What are the signs of summer?" List on the board several signs suggested by your students. After your students give several examples (e.g., hot, late sunsets, green grass, green-leafed trees, beach days, sleeveless shirts, shorts, bare feet, end of school, and tall sunflowers), ask, "What season follows summer?" Follow with: "What changes occur when fall replaces summer?" If your students need support, refer to your list and say, for example, "In the summer we wear sleeveless shirts to keep cool. What kind of shirt would you most likely wear in the fall?" Follow with: "Why would you wear shirts with sleeves?" When they mention it's cooler

in the fall, say, "Because there's a *change* in the weather." Follow the same procedure to discuss the changes observed in winter and in spring.

☀ Introduce the poem by saying, "The poet, Charlotte Zolotow, describes some of the same things you've mentioned about each of these seasons, but she adds a subtle twist." Invite your students to read the poem silently. Then say, "When you finish, take a few minutes to think about the poem. The last line is especially powerful. I'll share my own thoughts about this line after I hear your ideas." Remove the paper clips from the sides of the chart paper, and say, "Please begin reading."

☀ After your students have finished reading, review two words: *autumn* and *crimson*. Point to the word *autumn* and ask, "Who knows this word?" Call on a student to identify it. Then ask, "What's another word that many people use to refer to this season?" Then point to the word *crimson* and ask, "What's this word?" After your students successfully read it aloud, follow with: "What is the color of crimson?" Confirm a student's accuracy by elaborating on his or her answer. Say, "Yes, it *is* red—a deep red, like the color of blood." Then ask, "What was the poet describing as golden and crimson?" Call on a student to answer. Affirm your student's response by saying, "Yes, the poet *is* describing the yellow and red leaves that fall from trees in autumn."

☀ Invite your students to read this poem aloud with you. Point to the white space after each stanza: "The white space signals the reader to pause. When we come to the white space just before the last stanza of the poem, let's pause a bit longer so that the last line will have more impact." Then read the poem chorally.

☀ Discuss the meaning of the poem. Ask, "How does Zolotow build up the poem to its powerful last line?" Prompt them if necessary by directing their attention to the poem. Say, "She uses repetition. Which line is repeated?" Follow with: "Why does she say this about the seasons of the year?" Discuss how each season's uniqueness remains the same year after year. Then invite them: "Please read the last line aloud with me." After you and your students finish reading, ask, "What does this line mean to you?" Follow with: "How have you changed this year?" After your students discuss their physical changes, say, "I know I've changed as a teacher. Poetry has helped me become a better teacher of reading, and in the process, I've discovered poems I truly love." Then ask, "How have you changed as a reader?"

❧ Final Reflection ❧

When my students began to discuss how they had changed, they talked about all the physical changes that they noticed about themselves. However, no one considered they had changed as students until I brought up the subject. Although several students then provided wonderful insights, MacAllister summed up our year beautifully by saying, "The last line shouldn't be 'It's only I who have changed.' Instead it should be 'It's only *we* who have changed,' because we're *all* great readers now." And she was right.

I must admit I never would have considered using poetry with kindergartners— that is, not until Nancie provided the impetus by suggesting that I should include poetry as a component of my reading program. I remember how hesitant I was to make the change from singing songs as a vehicle of literacy to reading poems. At first I wondered if poems could engage my students as well as melodies did. But was I ever wrong in my thinking!

The rhythms of poetry and the sounds of language not only keep my students' attention, but also positively impact their reading development. Their reading achievement has soared; by June every child in my class is now a confident, joyful reader. Poetry has become and will continue to be a daily staple in my classroom; my students have thrived as readers, writers, and people. Now I can't imagine a day without the songs of poetry filling our hearts and minds.

Silent Reading Checklist

Name: _____

		Date:	Date:	Date:	Date:	Date:
Habits	Easily distracted					
	Persists					
	Gives up easily					
	Excessive head movement					
Vocalization	Whispers loudly					
	Whispers softly					
	Reads silently					
Rate	Reads slowly					
	Reads quickly					
	Reads at an appropriate rate					
Comprehension	Understands main idea					
	Recalls details					
	Recalls sequence					
	Locates information					
	Makes predictions					
	Makes connections:					
	Text-to-self					
	Text-to-text					
	Text-to-world					
	Interprets figurative language					
	Evaluates critically					

Every Child a Reader: Month-by-Month Lessons to Teach Beginning Reading, Helene Coffin: Scholastic 2009 page 331

Oral Reading Checklist

Name: _____

		Date:	Date:	Date:	Date:	Date:
Fluency	Consistently reads word-by-word					
	Consistently reads in meaningful chunks					
	Reads in meaningful chunks at times					
	Attends to punctuation					
	Reads with appropriate intonation					
Rate	Reads hesitantly					
	Reads too quickly					
	Reads at an appropriate rate					
Word Recognition	Recognizes words in context					
	Recognizes words in isolation					
Strategies	Uses picture clues					
	Uses letters and sounds					
	Uses context					
	Uses sentence structure					
	Integrates reading strategies					
Miscues	Self-corrects					
	Confuses letters in words					
	Confuses similar words					
	Reverses words					
	Adds words					
	Omits words					
Comprehension	Word calling					
	Reads for meaning					
	Rereads to maintain meaning					
	Rereads to establish meaning					

High-Frequency Words

the	I	was	for
to	you	said	on
and	it	his	they
he	of	that	but
a	in	she	had
at	look	out	we
him	is	as	am
with	her	be	then
up	there	have	little
all	some	go	down
do	what	get	my
can	so	them	would
could	see	like	me
when	not	one	will
did	were	this	yes
big	now	very	ride
went	long	an	into
are	no	over	just
come	came	your	blue
if	ask	its	red
from	want	put	every
good	don't	too	pretty
any	how	got	jump
about	know	take	green
around	right	where	four

Every Child a Reader: Month-by-Month Lessons to Teach Beginning Reading, Helene Coffin: Scholastic 2009 page 333

Dear _____,

      This is _____'s poetry notebook, which s/he will bring home at the end of each week. We will add new poems after they have been shared in class. Every weekend, your child should read both the new poems and "old favorites" for fifteen minutes. By rereading these poems again and again, your child will gain fluency and expression.

      After s/he has read for fifteen minutes, invite him/her to select his/her favorite new poem to illustrate. Please discuss what should be included in the illustration to help depict the meaning of the poem. Remove the favorite poem from the sleeve and ask your child to point to where s/he wants to draw each item on the page. This will help create a plan before beginning to draw. Emphasize to your child that neat, careful work is expected. When s/he is finished, please re-sleeve the illustrated poem.

      At first, your child will memorize the words. This "memory reading" establishes the foundation for learning how written language works. During this stage of reading, it is imperative that your child touch each word as s/he "reads." In a short time, your child will learn to connect the spoken word to the printed text and will then begin to attend to the print.

      Working together, we will share the joy of watching _____ blossom into an independent reader. More importantly, we will be laying a solid foundation for developing a lifelong love of reading.

                      With much appreciation,

Every Child a Reader: Month-by-Month Lessons to Teach Beginning Reading, Helene Coffin: Scholastic 2009 page 334

REFERENCES

Atwell, N. (2007). *The reading zone: How to help kids become skilled, passionate, habitual, critical readers.* New York: Scholastic.

Cunningham, P. M. (1995). *Phonics they use: Words for reading and writing* (2nd Ed.). New York: HarperCollins.

CREDITS (continued from copyright page)

NOTES